HISTORY'S GREATEST GAMES

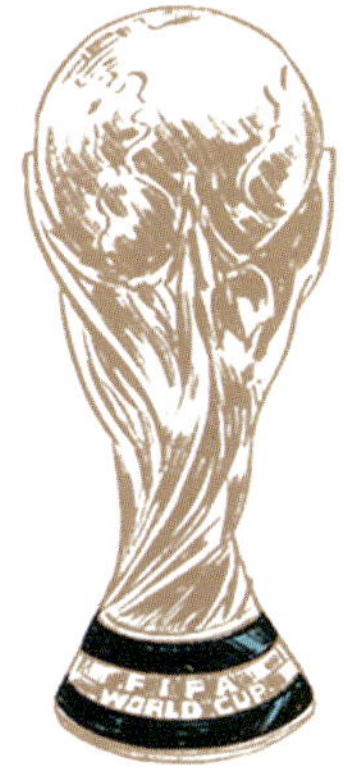
FIFA
WORLD CUP

HISTORY'S GREATEST GAMES

LIONEL MESSI'S WORLD CUP TRIUMPH

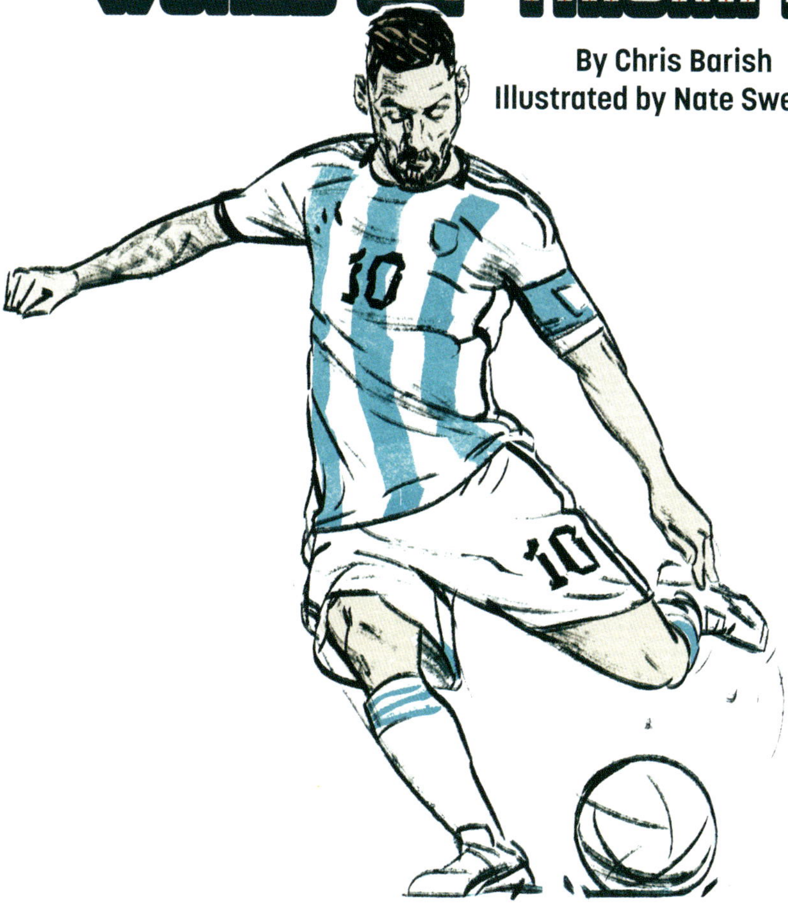
10
10

By Chris Barish
Illustrated by Nate Sweitzer

ABRAMS FANFARE
NEW YORK

Editor: Erica Finkel
Design Manager: Deena Micah Fleming
Designer: Brann Garvey
Managing Editor: Krista Keplinger
Production Manager: Katie Gaffney

Library of Congress Control Number 2025941044

Hardcover ISBN 978-1-4197-7939-8
Paperback ISBN 978-1-4197-7940-4

Published in 2026 by Abrams Fanfare, an imprint of ABRAMS. All rights reserved. No portion of this book may be reproduced, stored in a retrieval system, or transmitted in any form or by any means, mechanical, electronic, photocopying, recording, or otherwise, without written permission from the publisher.

Printed and bound in China
10 9 8 7 6 5 4 3 2 1

Abrams Fanfare are available at special discounts when purchased in quantity for premiums and promotions as well as fundraising or educational use. Special editions can also be created to specification. For details, contact specialsales@abramsbooks.com or the address below.

Abrams Fanfare® is a registered trademark of Harry N. Abrams, Inc.

ABRAMS The Art of Books
195 Broadway, New York, NY 10007
abramsbooks.com

ABRAMS is represented in the UK and Europe by Abrams & Chronicle Books, 1 West Smithfield, London EC1A 9JU and Média Participations, 57 rue Gaston Tessier, 75166 Paris, France.
abramsandchronicle.co.uk and media-participations.com
info@abramsandchronicle.com

PREGAME

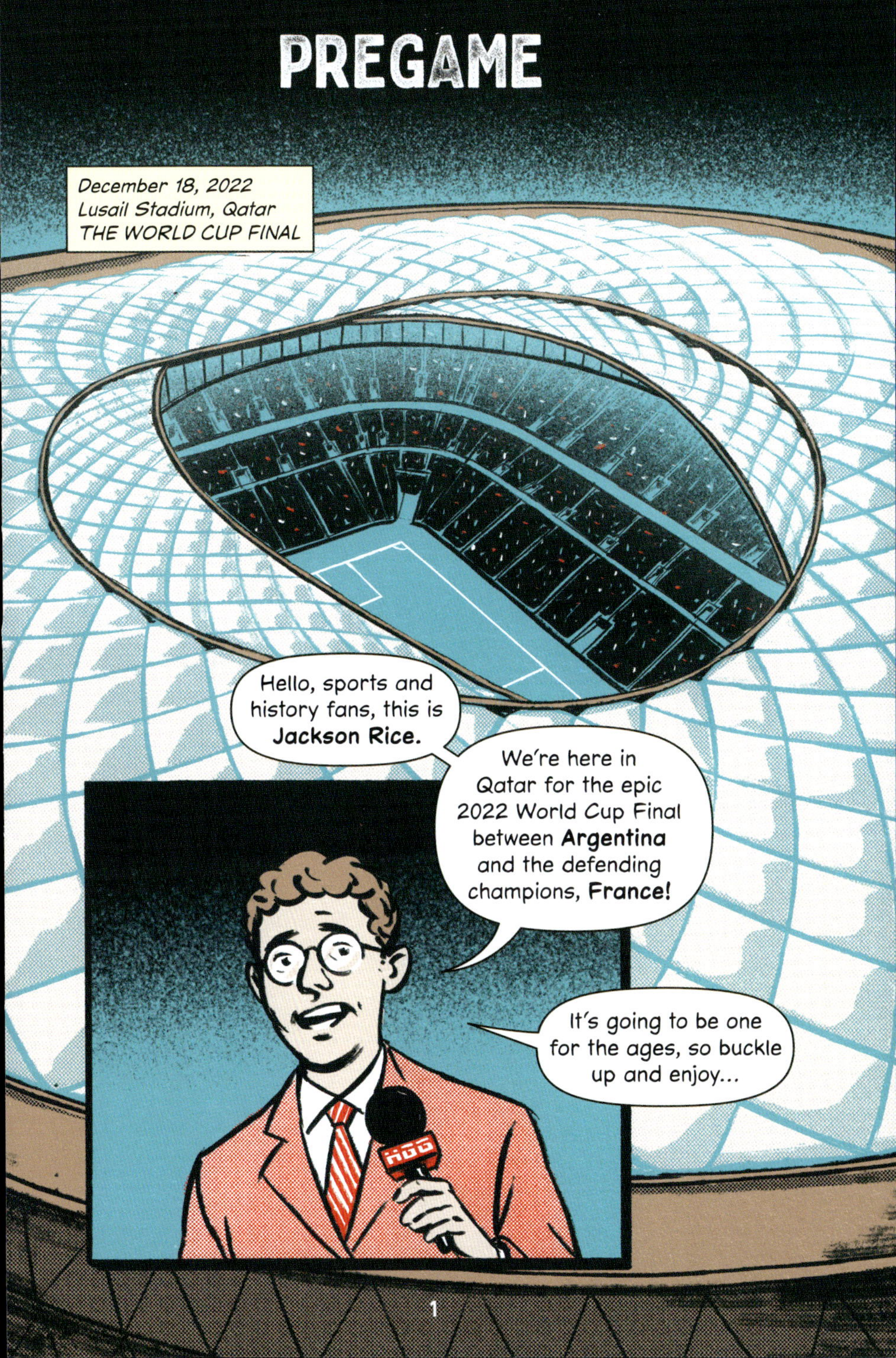
December 18, 2022
Lusail Stadium, Qatar
THE WORLD CUP FINAL
Hello, sports and history fans, this is **Jackson Rice.**
We're here in Qatar for the epic 2022 World Cup Final between **Argentina** and the defending champions, **France!**
It's going to be one for the ages, so buckle up and enjoy...

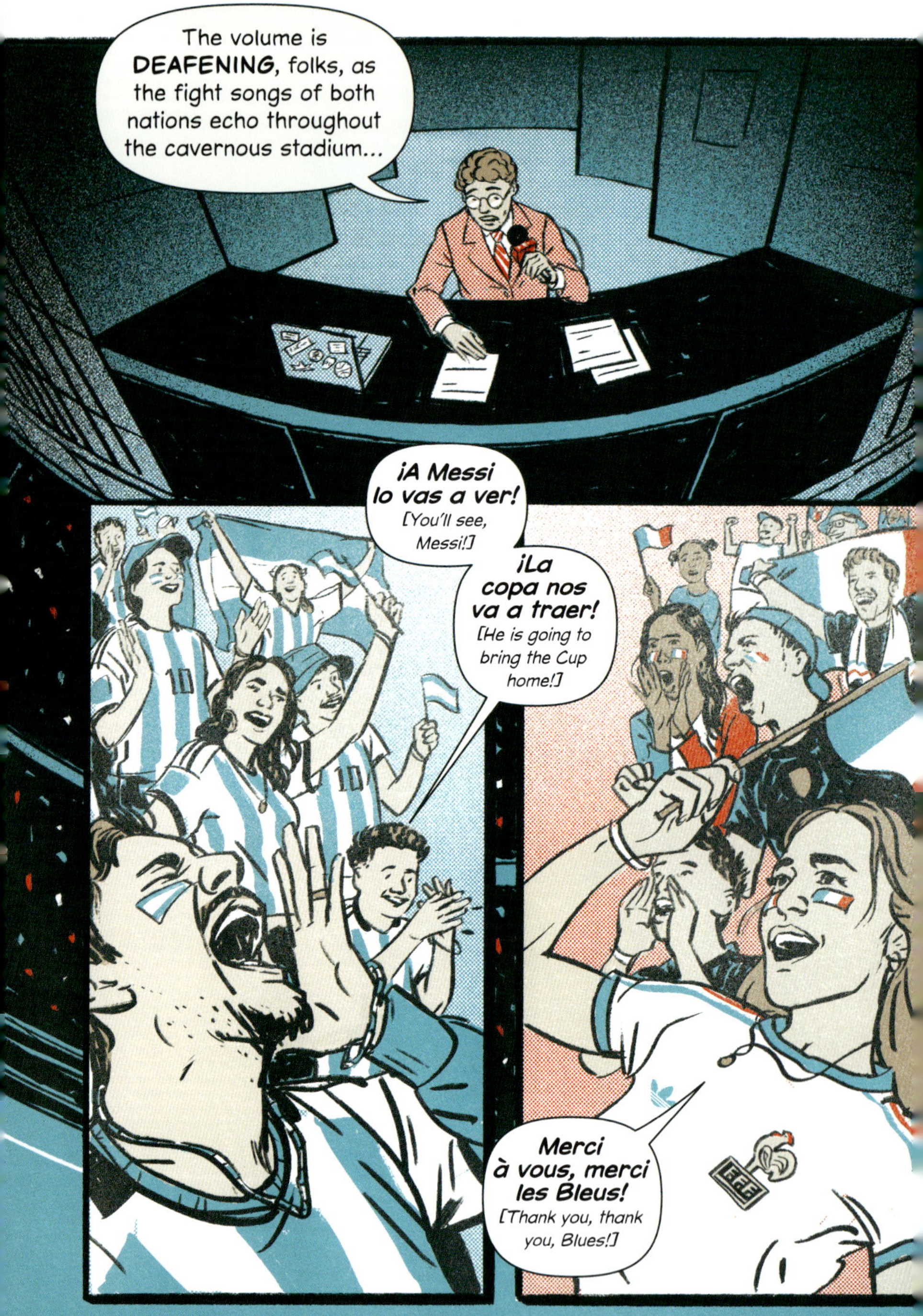
The volume is DEAFENING, folks, as the fight songs of both nations echo throughout the cavernous stadium...
¡A Messi lo vas a ver!
[You'll see, Messi!]
¡La copa nos va a traer!
[He is going to bring the Cup home!]
Merci à vous, merci les Bleus!
[Thank you, thank you, Blues!]

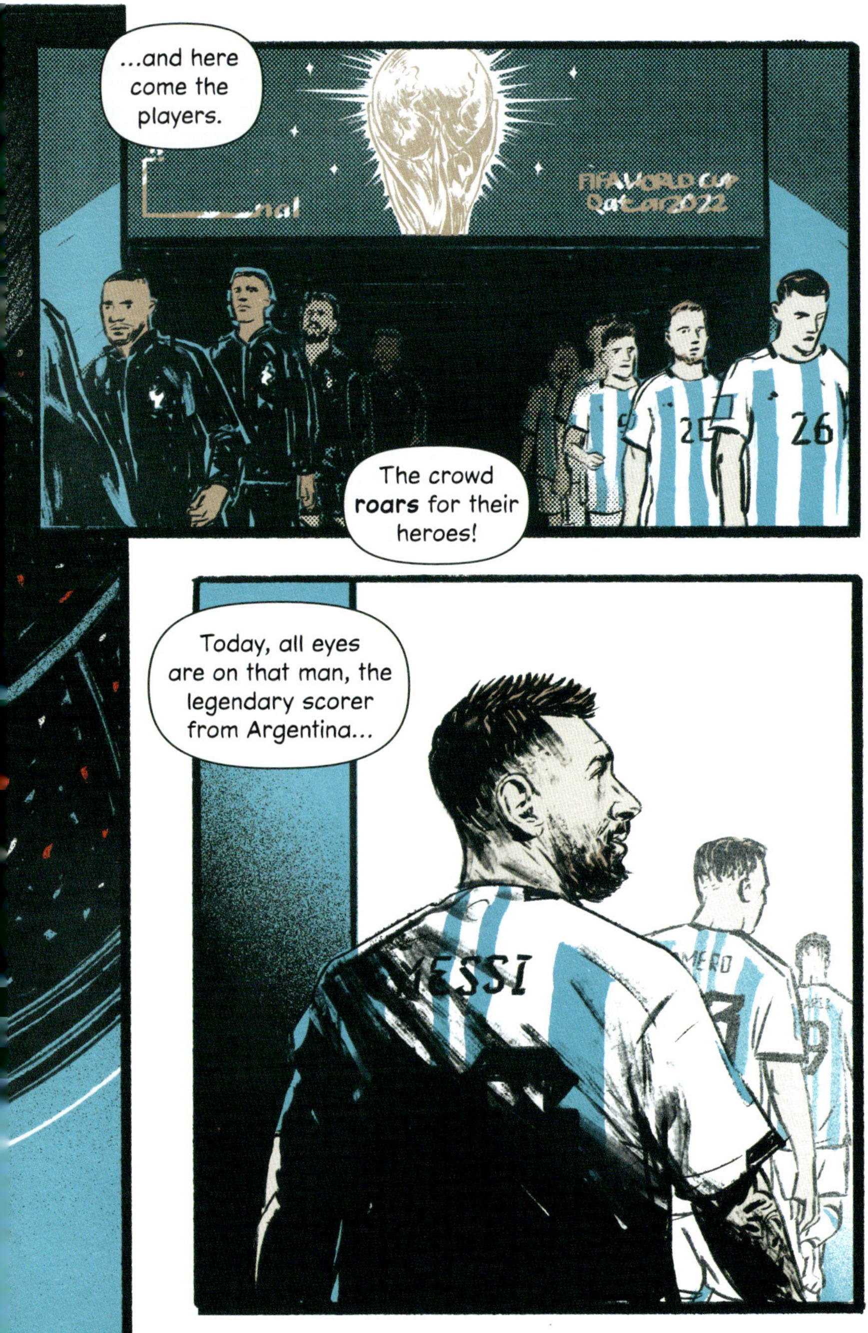
...and here come the players.
FIFA WORLD CUP Qatar2022
The crowd **roars** for their heroes!
Today, all eyes are on that man, the legendary scorer from Argentina...
MESSI

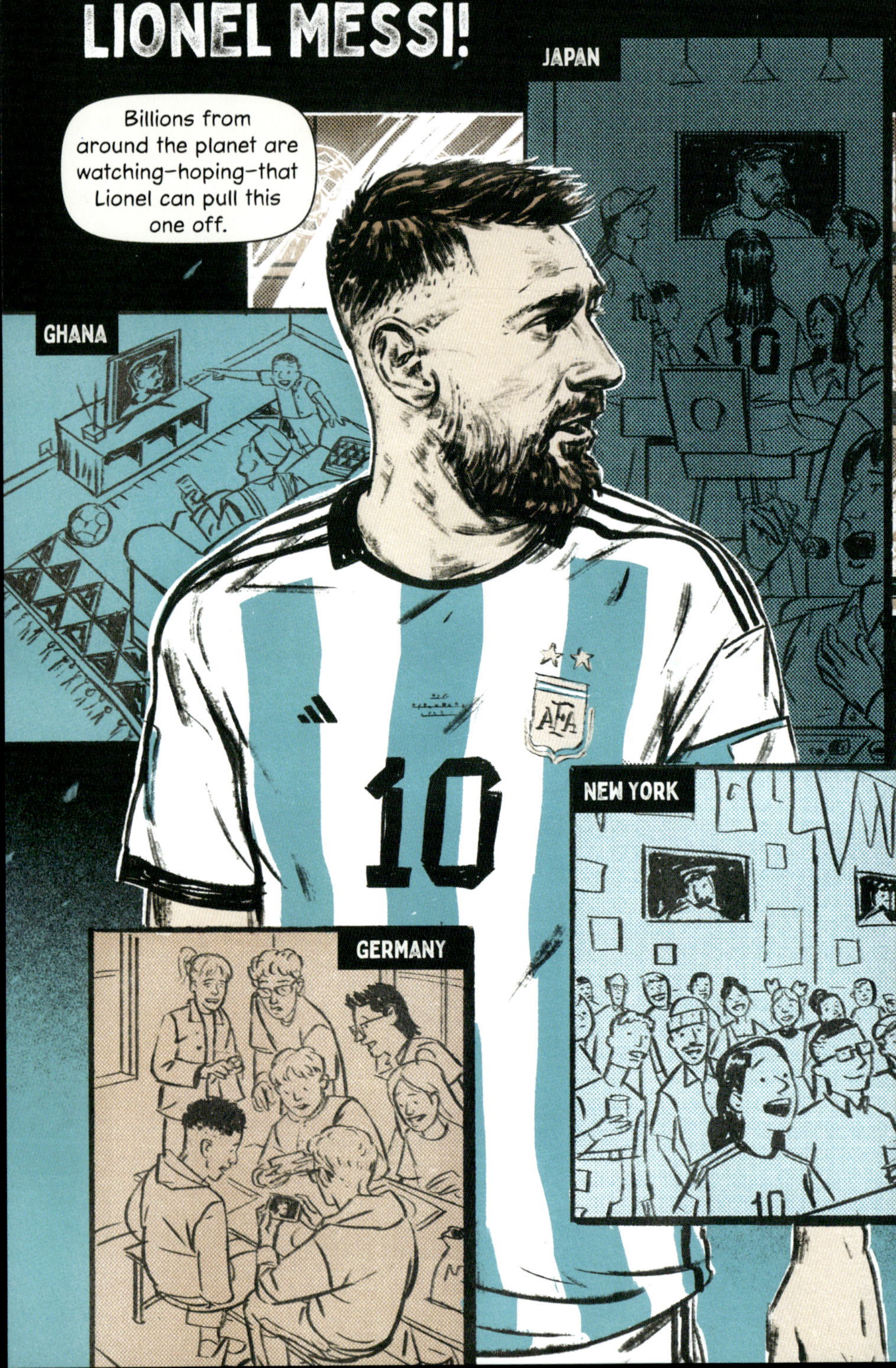
LIONEL MESSI!
Billions from around the planet are watching—hoping—that Lionel can pull this one off.
JAPAN
GHANA
NEW YORK
GERMANY
AFA
10

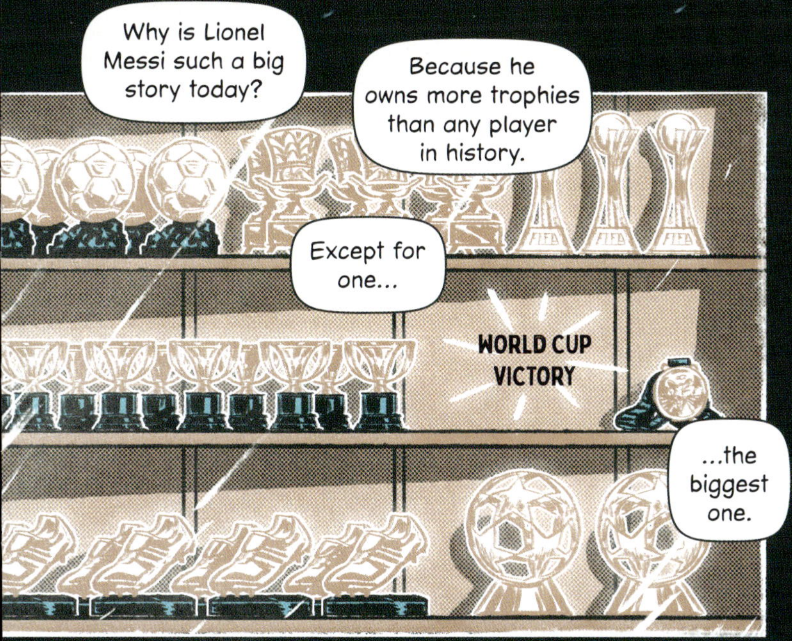

Why is Lionel Messi such a big story today?
Because he owns more trophies than any player in history.
Except for one...
WORLD CUP VICTORY
...the biggest one.

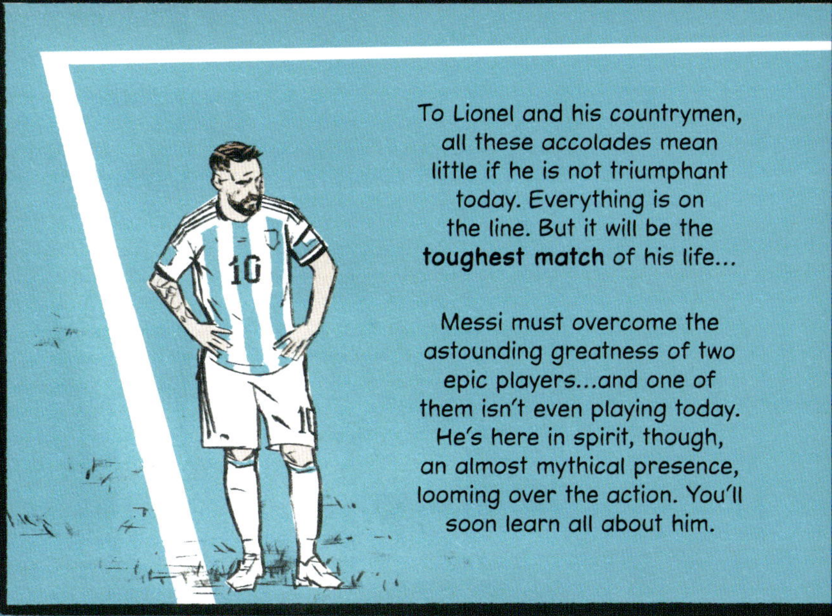

To Lionel and his countrymen, all these accolades mean little if he is not triumphant today. Everything is on the line. But it will be the **toughest match** of his life...
Messi must overcome the astounding greatness of two epic players...and one of them isn't even playing today. He's here in spirit, though, an almost mythical presence, looming over the action. You'll soon learn all about him.

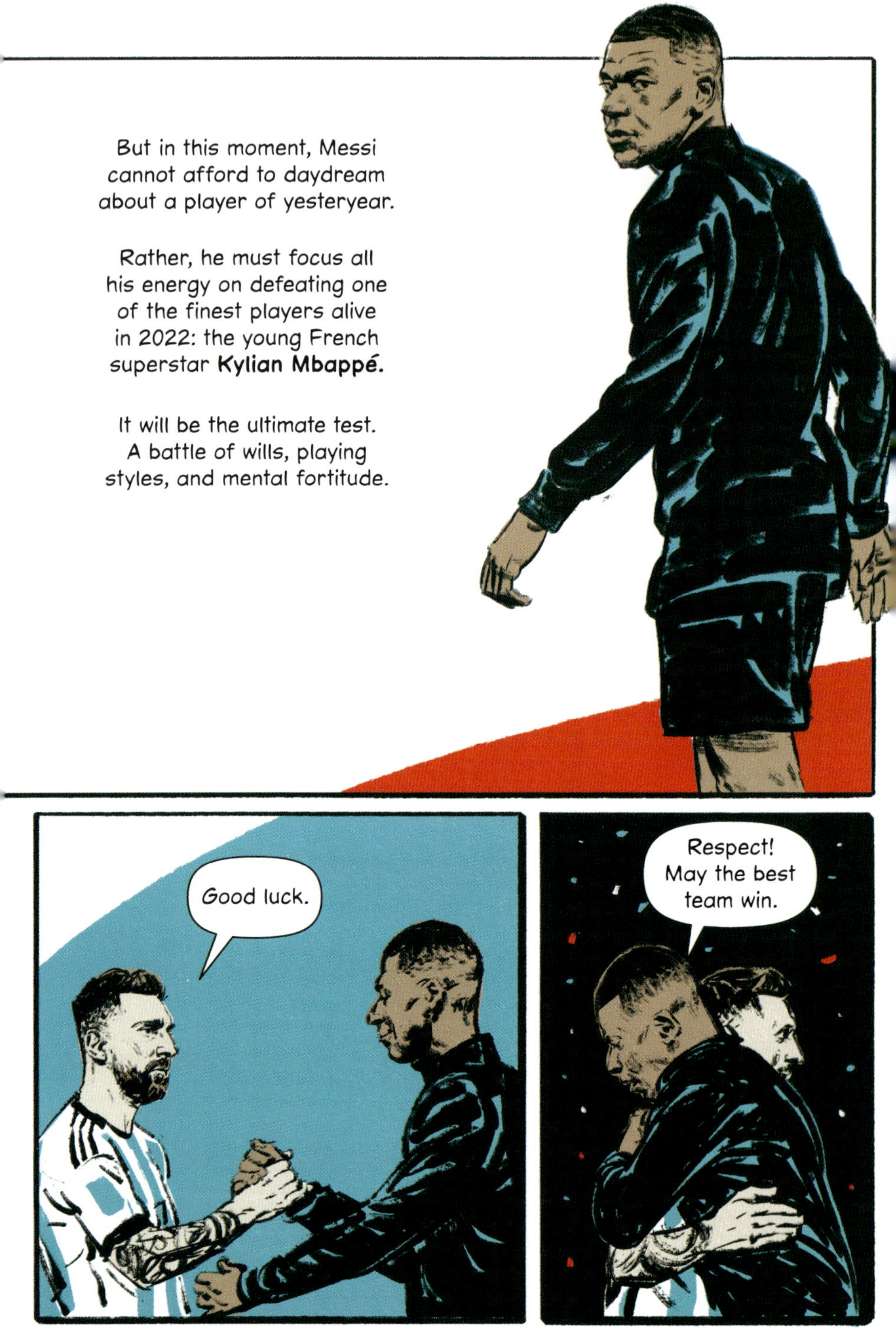
But in this moment, Messi cannot afford to daydream about a player of yesteryear.
Rather, he must focus all his energy on defeating one of the finest players alive in 2022: the young French superstar **Kylian Mbappé.**
It will be the ultimate test. A battle of wills, playing styles, and mental fortitude.
Good luck.
Respect! May the best team win.

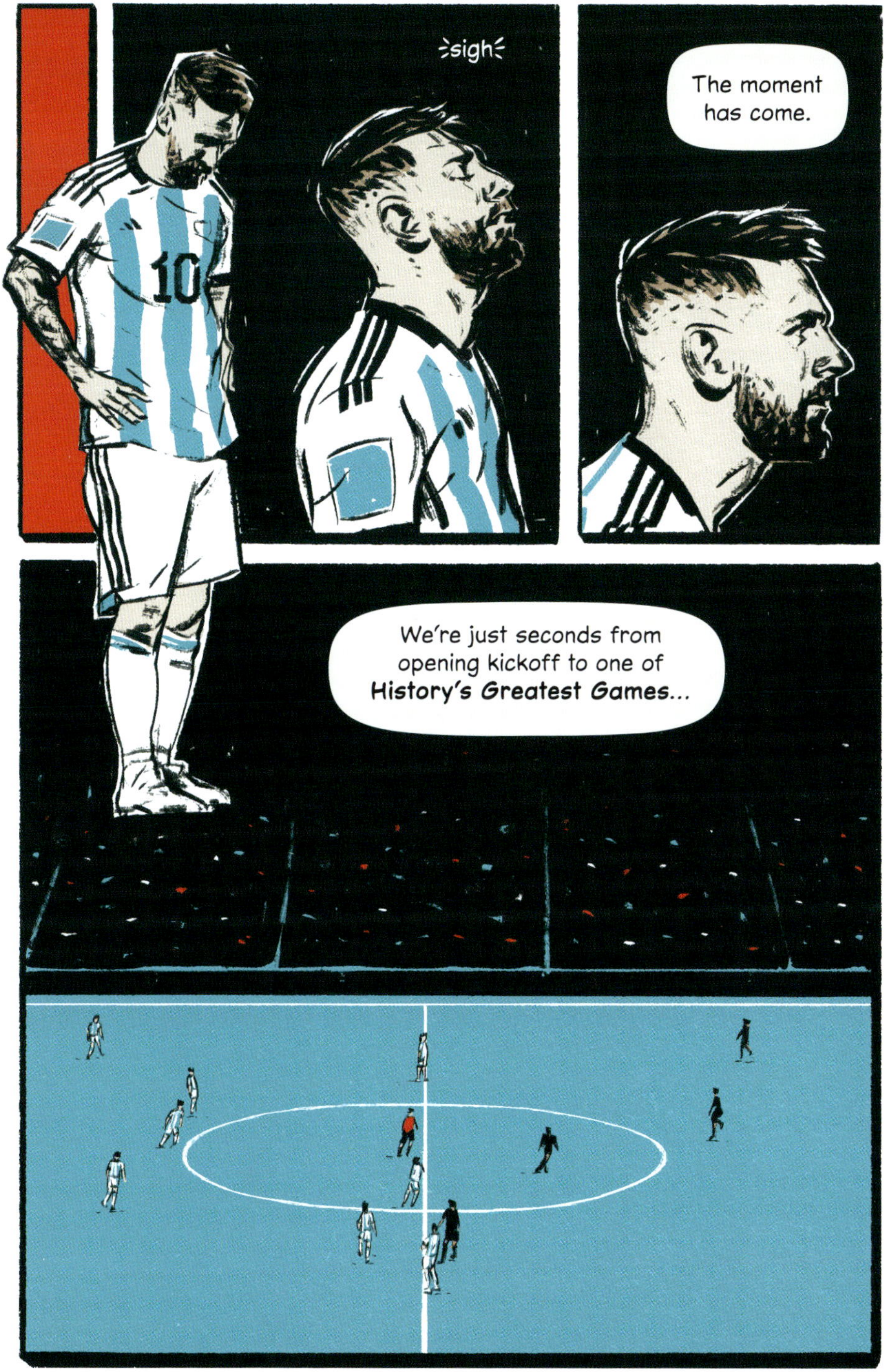
sigh
The moment has come.
We're just seconds from opening kickoff to one of **History's Greatest Games...**

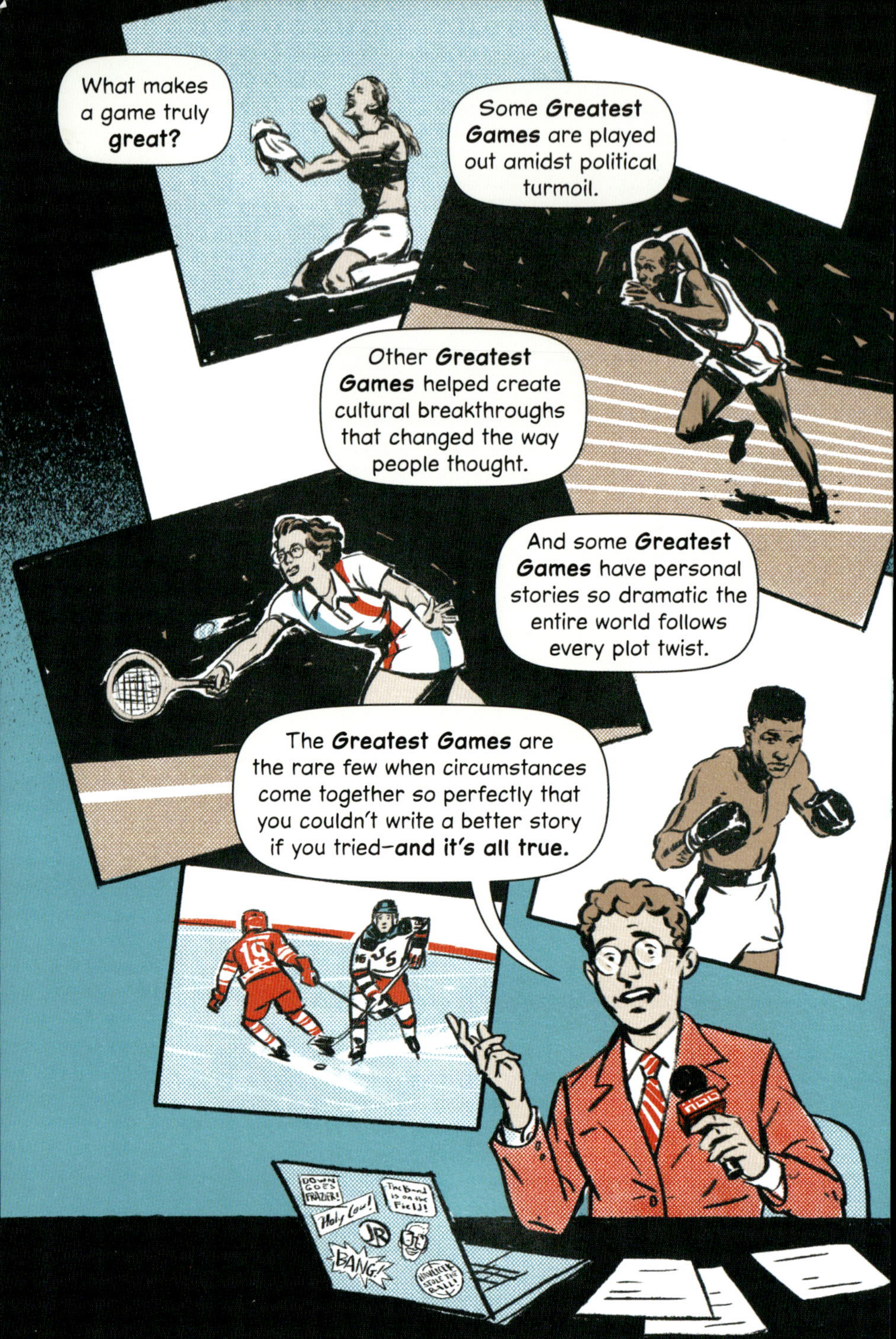
What makes a game truly **great?**
Some **Greatest Games** are played out amidst political turmoil.
Other **Greatest Games** helped create cultural breakthroughs that changed the way people thought.
And some **Greatest Games** have personal stories so dramatic the entire world follows every plot twist.
The **Greatest Games** are the rare few when circumstances come together so perfectly that you couldn't write a better story if you tried—**and it's all true.**
DOWN GOES FRAZIER!
The Band is on the Field!
Holy Cow!
JR
BANG!
HAVLICEK STOLE THE BALL!

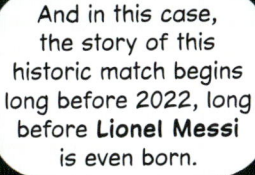

And in this case, the story of this historic match begins long before 2022, long before **Lionel Messi** is even born.

To understand why Messi's defining World Cup match was so momentous, we must first go back to the birth of the **World Cup** itself.

WATER BREAK!
HOW TO SAY "SOCCER" IN DIFFERENT LANGUAGES

Soccer, as the game is called in the United States, Canada, and Australia, is the world's sport. In the UK, however, it is most often referred to as football. Just knowing what to call it in another culture can connect you with a new friend:

Arabic	Kurat al-qadam
Croatian	Nogomet
Dutch	Voetbal
Finnish	Jalkapallo
French	Le football
Irish	Sacar
Italian	Calcio
Japanese	Sakkā
Luxembourgish	Fussball
Polish	Piłka nożna
Spanish	Fútbol

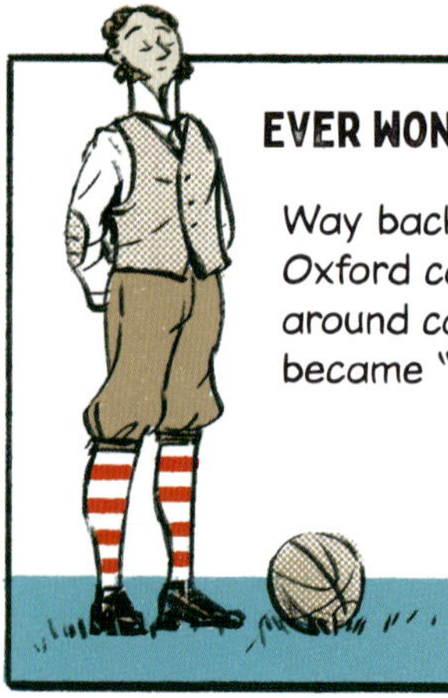

EVER WONDER WHERE THE WORD "SOCCER" ORIGINATED?

Way back in the 1880s, students from the University of Oxford called the sport "association football." The slang around campus turned it into "assoccer," which eventually became "soccer."

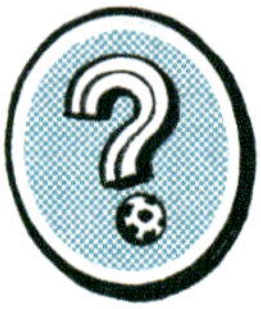

TRIVIA GOALS

What memorable event occurred during a World Cup match?

A) A player's pants fell down during a penalty kick in the semifinals.

B) The soccer ball popped after a winger blasted a shot on goal.

C) A player's shoe flew off and scored a goal in the upper right corner.

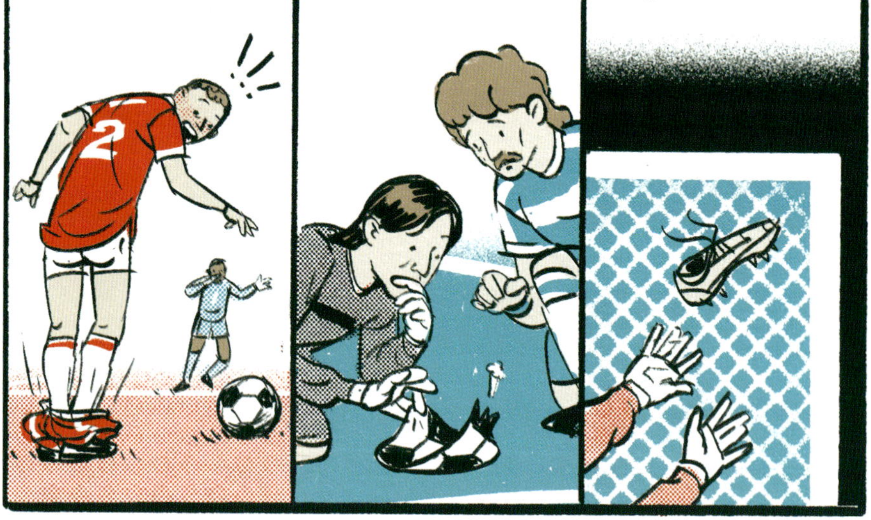

(You can find the correct answers to the trivia questions at the end of the book. Good luck!)

CHAPTER

1

THE WORLD'S SPORT

In 1930, countries from all around the globe were suffering from an unparalleled economic disaster called the *Great Depression*. Things took a terrible turn in *October 1929* when the stock market collapsed.

I invested all our savings in RCA stock at $114 per share... now it's worth $3. We're ruined.
What will we do to survive?
I don't know. I just don't know.

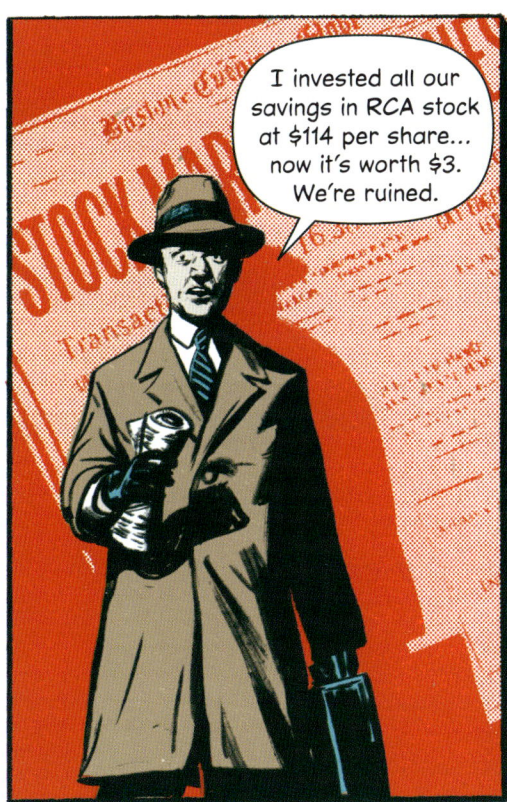

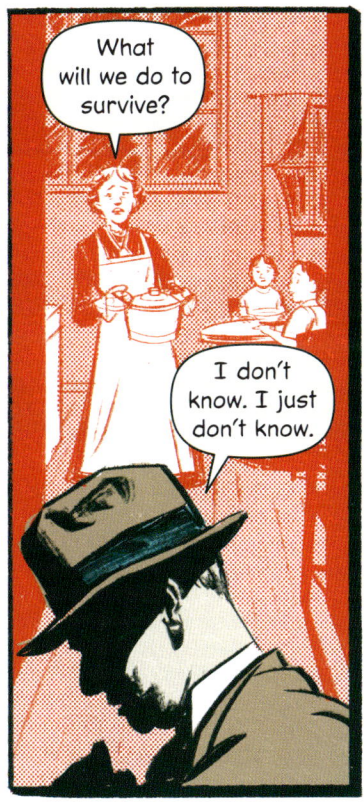

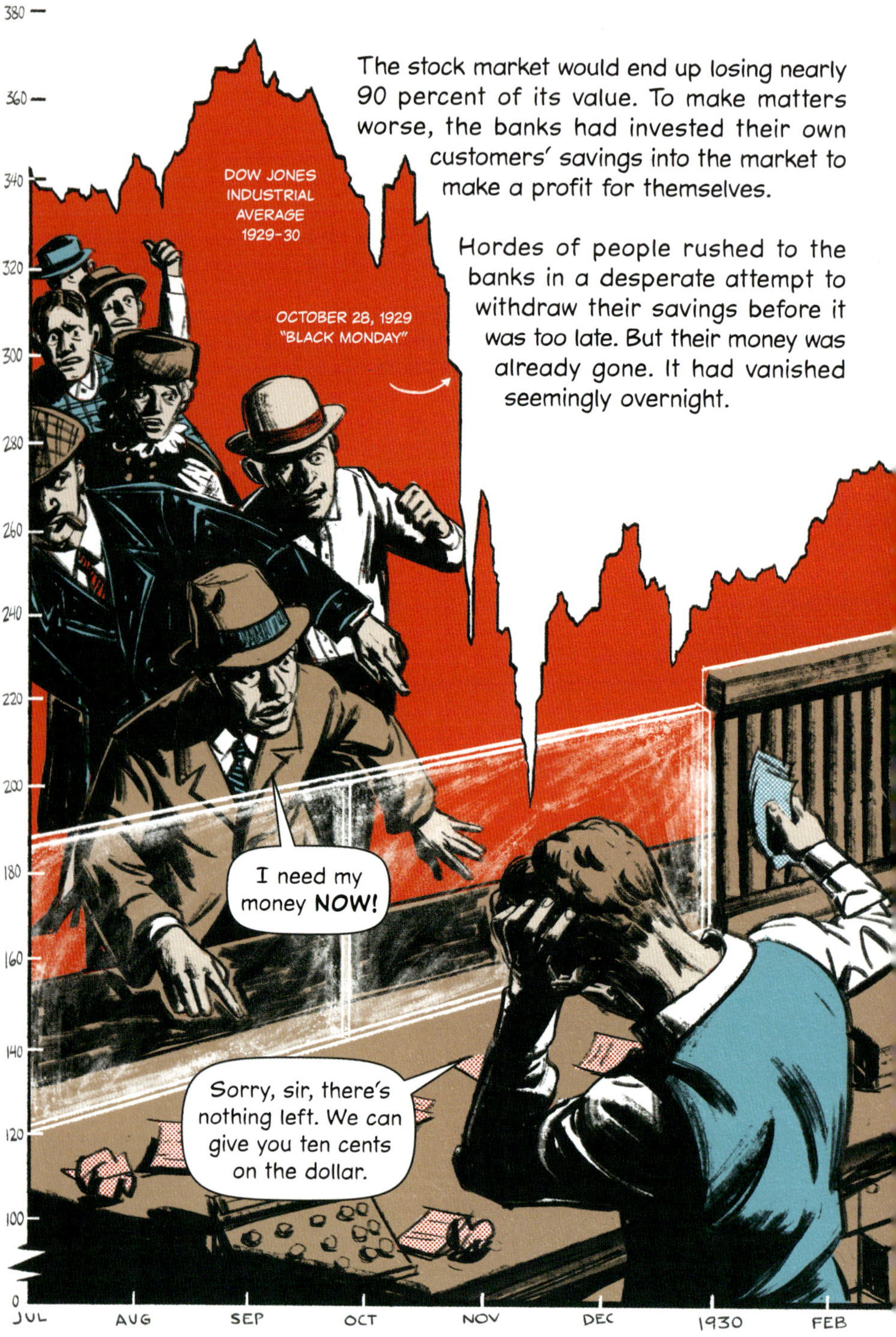
The stock market would end up losing nearly 90 percent of its value. To make matters worse, the banks had invested their own customers' savings into the market to make a profit for themselves.
Hordes of people rushed to the banks in a desperate attempt to withdraw their savings before it was too late. But their money was already gone. It had vanished seemingly overnight.
DOW JONES INDUSTRIAL AVERAGE 1929–30
OCTOBER 28, 1929 "BLACK MONDAY"
I need my money **NOW!**
Sorry, sir, there's nothing left. We can give you ten cents on the dollar.
380
360
340
320
300
280
260
240
220
200
180
160
140
120
100
0
JUL
AUG
SEP
OCT
NOV
DEC
1930
FEB

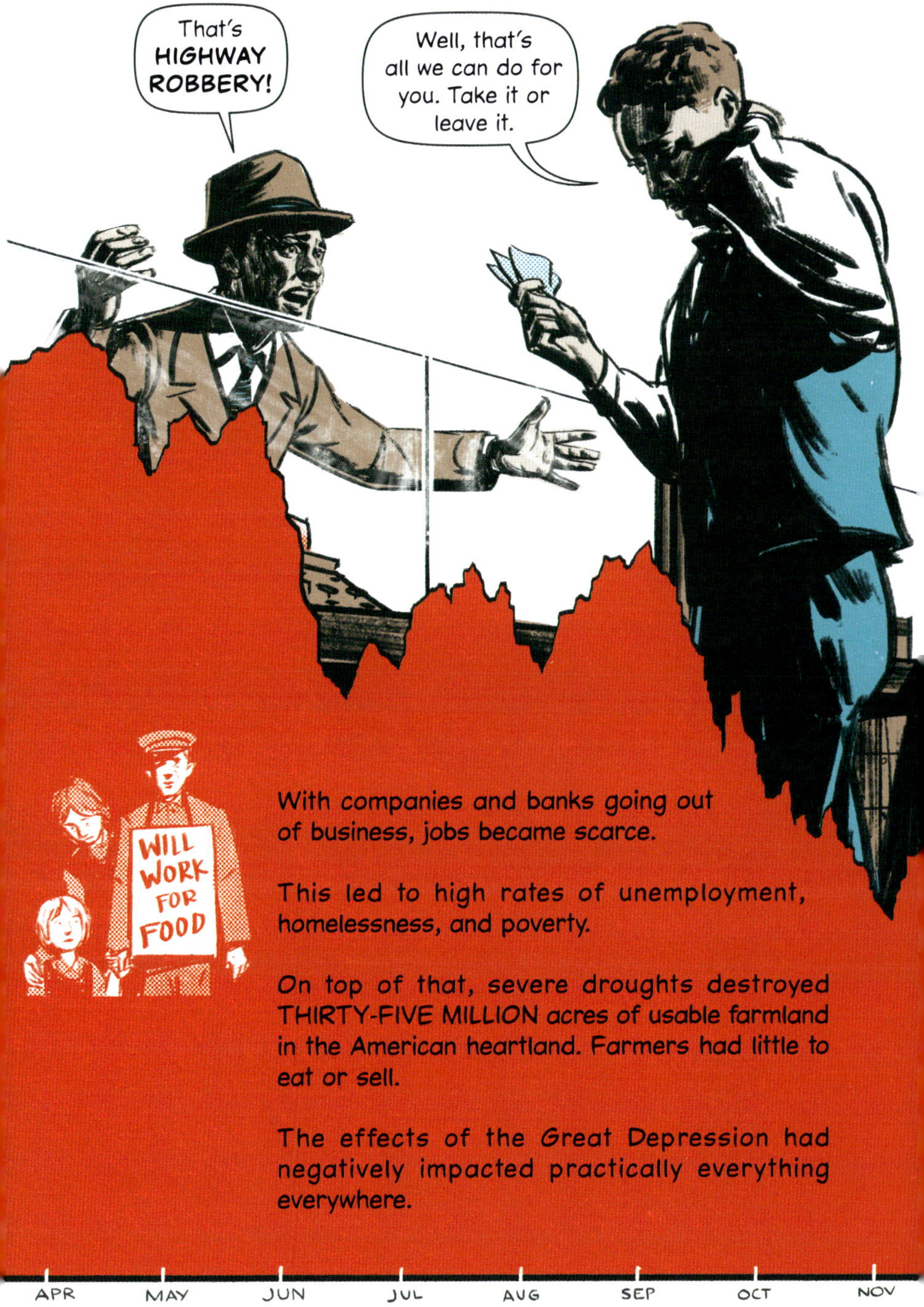
That's HIGHWAY ROBBERY!
Well, that's all we can do for you. Take it or leave it.
WILL WORK FOR FOOD
With companies and banks going out of business, jobs became scarce.
This led to high rates of unemployment, homelessness, and poverty.
On top of that, severe droughts destroyed THIRTY-FIVE MILLION acres of usable farmland in the American heartland. Farmers had little to eat or sell.
The effects of the Great Depression had negatively impacted practically everything everywhere.
APR
MAY
JUN
JUL
AUG
SEP
OCT
NOV

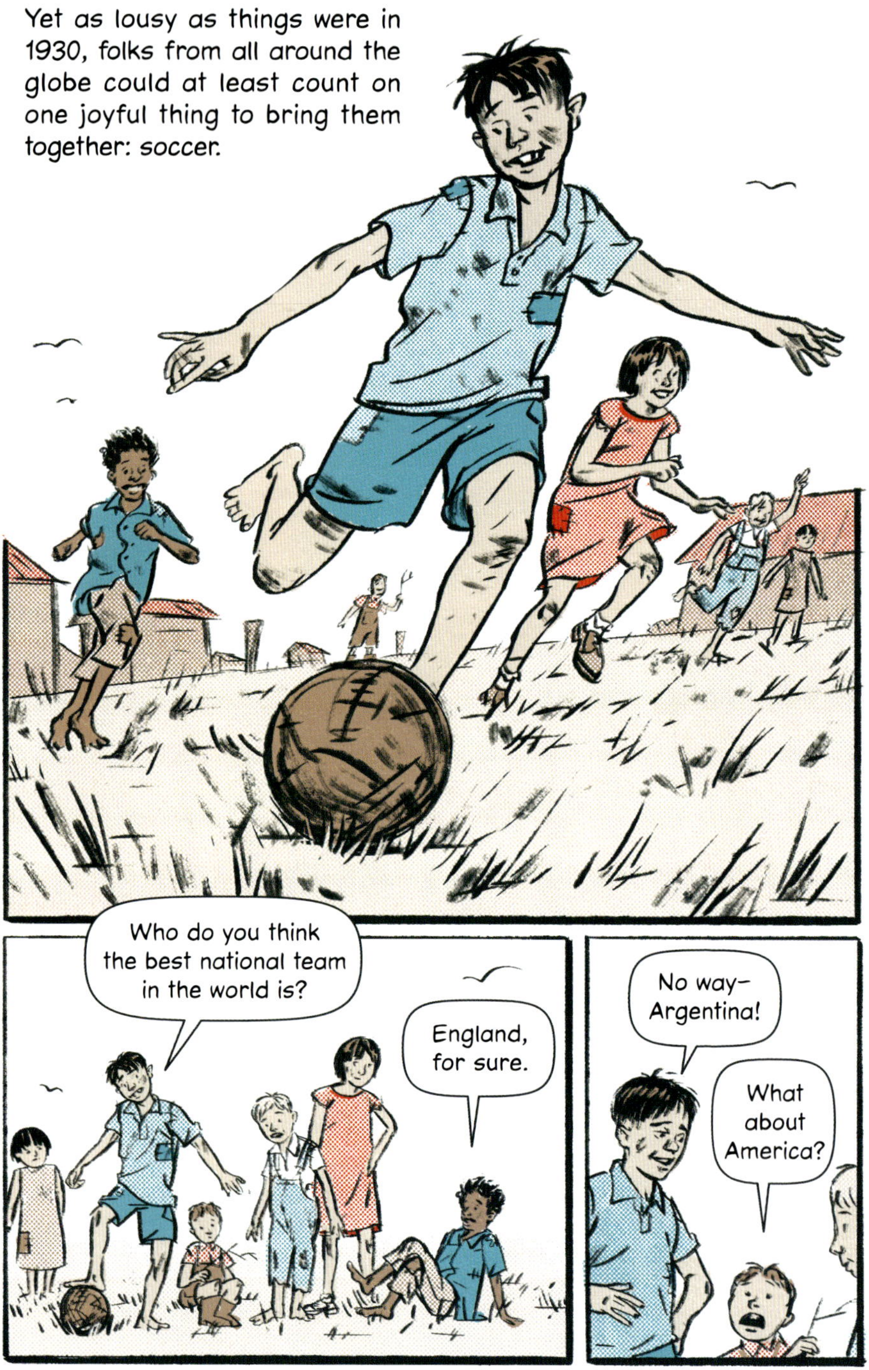
Yet as lousy as things were in 1930, folks from all around the globe could at least count on one joyful thing to bring them together: *soccer.*
Who do you think the best national team in the world is?
England, for sure.
No way—Argentina!
What about America?

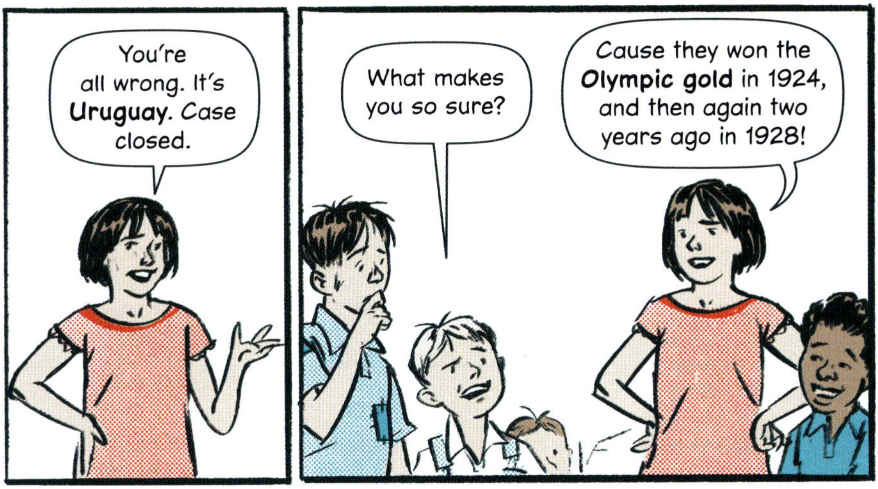
You're all wrong. It's **Uruguay**. Case closed.
What makes you so sure?
Cause they won the **Olympic gold** in 1924, and then again two years ago in 1928!

Soccer is the world's sport because nearly anyone can play, practically anytime, anywhere. The beauty is in its simplicity. You don't need piles of expensive equipment, like in American football.

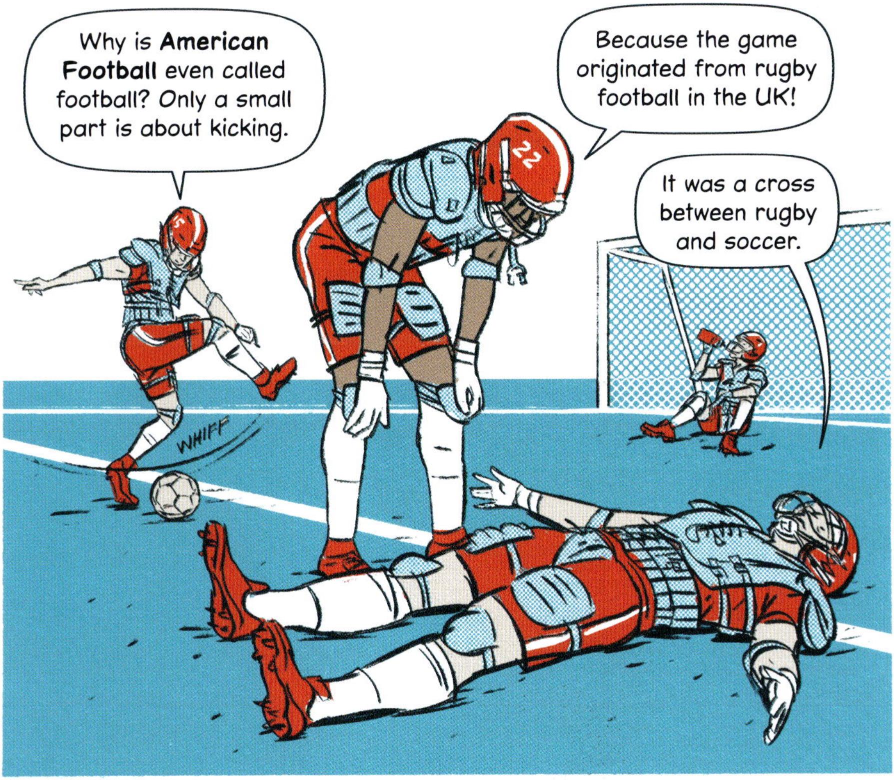
Why is **American Football** even called football? Only a small part is about kicking.
Because the game originated from rugby football in the UK!
It was a cross between rugby and soccer.
WHIFF

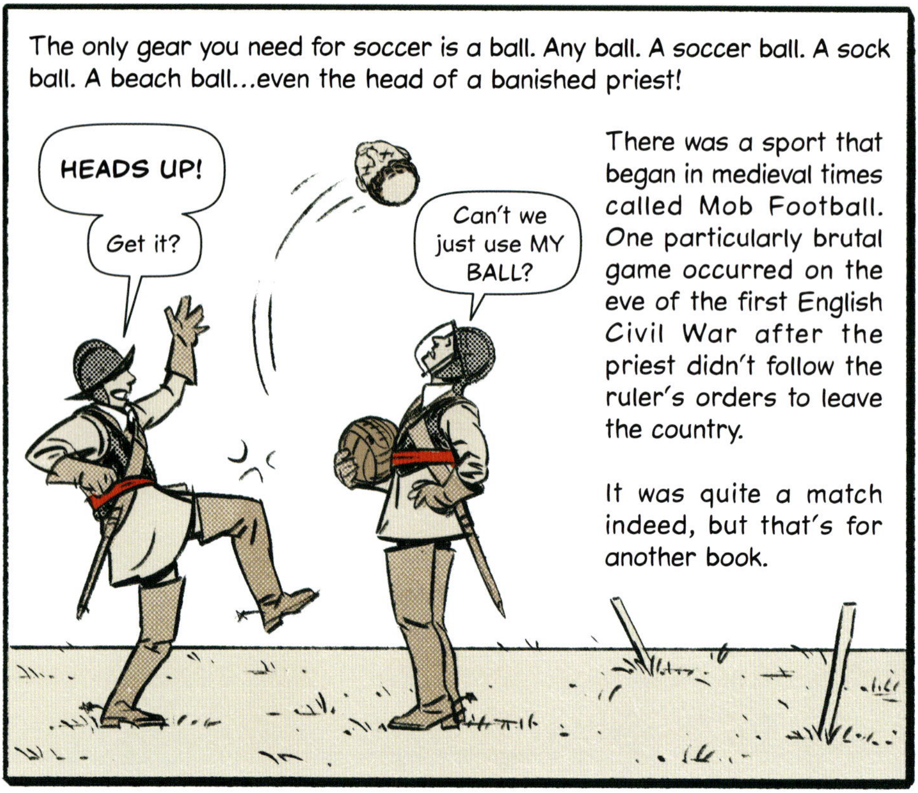
The only gear you need for soccer is a ball. Any ball. A soccer ball. A sock ball. A beach ball...even the head of a banished priest!
HEADS UP!
Get it?
Can't we just use MY BALL?
There was a sport that began in medieval times called Mob Football. One particularly brutal game occurred on the eve of the first English Civil War after the priest didn't follow the ruler's orders to leave the country.
It was quite a match indeed, but that's for another book.

And in soccer, you don't need a fancy place to play, like an ice hockey rink.

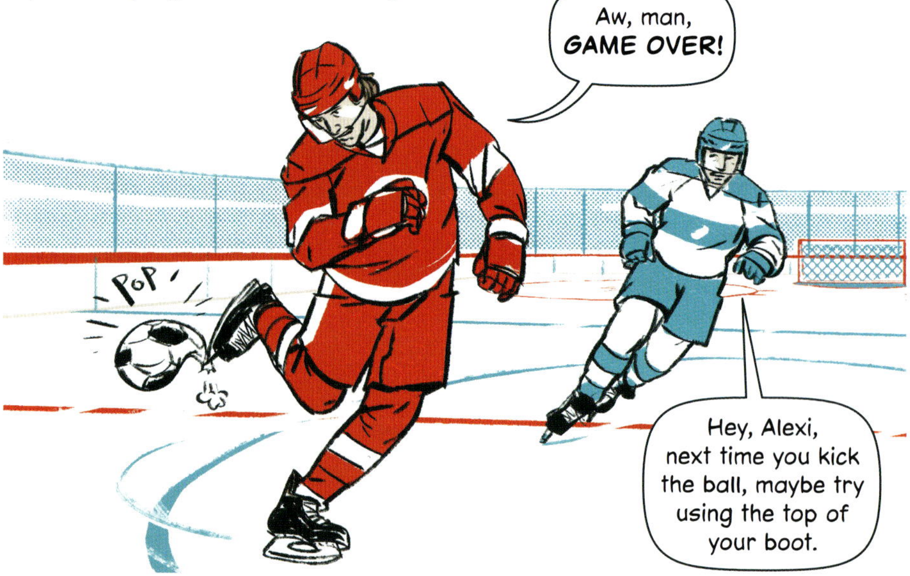
Aw, man, GAME OVER!
POP
Hey, Alexi, next time you kick the ball, maybe try using the top of your boot.

In soccer, all you need is a field. Any space will do. A pitch. A beach. A boardroom. A bedroom.

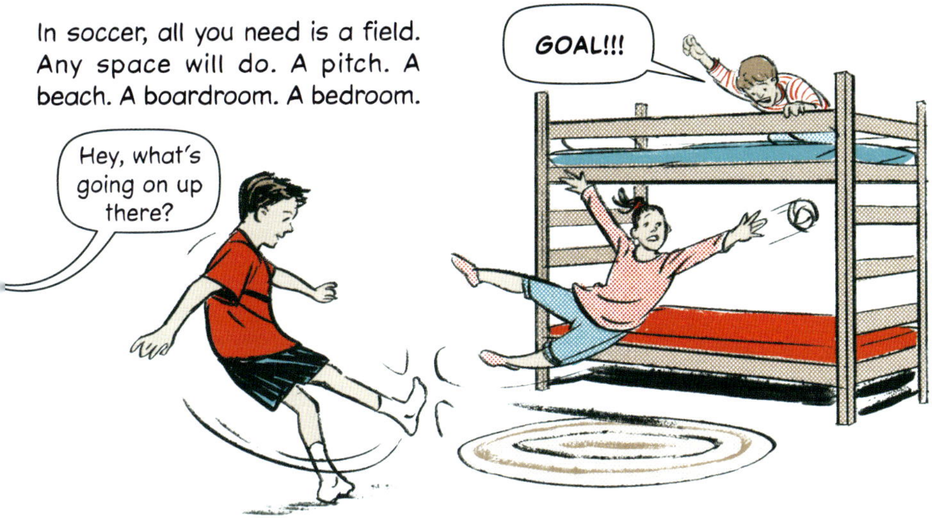
GOAL!!!
Hey, what's going on up there?

And you don't need a wordy rule book, like in baseball...

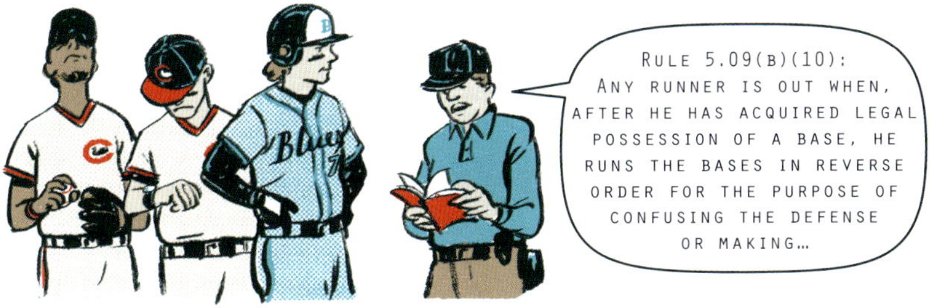
RULE 5.09(B)(10): ANY RUNNER IS OUT WHEN, AFTER HE HAS ACQUIRED LEGAL POSSESSION OF A BASE, HE RUNS THE BASES IN REVERSE ORDER FOR THE PURPOSE OF CONFUSING THE DEFENSE OR MAKING...

Soccer speaks a common language understood by all. A language that transcends borders, barriers, and cultures.

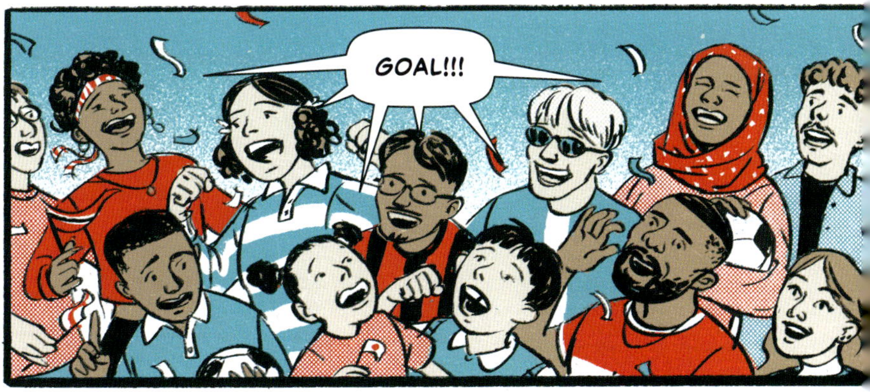
GOAL!!!

And because the sport was so popular during the Great Depression, one man had the idea to create an international tournament to showcase the world's favorite game. He was a soccer visionary named Jules Rimet, the president of the French Football Federation and of FIFA (Fédération Internationale de Football Association), the international committee for world soccer.

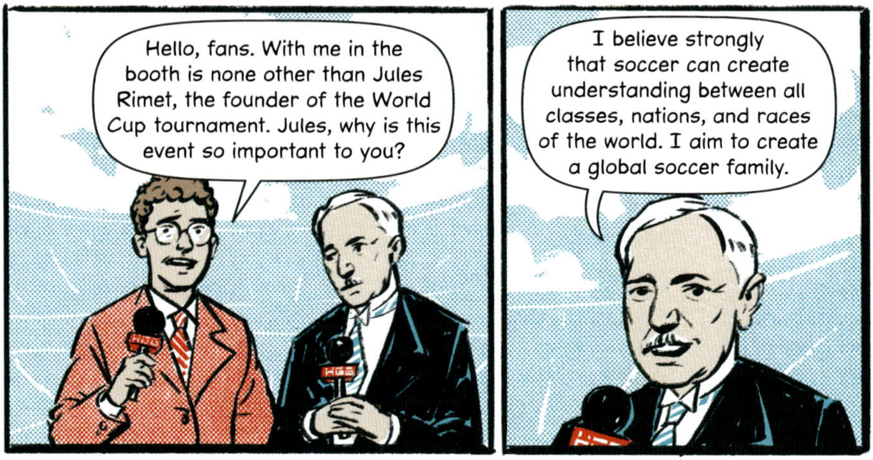
Hello, fans. With me in the booth is none other than Jules Rimet, the founder of the World Cup tournament. Jules, why is this event so important to you?
I believe strongly that soccer can create understanding between all classes, nations, and races of the world. I aim to create a global soccer family.

The event would be open to all nations that were members of FIFA. Teams were free to field professional players, not just amateurs, as was the case in the Olympics. Every four years, the entire globe could bond over the drama on the pitch and the feeling of national pride that the players and teams brought to their countries.

But what nation would have the honor of being the tournament's first host?

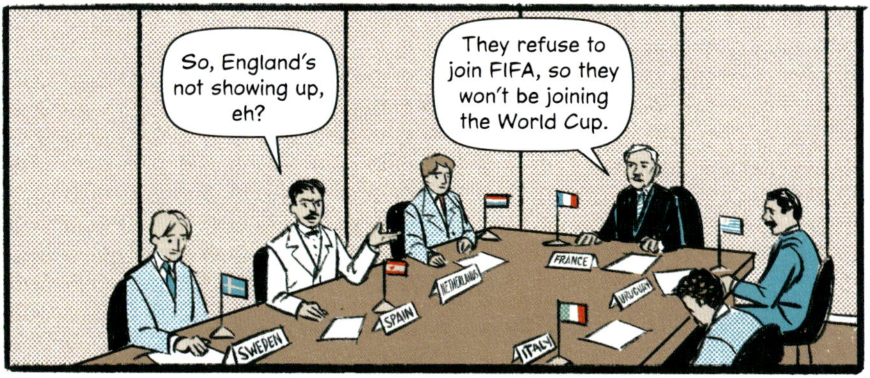
So, England's not showing up, eh?
They refuse to join FIFA, so they won't be joining the World Cup.
SWEDEN
SPAIN
NETHERLANDS
FRANCE
URUGUAY
ITALY

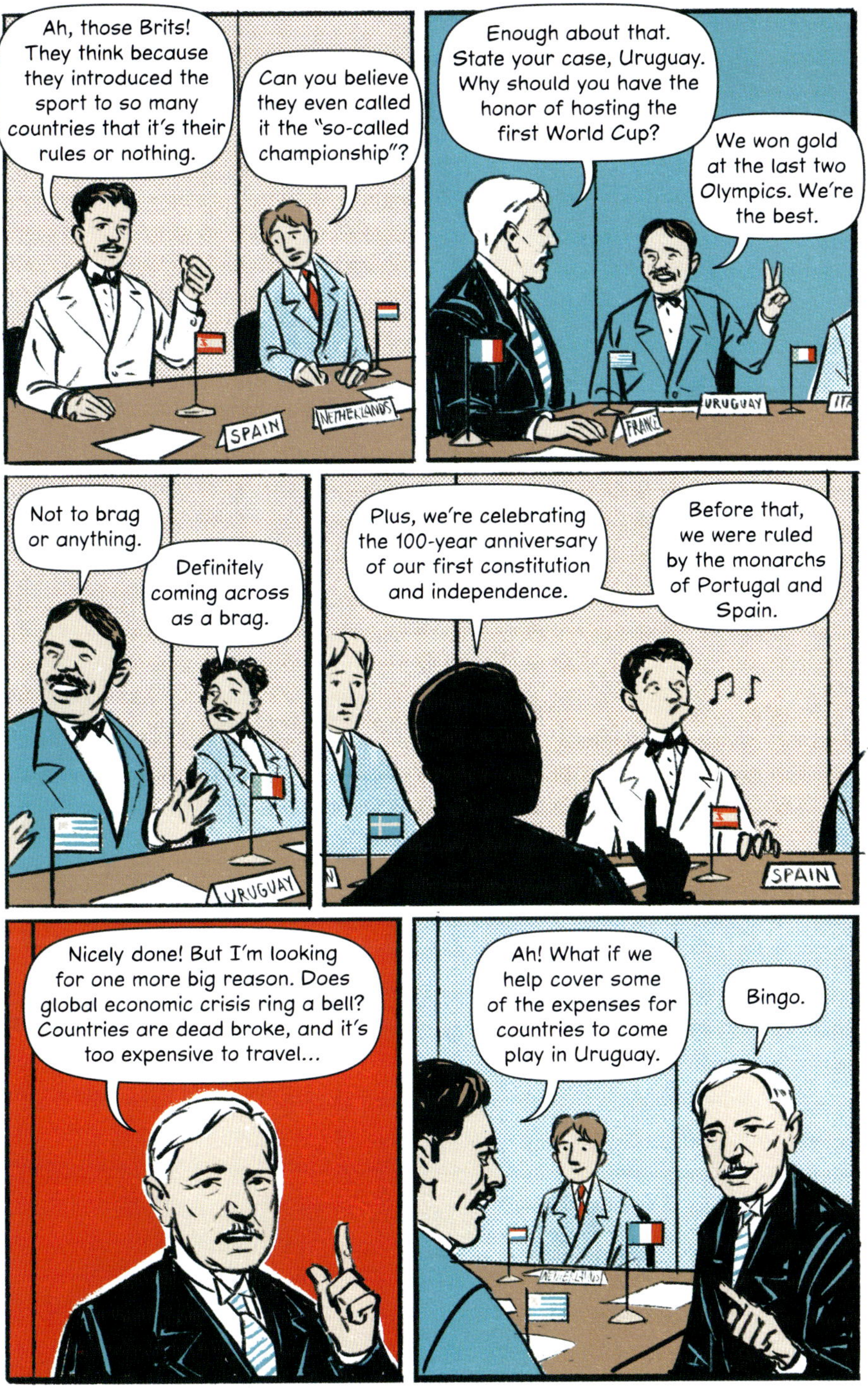

Ah, those Brits! They think because they introduced the sport to so many countries that it's their rules or nothing.
Can you believe they even called it the "so-called championship"?
SPAIN
NETHERLANDS
Enough about that. State your case, Uruguay. Why should you have the honor of hosting the first World Cup?
We won gold at the last two Olympics. We're the best.
FRANCE
URUGUAY
Not to brag or anything.
Definitely coming across as a brag.
URUGUAY
Plus, we're celebrating the 100-year anniversary of our first constitution and independence.
Before that, we were ruled by the monarchs of Portugal and Spain.
SPAIN
Nicely done! But I'm looking for one more big reason. Does global economic crisis ring a bell? Countries are dead broke, and it's too expensive to travel...
Ah! What if we help cover some of the expenses for countries to come play in Uruguay.
Bingo.

TIME-OUT FOR HISTORY

THE *CONTE VERDE*:
Cruising Toward the First World Cup

Set to take place during the depths of the Great Depression, the inaugural World Cup was rife with economic challenges that kept teams from participating, threatening to derail the tournament. Governments simply could not afford to send their squads on long, expensive journeys overseas, and most players did not have the luxury to take time away from work if they were lucky enough to have jobs at all. So, Uruguay and other heads of state helped bring in a handful of nations on an Italian steamship called the *Conte Verde*.

It was an interesting two-week journey.

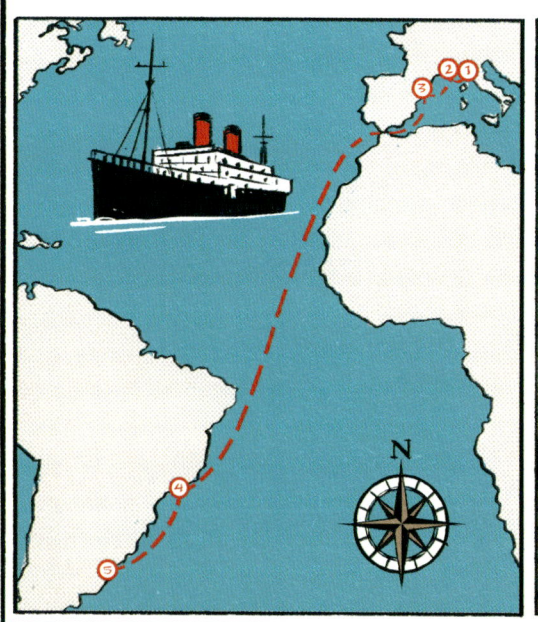

The Romanian team: Hops on the steamer first in Genoa, Italy.

"We all need to practice. Teams should use the top deck to get our training in."

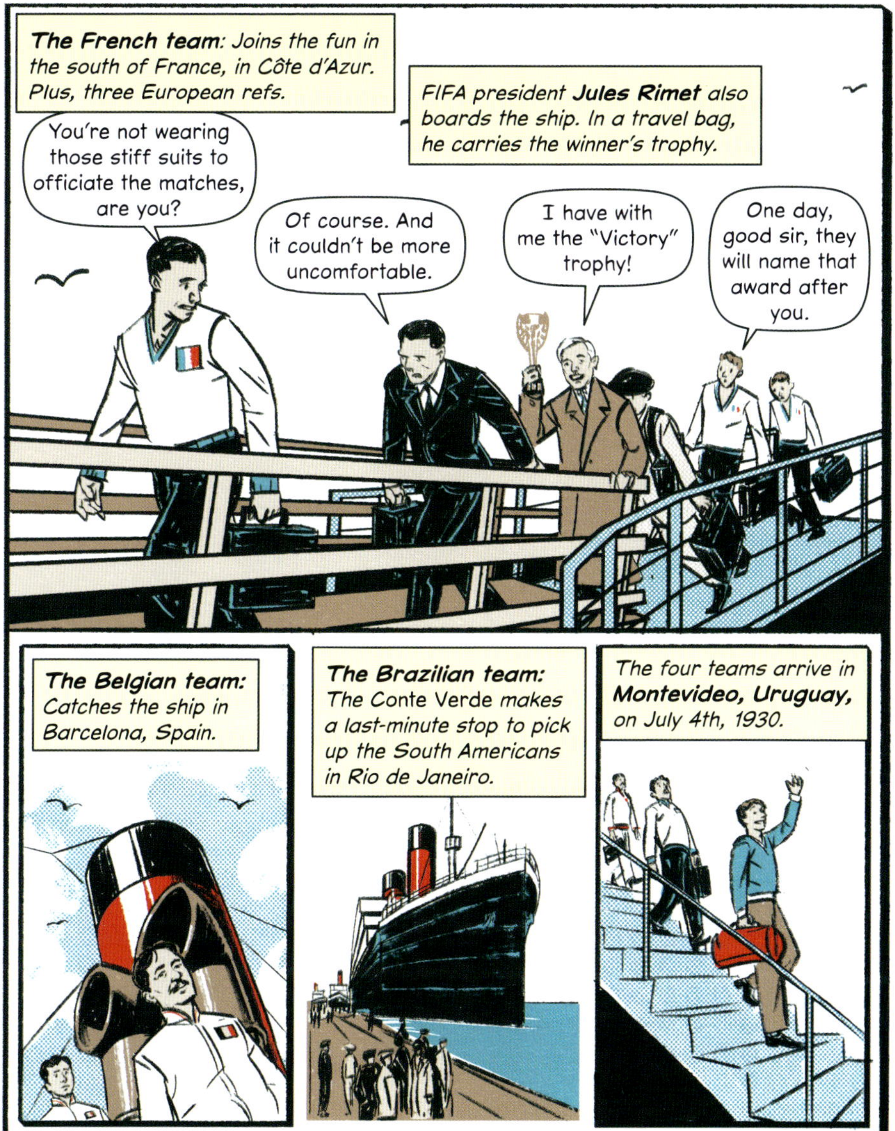
The French team: Joins the fun in the south of France, in Côte d'Azur. Plus, three European refs.
You're not wearing those stiff suits to officiate the matches, are you?
Of course. And it couldn't be more uncomfortable.
FIFA president Jules Rimet also boards the ship. In a travel bag, he carries the winner's trophy.
I have with me the "Victory" trophy!
One day, good sir, they will name that award after you.
The Belgian team: Catches the ship in Barcelona, Spain.
The Brazilian team: The Conte Verde makes a last-minute stop to pick up the South Americans in Rio de Janeiro.
The four teams arrive in Montevideo, Uruguay, on July 4th, 1930.

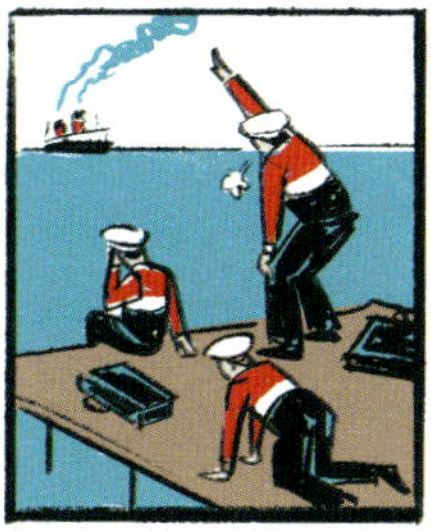

Egypt, however, was booked on a ship leaving from Marseille, France. Before they could board, they were caught in a disruptive storm in the Mediterranean. The team was a day late, and the ship sailed off without them. Sadly, Egypt was out of the World Cup without ever taking a shot.

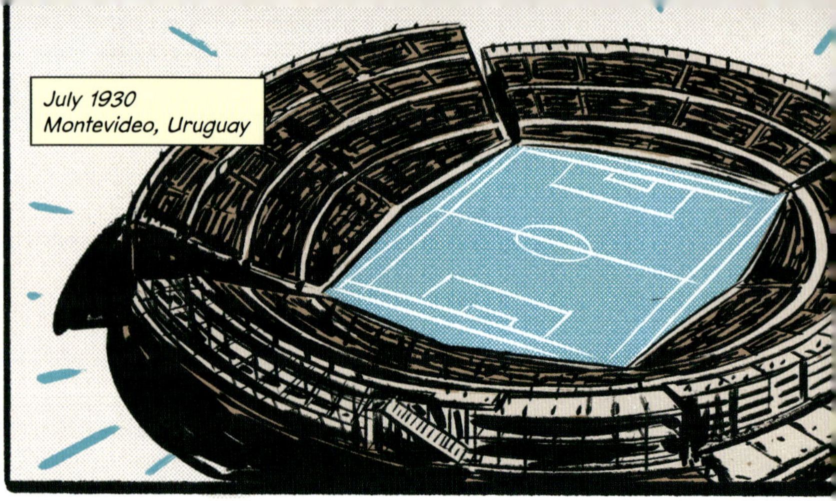
July 1930
Montevideo, Uruguay

In July 1930, the first-ever World Cup kicked off. The original tournament was in many ways like today's event. Teams were placed into group divisions and advanced to knockout rounds.

It came down to two semifinal matches. In match number one, Argentina easily defeated USA by a score of 6 to 1. However, during the rough and tumble match, a very bizarre injury occurred. Not to a player, but to a team doctor!

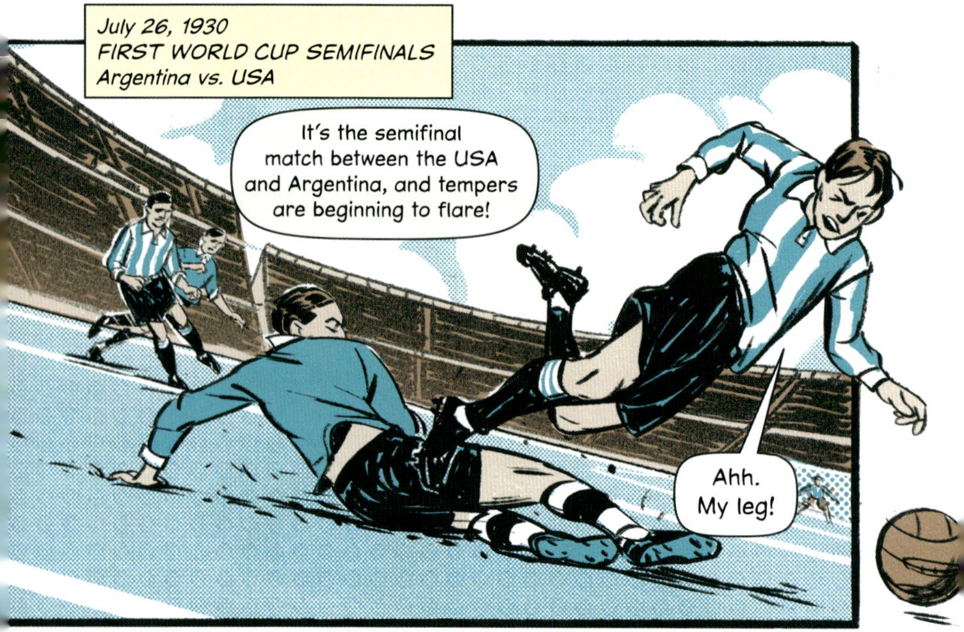
July 26, 1930
FIRST WORLD CUP SEMIFINALS
Argentina vs. USA
It's the semifinal match between the USA and Argentina, and tempers are beginning to flare!
Ahh. My leg!

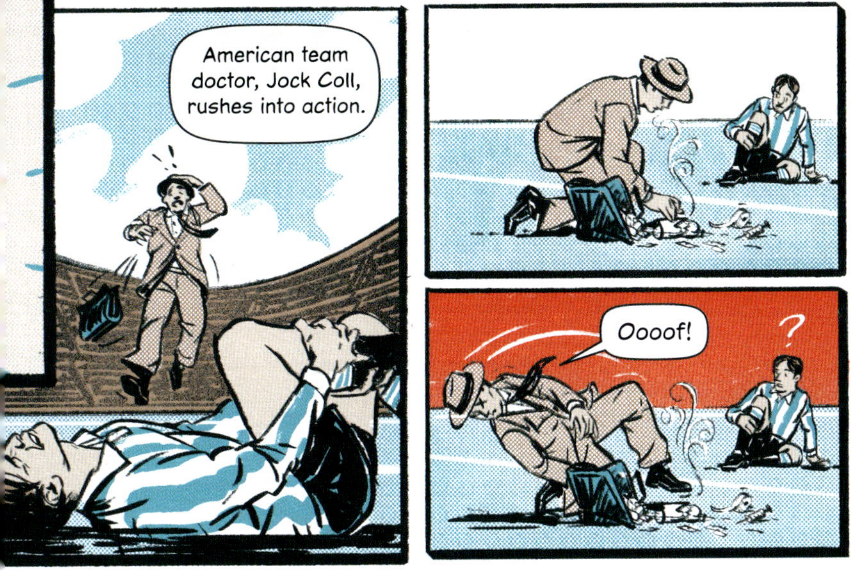
American team doctor, Jock Coll, rushes into action.
Oooof!
?

Reports stated that the doctor accidentally dropped his medical bag while running to treat the player. His bottle of chloroform smashed open and knocked him out cold. Before modern anesthesia, chloroform was commonly used for pain relief, and in larger doses, it would put patients to sleep.

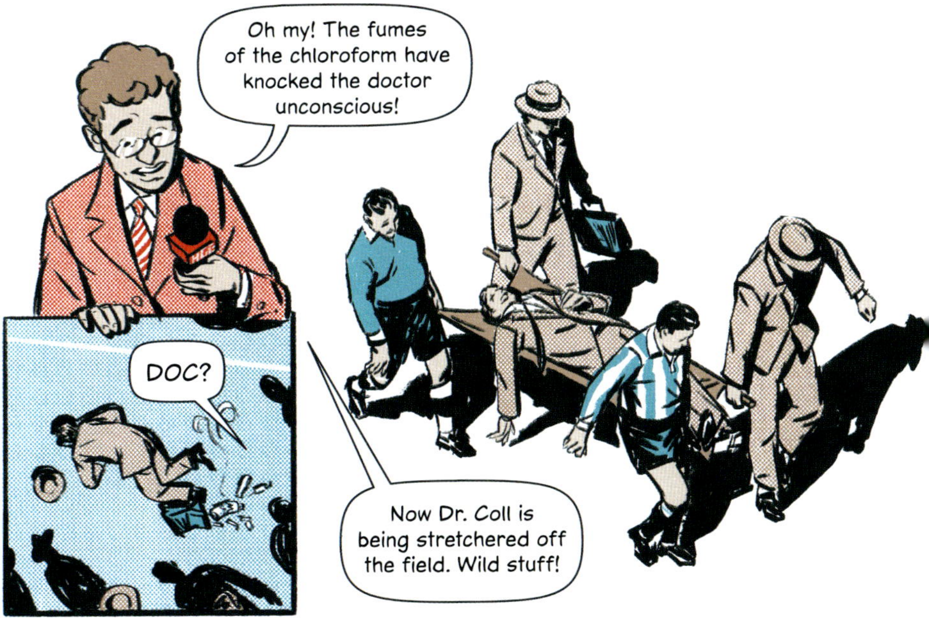
Oh my! The fumes of the chloroform have knocked the doctor unconscious!
DOC?
Now Dr. Coll is being stretchered off the field. Wild stuff!

In the second semifinal match, Uruguay defeated Yugoslavia. The very first World Cup Final matchup was set: Uruguay would be facing off against Argentina, one of the finalists in the 2022 World Cup and the homeland of Lionel Messi.

When the people in Argentina learned that their squad had reached the first World Cup Final, tens of thousands of fans flooded into Uruguay. An armada of ships crossed the River Plate, the body of water that borders Argentina and Uruguay. They chanted patriotic fight songs along the way.

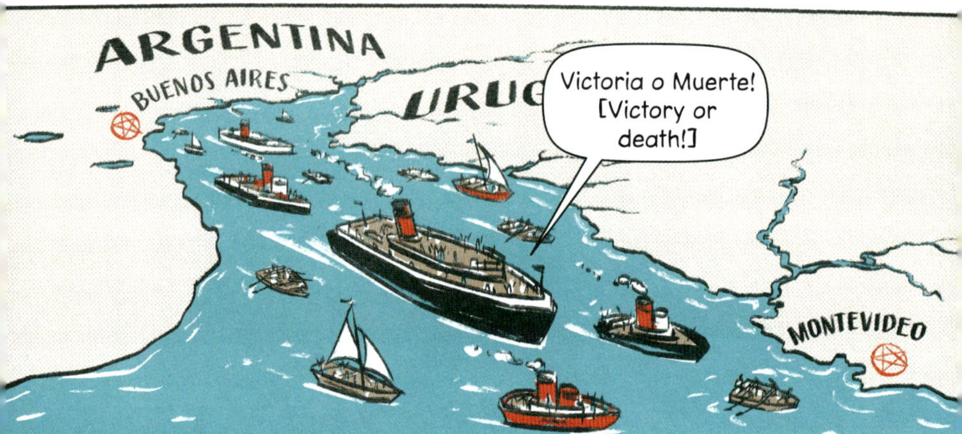

ARGENTINA
BUENOS AIRES
Victoria o Muerte! [Victory or death!]
MONTEVIDEO

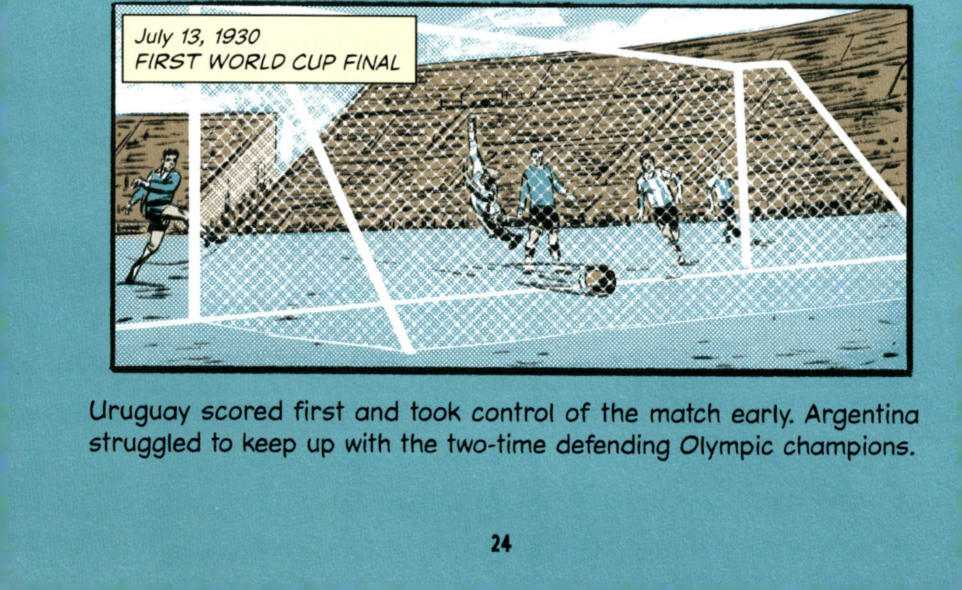

July 13, 1930
FIRST WORLD CUP FINAL

Uruguay scored first and took control of the match early. Argentina struggled to keep up with the two-time defending Olympic champions.

Uruguay's fourth and final goal was scored by the sensational Héctor "El Manco" Castro, a one-armed star who also struck Uruguay's first goal of the tournament! Castro had lost his arm in a chainsaw accident when he was just thirteen.

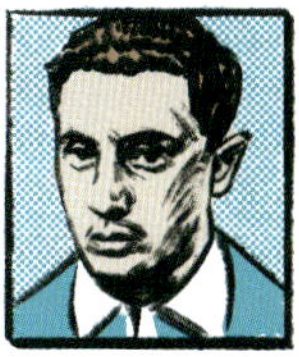

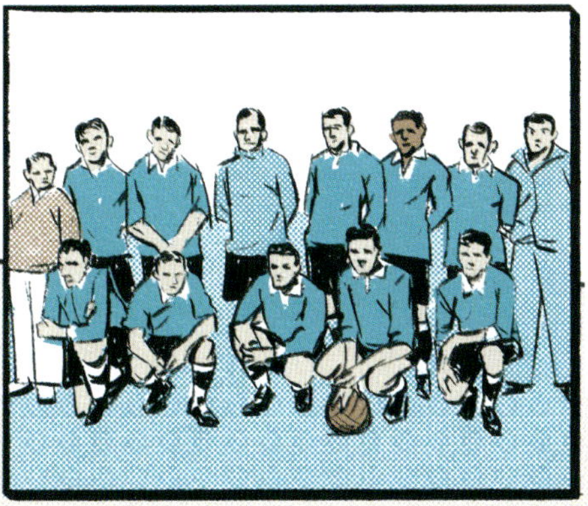

Uruguay defeated Argentina 4 to 2, and the hosts of the first World Cup were the champions. There were tremendous celebrations in Uruguay, and a public holiday was announced. The Argentines didn't take the loss quite as well, and riots ensued.

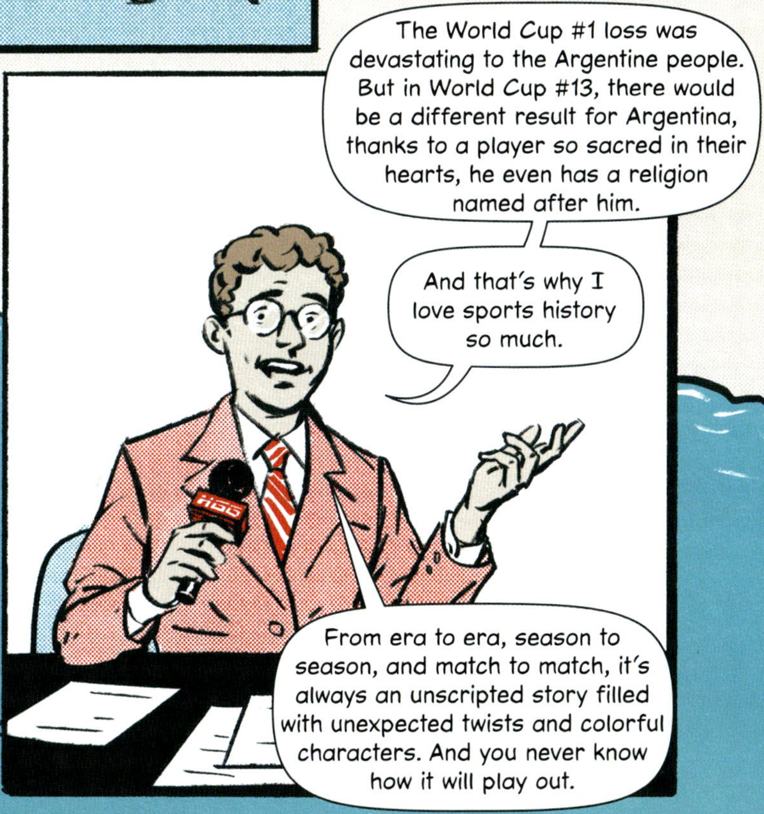
The World Cup #1 loss was devastating to the Argentine people. But in World Cup #13, there would be a different result for Argentina, thanks to a player so sacred in their hearts, he even has a religion named after him.
And that's why I love sports history so much.
From era to era, season to season, and match to match, it's always an unscripted story filled with unexpected twists and colorful characters. And you never know how it will play out.

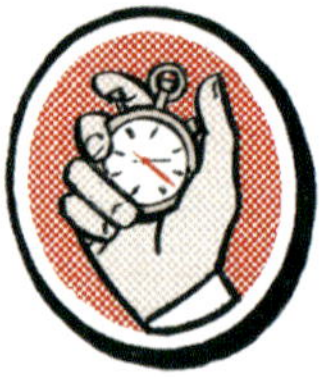

TIME-OUT FOR HISTORY

KICKING IT ON THE WESTERN FRONT

World War I brought a horrifying new level of carnage and destruction to warfare. Machine guns. Tanks. Grenades. Poison gas. Aircraft bombings. Barbed wire. And a new way of fighting, called trench warfare.

On Christmas morning 1914, English and German soldiers were trading attacks from their fortified trenches.

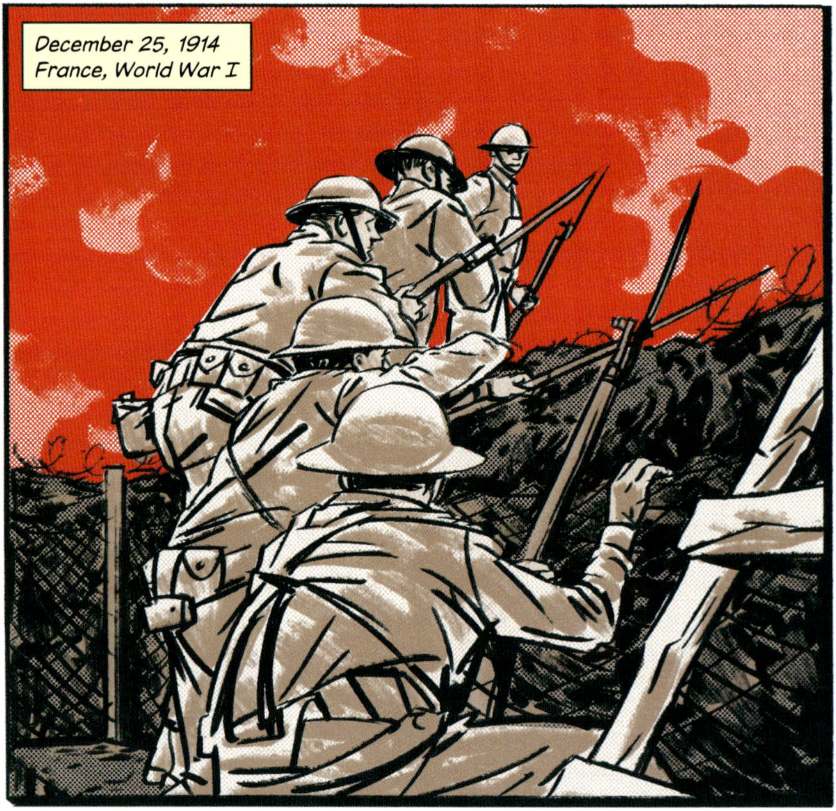
December 25, 1914
France, World War I

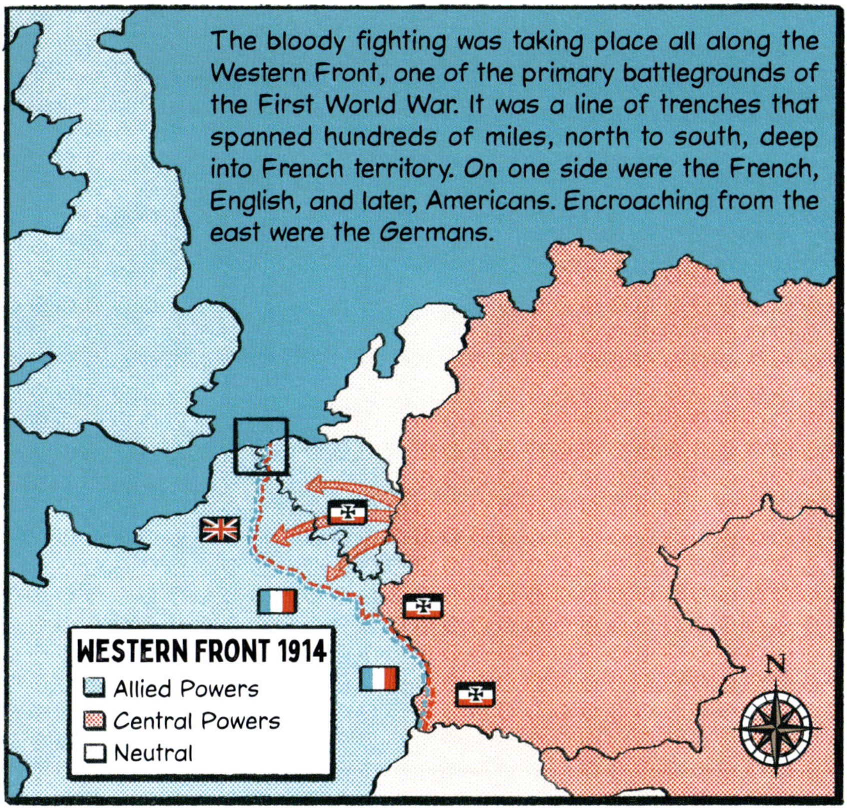
The bloody fighting was taking place all along the Western Front, one of the primary battlegrounds of the First World War. It was a line of trenches that spanned hundreds of miles, north to south, deep into French territory. On one side were the French, English, and later, Americans. Encroaching from the east were the *Germans*.
WESTERN FRONT 1914
Allied Powers
Central Powers
Neutral
N

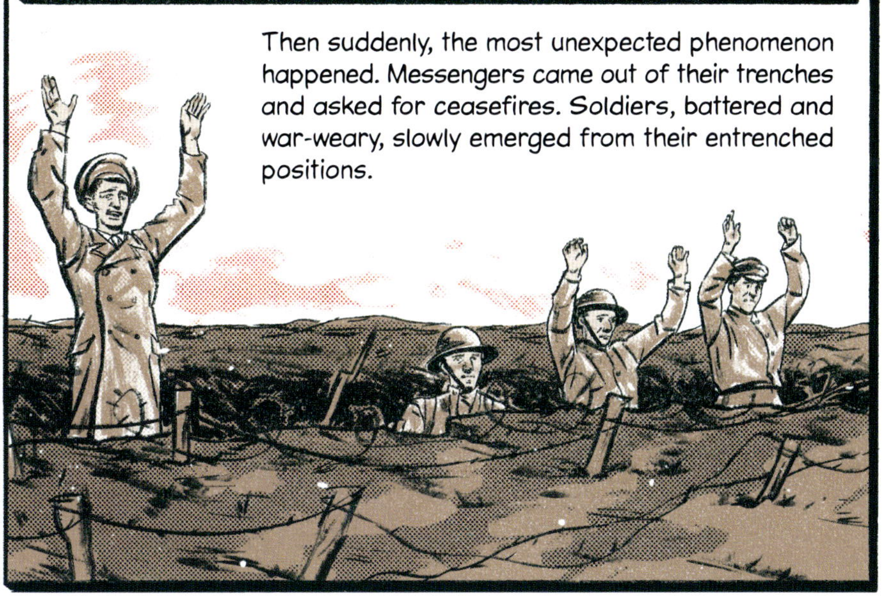
Then suddenly, the most unexpected phenomenon happened. Messengers came out of their trenches and asked for ceasefires. Soldiers, battered and war-weary, slowly emerged from their entrenched positions.

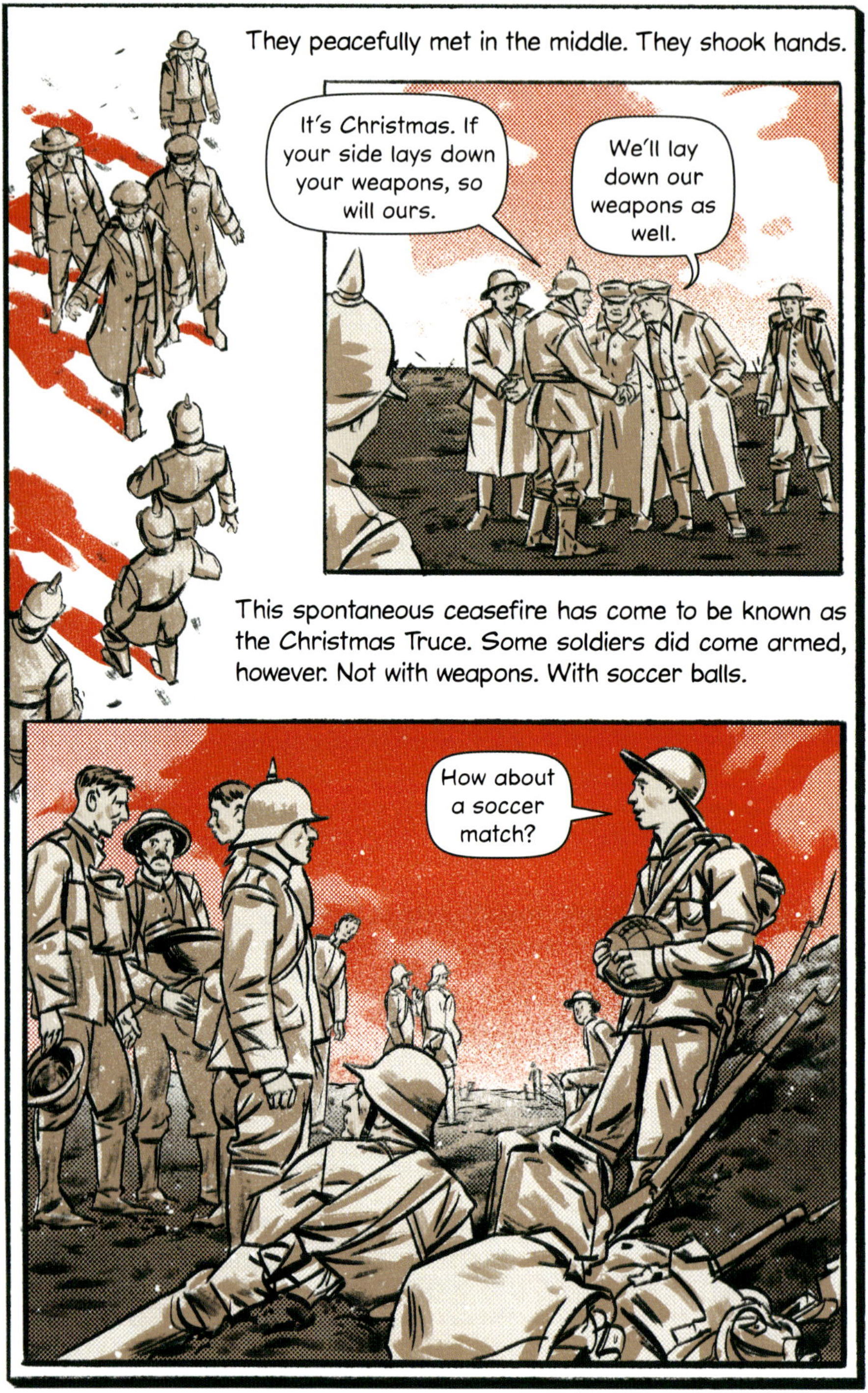
They peacefully met in the middle. They shook hands.
It's Christmas. If your side lays down your weapons, so will ours.
We'll lay down our weapons as well.
This spontaneous ceasefire has come to be known as the Christmas Truce. Some soldiers did come armed, however. Not with weapons. With soccer balls.
How about a soccer match?

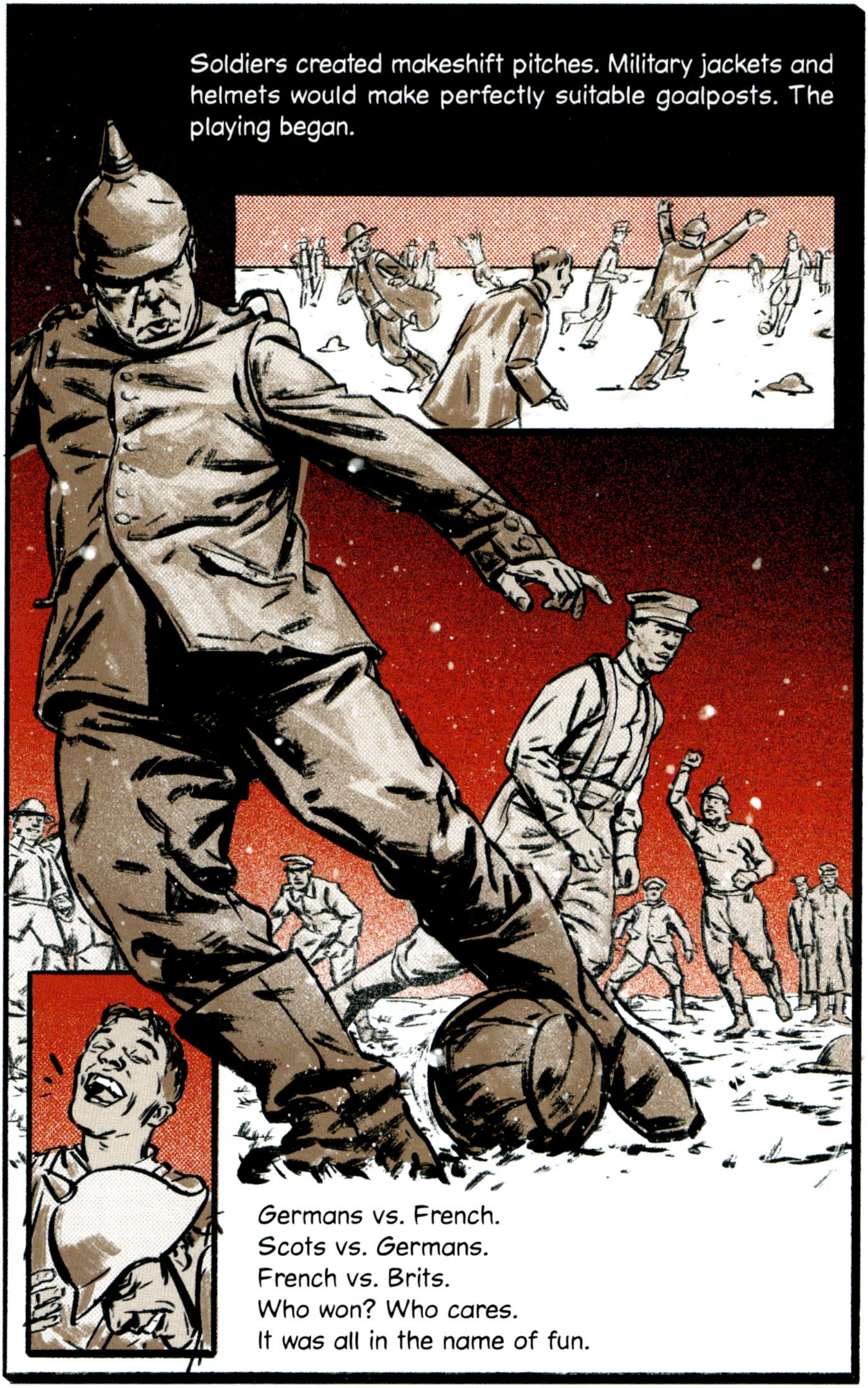
Soldiers created makeshift pitches. Military jackets and helmets would make perfectly suitable goalposts. The playing began.
Germans vs. French.
Scots vs. Germans.
French vs. Brits.
Who won? Who cares.
It was all in the name of fun.

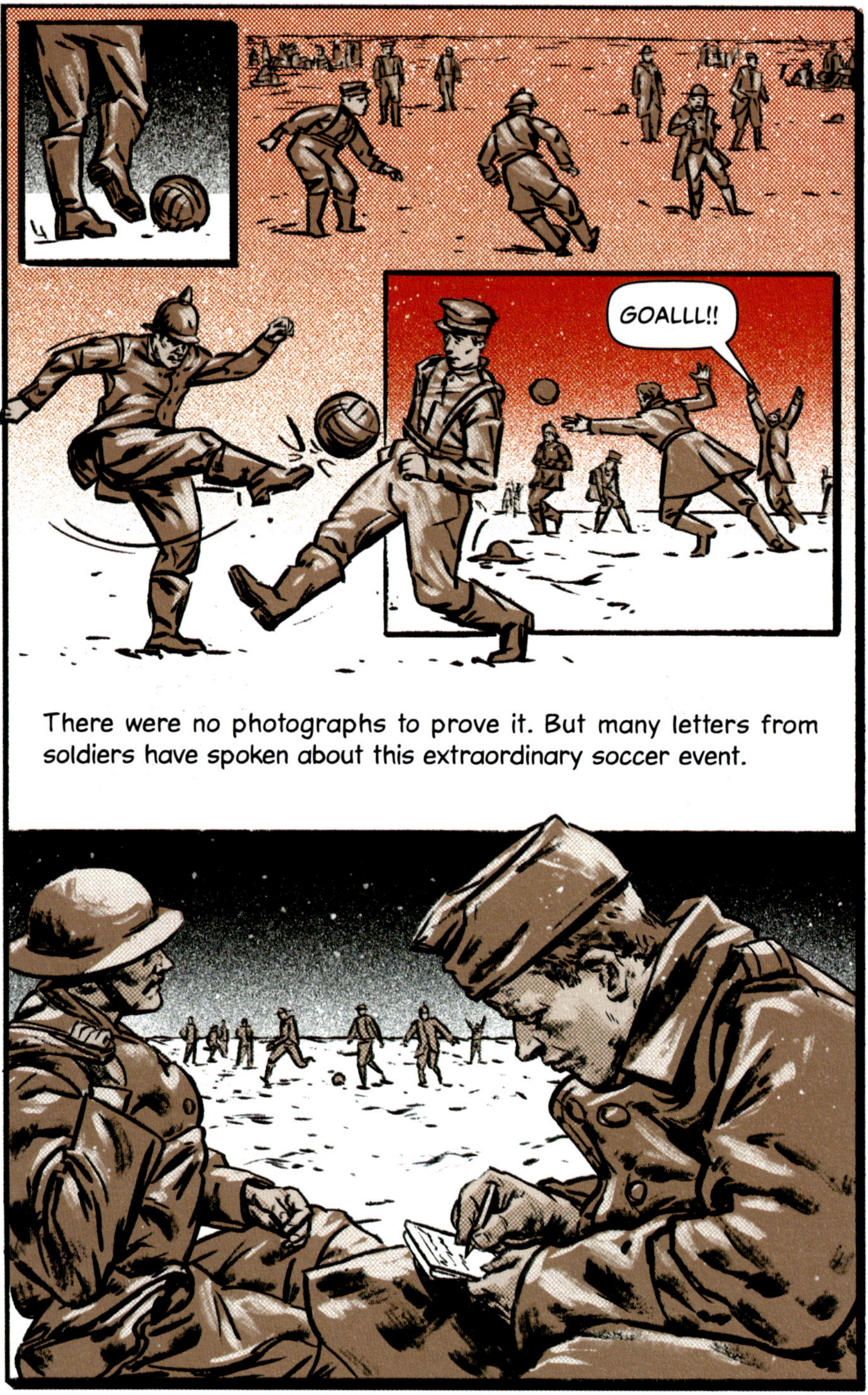
GOALLL!!
There were no photographs to prove it. But many letters from soldiers have spoken about this extraordinary soccer event.

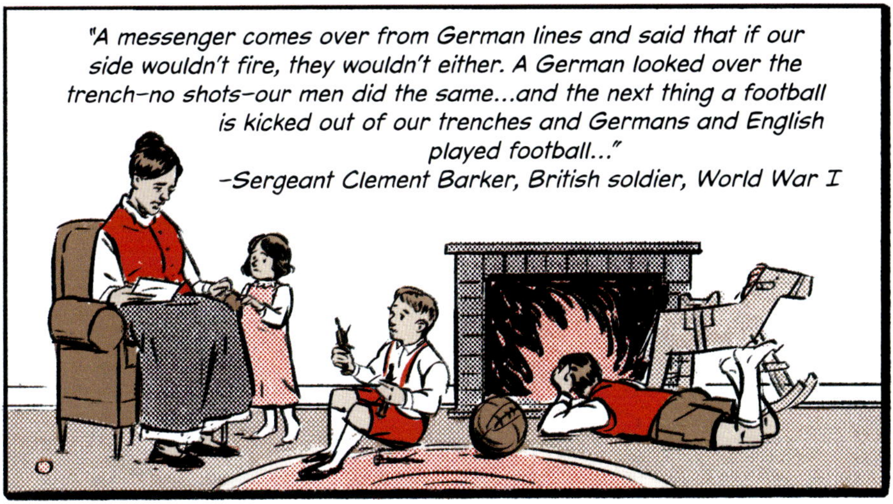
"A messenger comes over from German lines and said that if our side wouldn't fire, they wouldn't either. A German looked over the trench—no shots—our men did the same...and the next thing a football is kicked out of our trenches and Germans and English played football..."
—Sergeant Clement Barker, British soldier, World War I

TRIVIA GOALS

During the first World Cup finals between Uruguay and Argentina, which is true?

A) The nations each wanted to use their own ball. So, as a compromise, both balls were used, one per half.

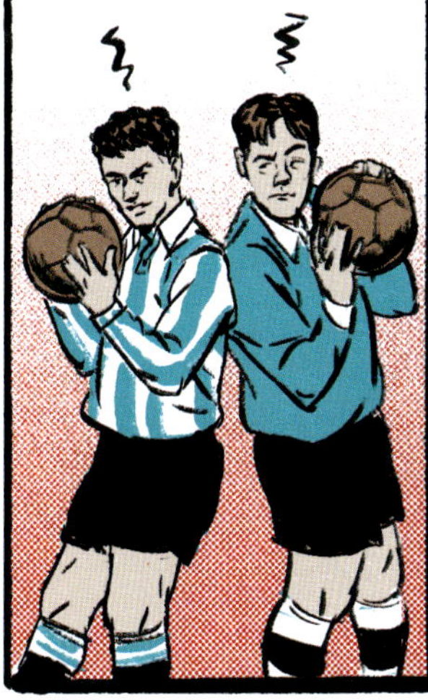

B) A family of cats ran onto the pitch and refused to leave. Finally, they were lured away by plates of a Uruguayan fish delicacy called bacalao.

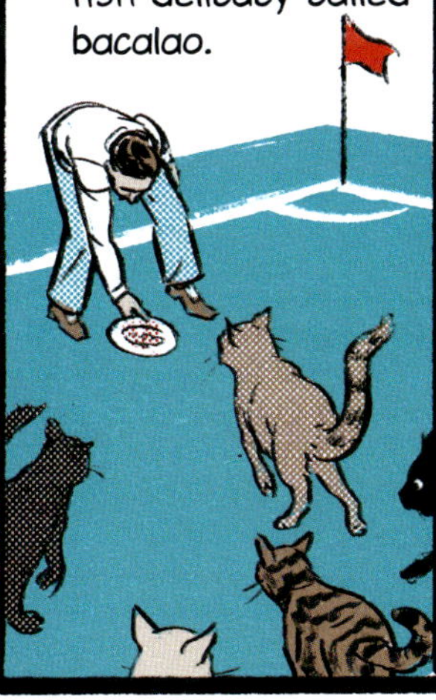

C) A bolt of lightning struck the goal post just a few hours before the match began.

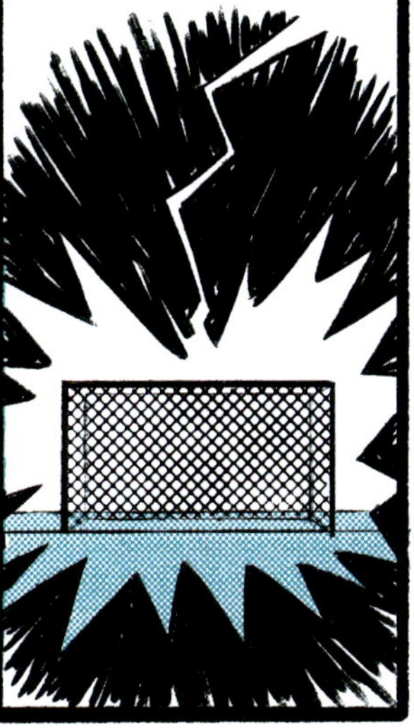

CHAPTER

2

THE FOOTBALLER "FROM THE GODS"

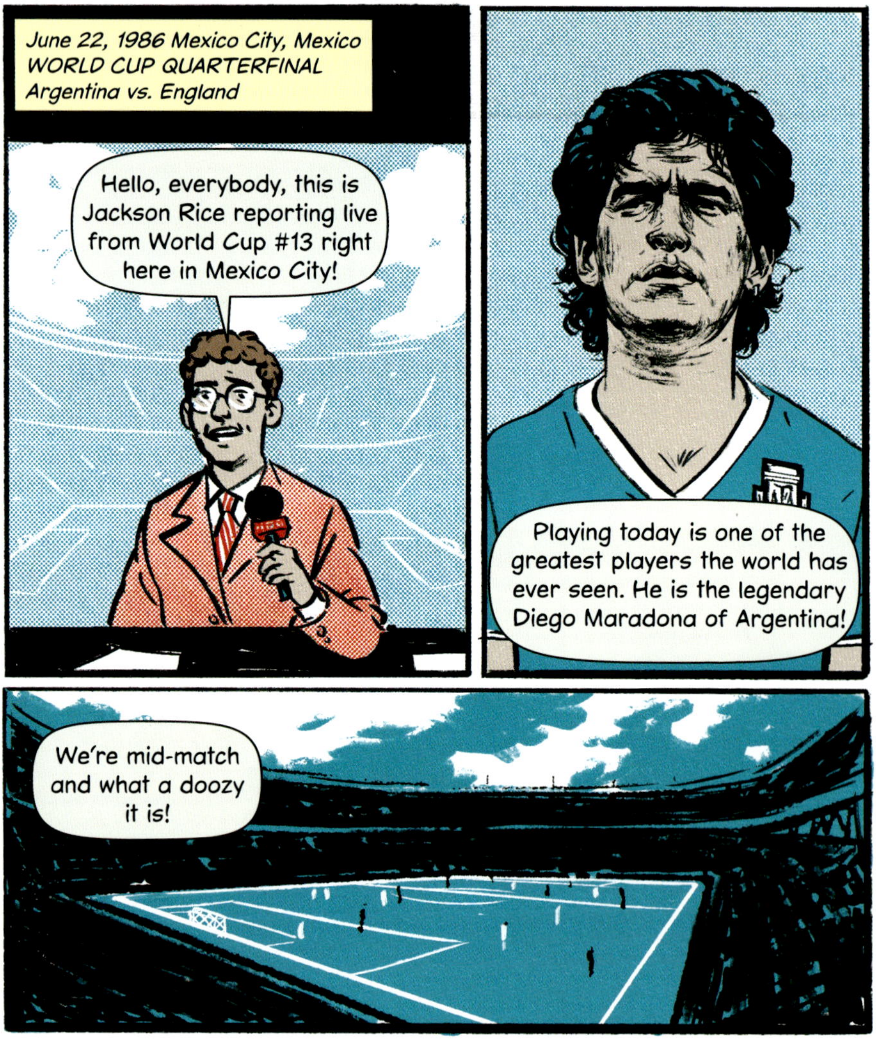
June 22, 1986 Mexico City, Mexico
WORLD CUP QUARTERFINAL
Argentina vs. England
Hello, everybody, this is Jackson Rice reporting live from World Cup #13 right here in Mexico City!
Playing today is one of the greatest players the world has ever seen. He is the legendary Diego Maradona of Argentina!
We're mid-match and what a doozy it is!

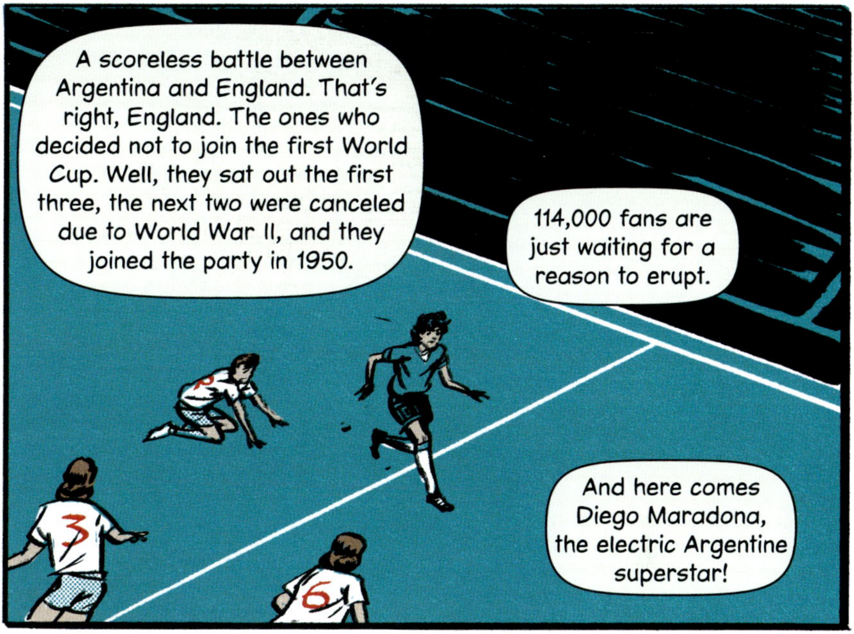
A scoreless battle between Argentina and England. That's right, England. The ones who decided not to join the first World Cup. Well, they sat out the first three, the next two were canceled due to World War II, and they joined the party in 1950.
114,000 fans are just waiting for a reason to erupt.
And here comes Diego Maradona, the electric Argentine superstar!

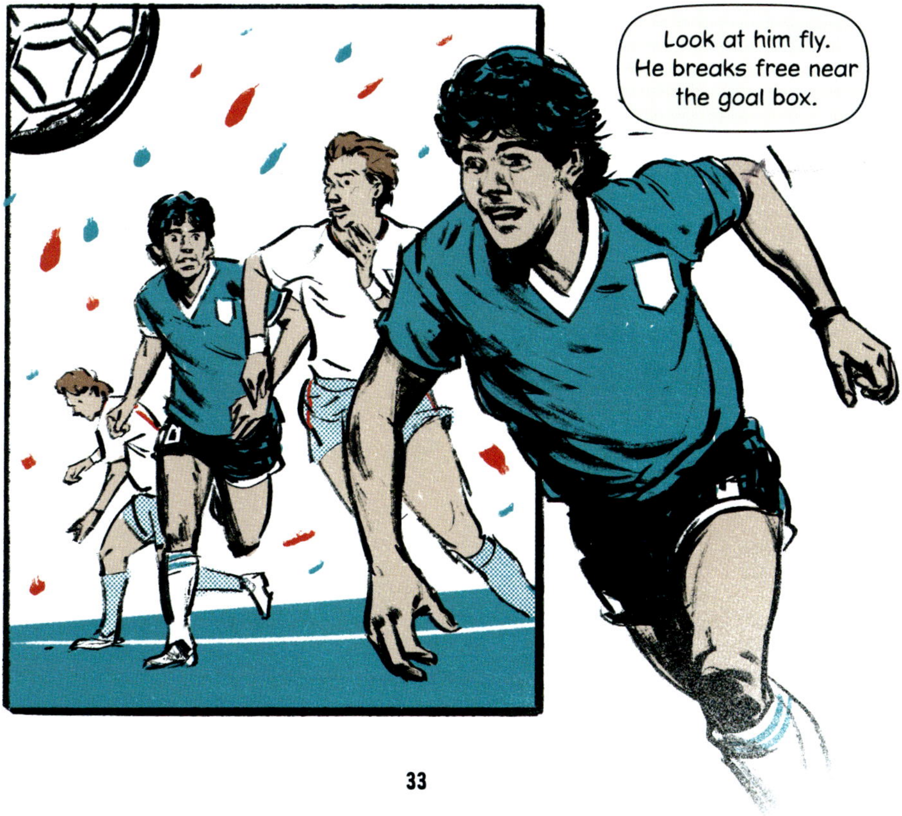
Look at him fly. He breaks free near the goal box.

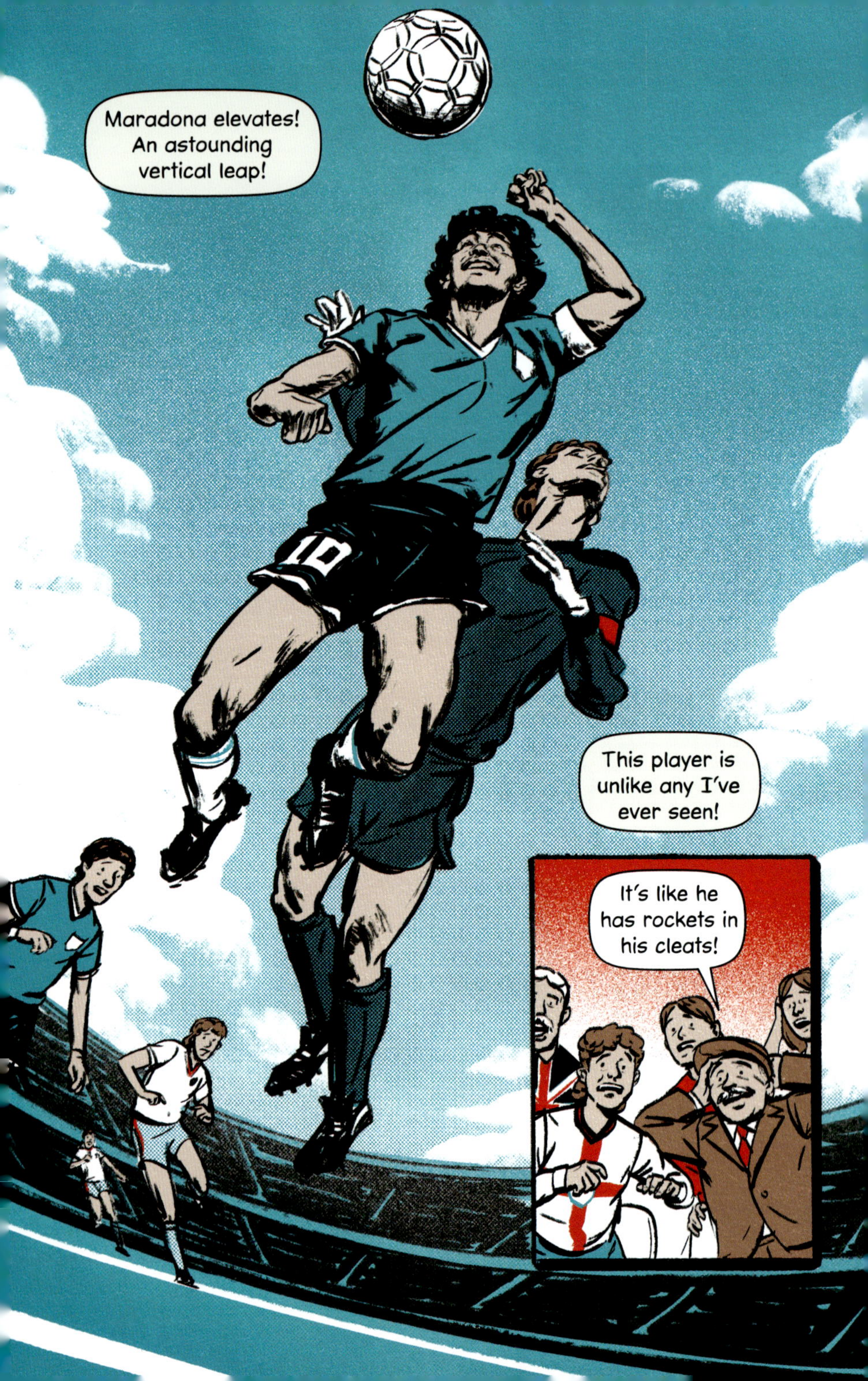
Maradona elevates! An astounding vertical leap!
This player is unlike any I've ever seen!
It's like he has rockets in his cleats!

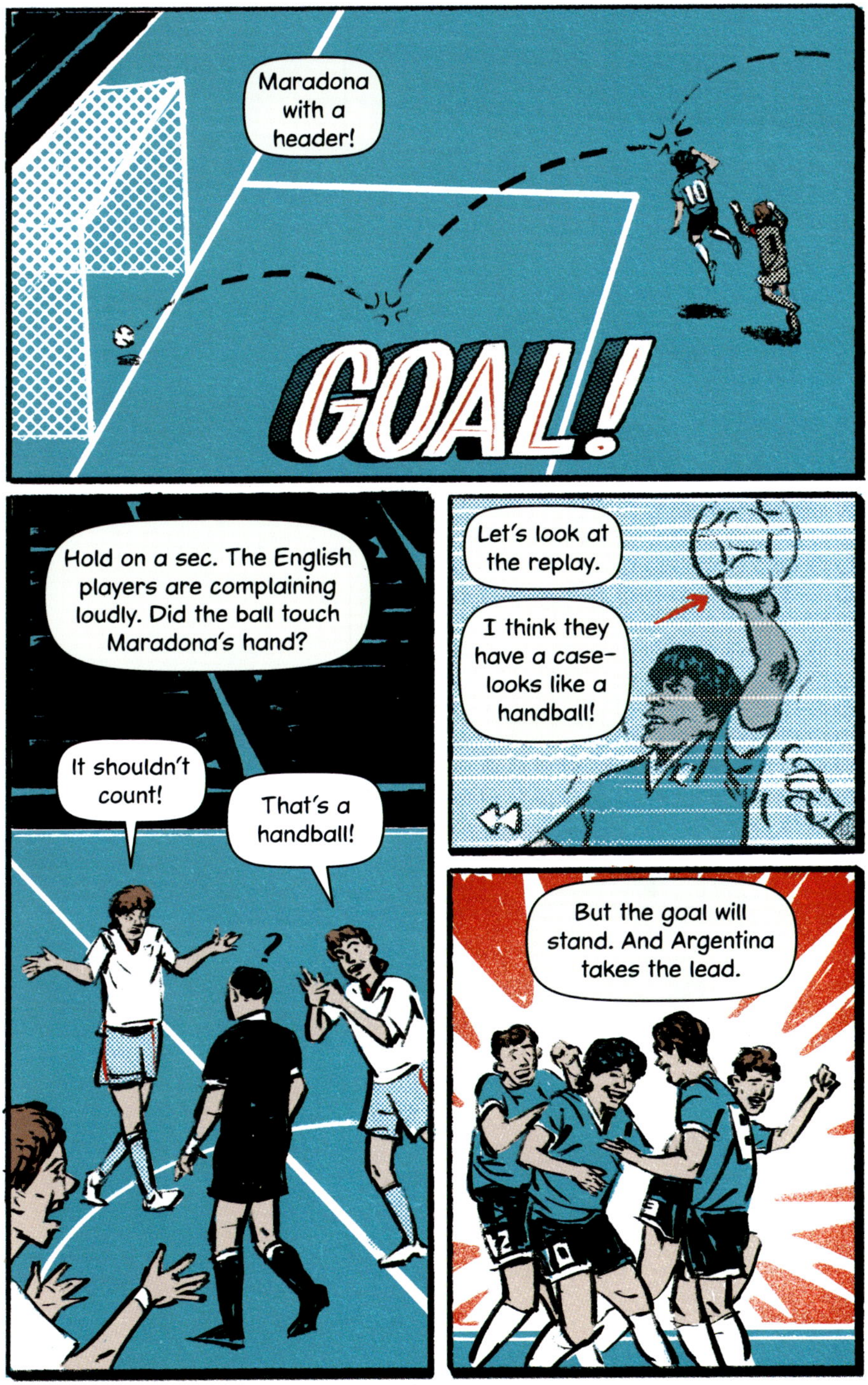
Maradona with a header!
GOAL!
Hold on a sec. The English players are complaining loudly. Did the ball touch Maradona's hand?
It shouldn't count!
That's a handball!
Let's look at the replay.
I think they have a case–looks like a handball!
But the goal will stand. And Argentina takes the lead.

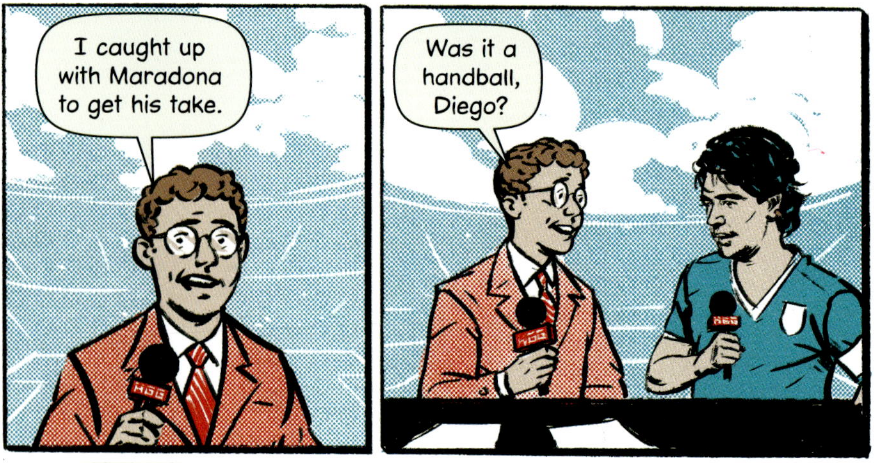
I caught up with Maradona to get his take.
Was it a handball, Diego?

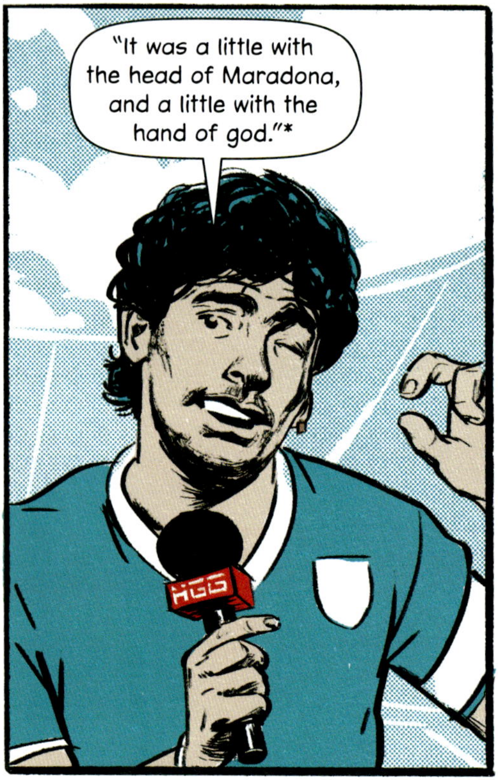
"It was a little with the head of Maradona, and a little with the hand of god."*

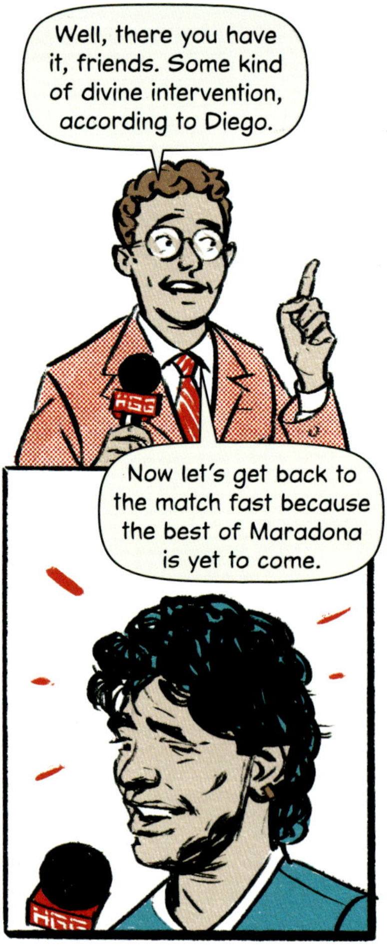
Well, there you have it, friends. Some kind of divine intervention, according to Diego.
Now let's get back to the match fast because the best of Maradona is yet to come.

*Note to readers: Dialogue in quotation marks are true quotes from historical figures.

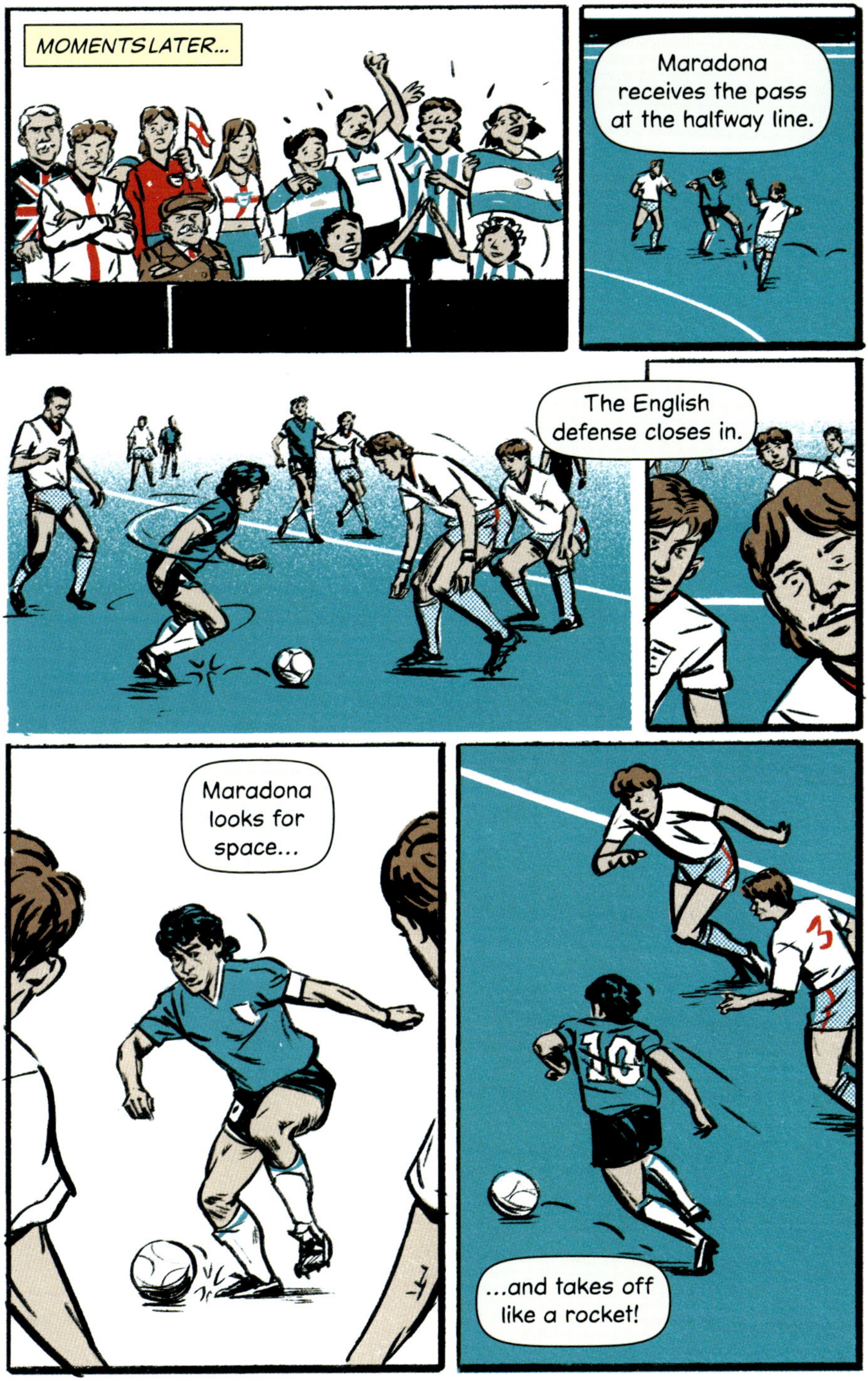
MOMENTS LATER...
Maradona receives the pass at the halfway line.
The English defense closes in.
Maradona looks for space...
...and takes off like a rocket!

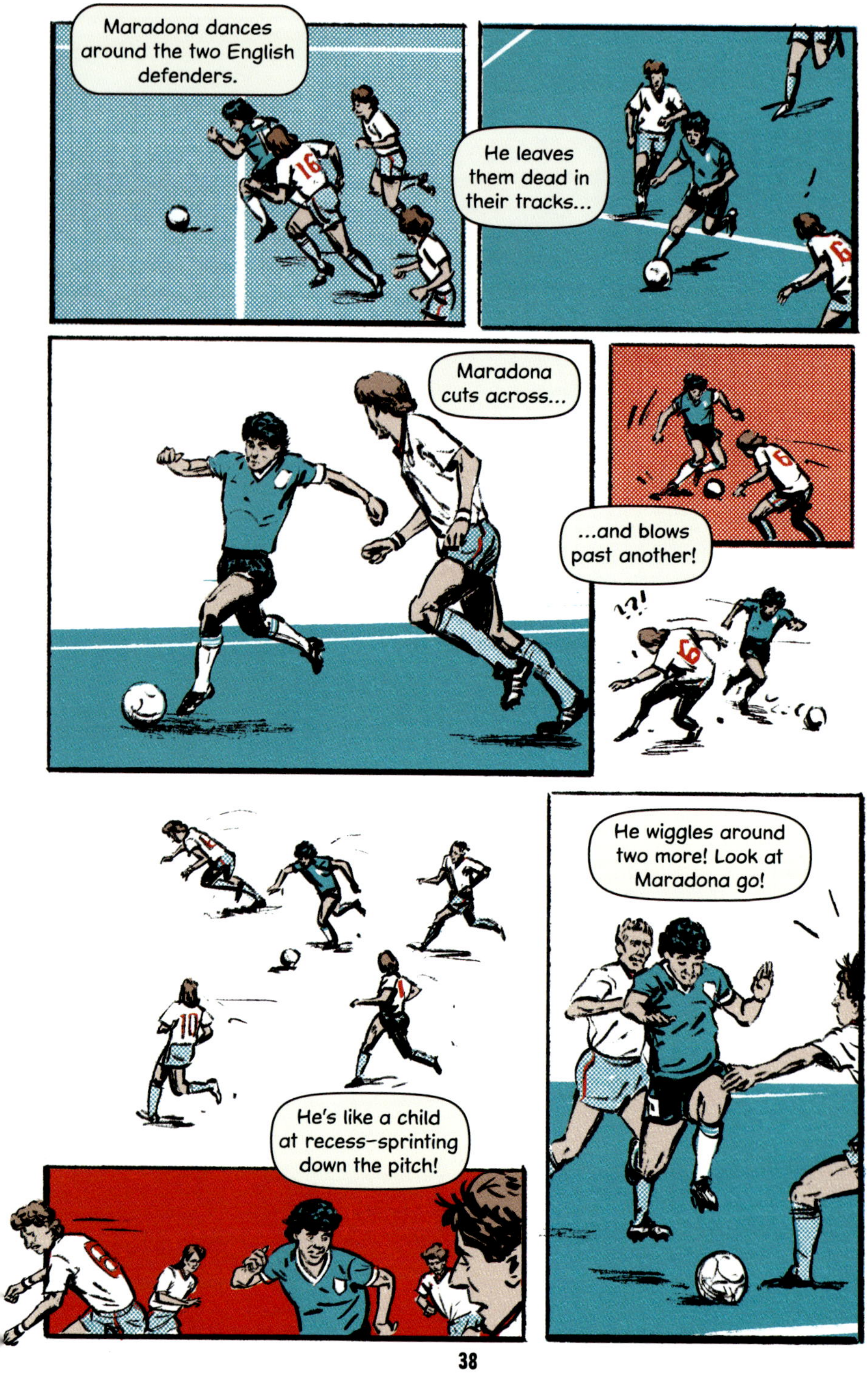
Maradona dances around the two English defenders.
He leaves them dead in their tracks...
Maradona cuts across...
...and blows past another!
??!
He wiggles around two more! Look at Maradona go!
He's like a child at recess–sprinting down the pitch!

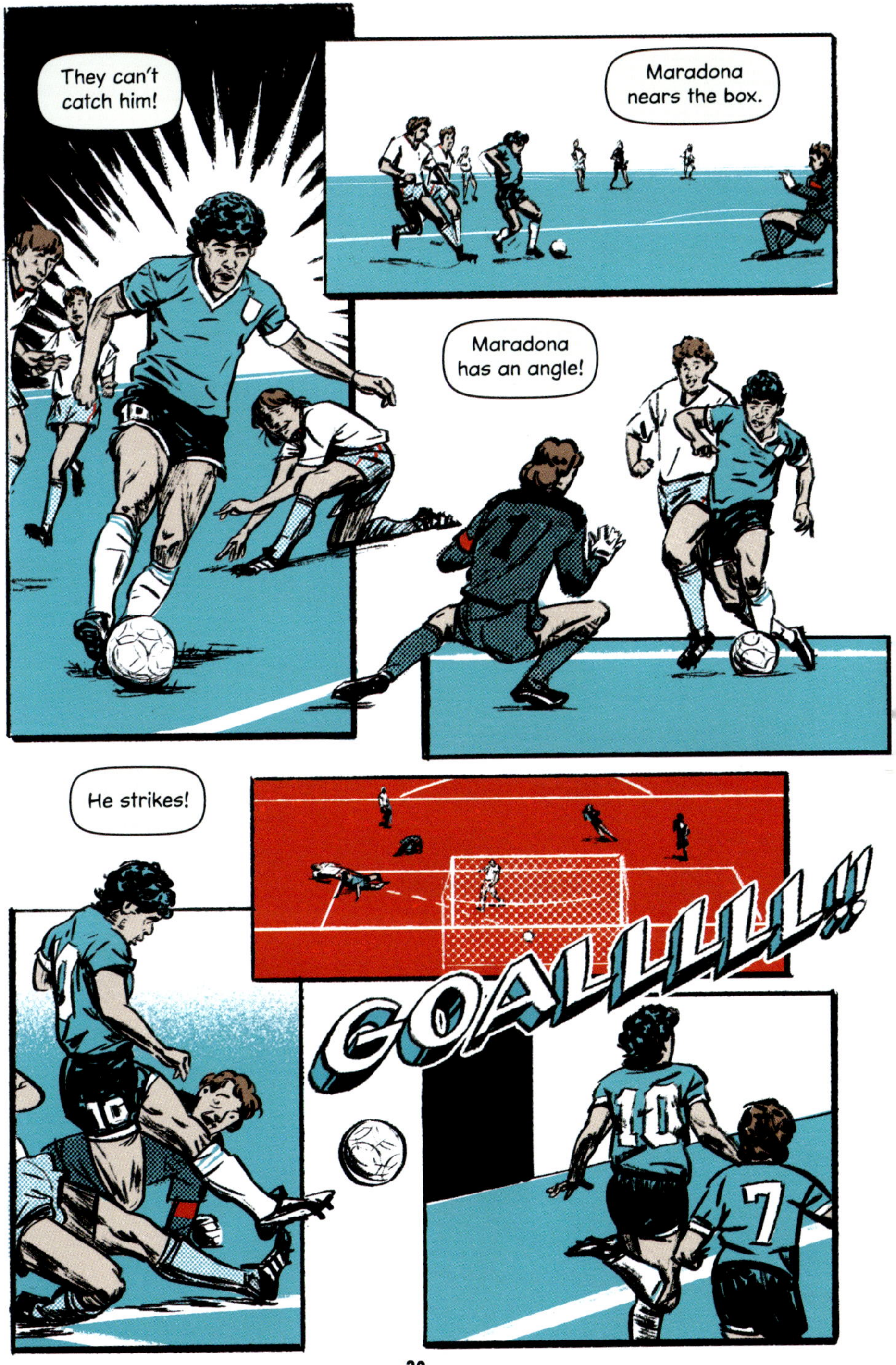

They can't catch him!
Maradona nears the box.
Maradona has an angle!
He strikes!
GOALLLLL!!

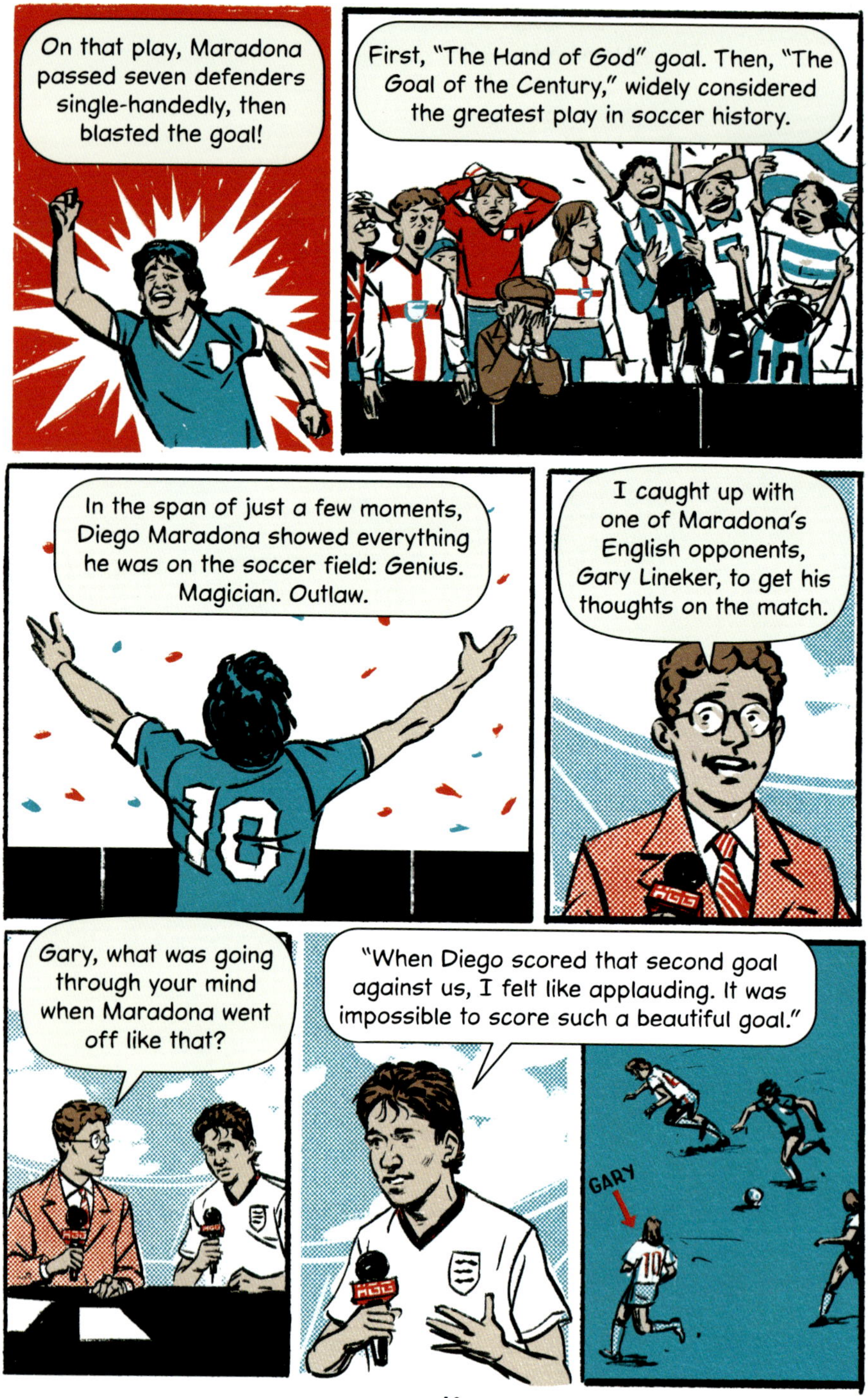

On that play, Maradona passed seven defenders single-handedly, then blasted the goal!
First, "The Hand of God" goal. Then, "The Goal of the Century," widely considered the greatest play in soccer history.
In the span of just a few moments, Diego Maradona showed everything he was on the soccer field: Genius. Magician. Outlaw.
I caught up with one of Maradona's English opponents, Gary Lineker, to get his thoughts on the match.
Gary, what was going through your mind when Maradona went off like that?
"When Diego scored that second goal against us, I felt like applauding. It was impossible to score such a beautiful goal."
GARY

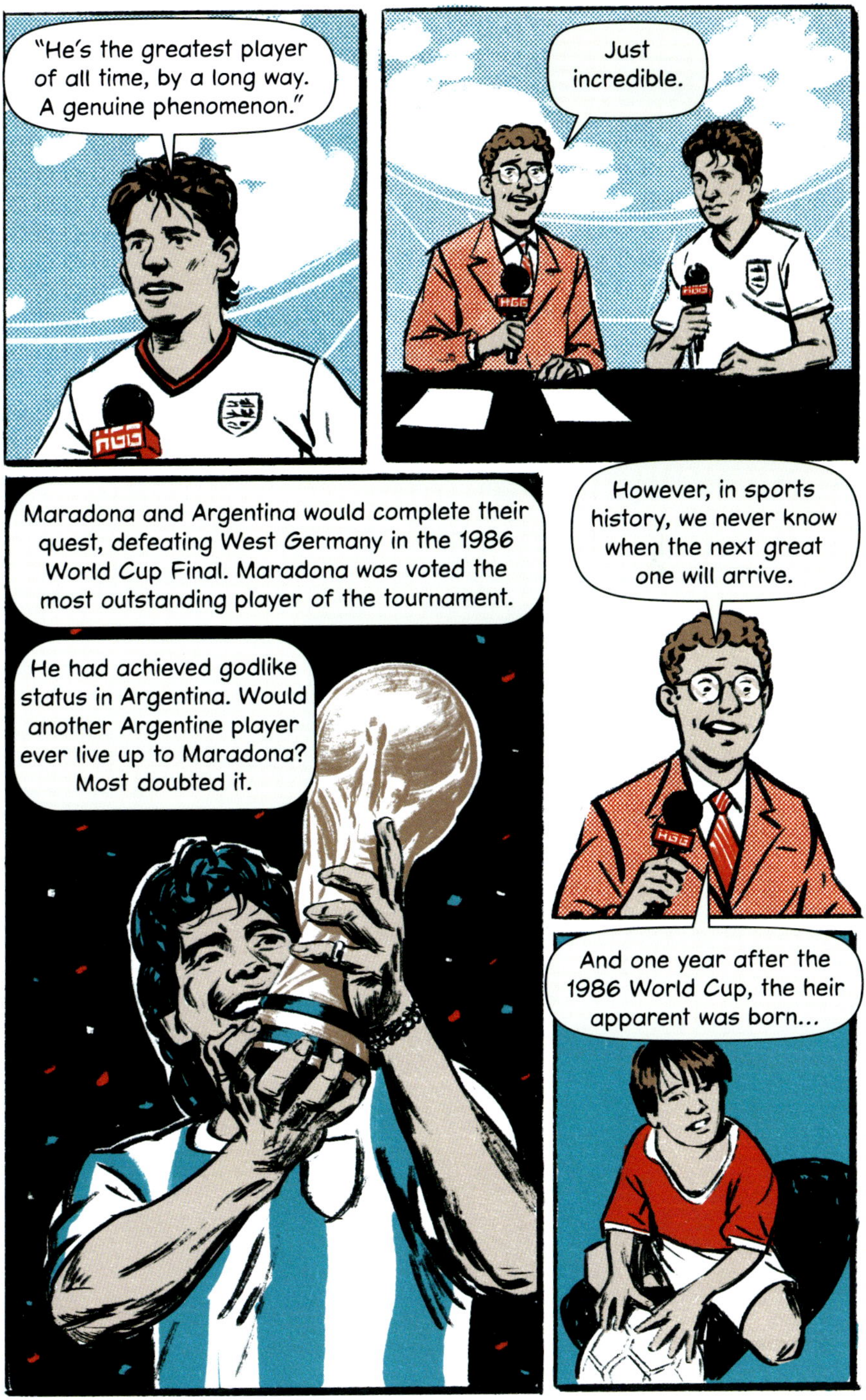
"He's the greatest player of all time, by a long way. A genuine phenomenon."
Just incredible.
HGG
Maradona and Argentina would complete their quest, defeating West Germany in the 1986 World Cup Final. Maradona was voted the most outstanding player of the tournament.
He had achieved godlike status in Argentina. Would another Argentine player ever live up to Maradona? Most doubted it.
However, in sports history, we never know when the next great one will arrive.
And one year after the 1986 World Cup, the heir apparent was born...

WATER BREAK!
THE CHURCH OF MARADONA

In 1998, fans in Buenos Aires began a new philosophy named after their patron saint of soccer. Today, there are tens of thousands of members, and it has since spread to Italy, Scotland, Peru, Brazil, Japan, Afghanistan, Chile, Mexico, and the United States. Though it's not meant to be taken too seriously, here are its ten commandments:

1. The ball is never soiled.
2. Love football above all else.
3. Declare unconditional love for Diego and the beauty of football.
4. Defend the Argentine shirt.
5. Spread the news of Diego's miracles throughout the universe.
6. Honor the temples where he played and his sacred shirts.
7. Don't proclaim Diego as a member of any single team.
8. Preach and spread the principles of the Church of Maradona.
9. Make Diego your middle name.
10. Name your first son Diego.

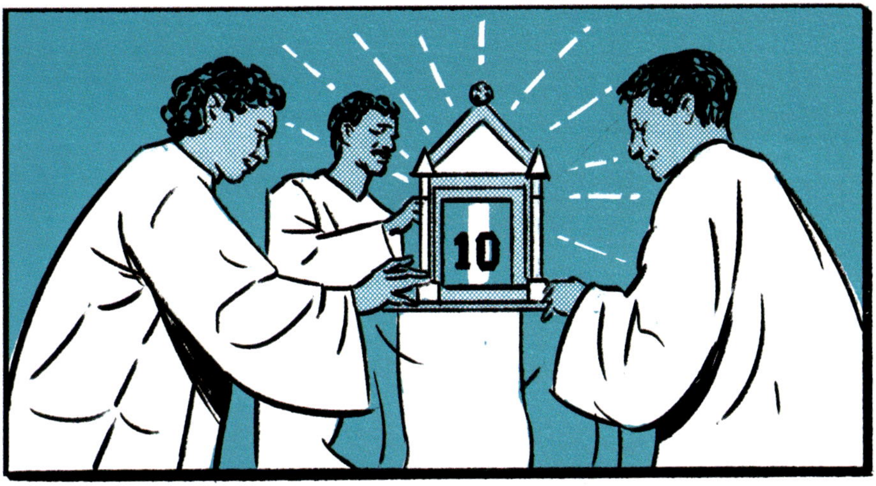
10

TRIVIA GOALS

Diego Maradona set many records during his sparkling career. Which one of these is true?

A) He is the only player to play every position in a single match.

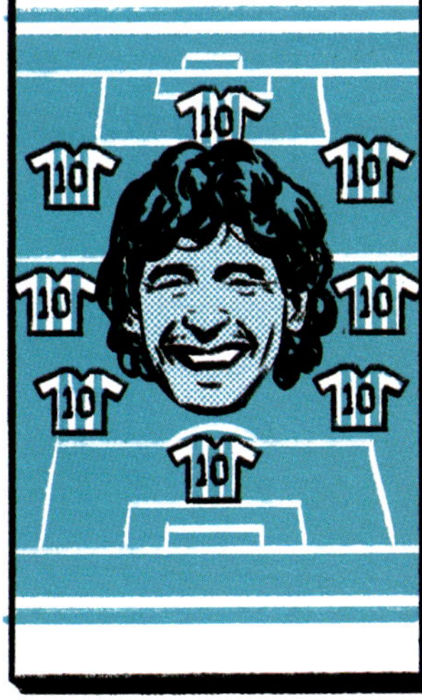

B) He was once fouled 23 times in a World Cup match, the most ever.

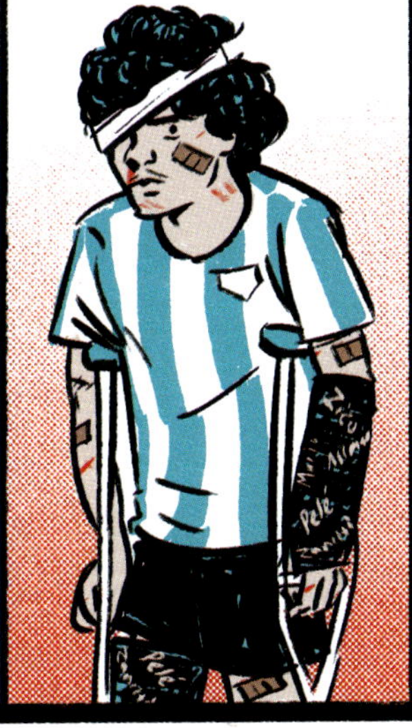

C) He is the first and only player to score a goal while doing a backflip.

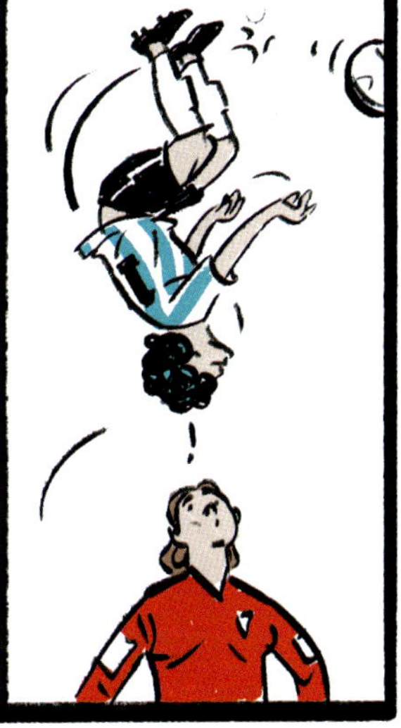

CHAPTER 3
BORN TO PLAY

*June 1987
La Bajada, Argentina*

One year after Maradona's epic World Cup tournament in 1986, Lionel Messi arrived. He came from a modest, middle-class neighborhood called La Bajada, within the larger city of Rosario, Argentina.

Young Leo was born to play soccer. From the earliest age, it was all he wanted to do.

At age six, little Leo joins Newell's Old Boys, teaming up with the best youth players in the region. He's the smallest kid on the squad, yet he's head and shoulders above them all in soccer talent. In his very first match, little Messi scores four goals!

Just like the great Diego Maradona, Lionel Messi is undersize. Both are even left-footed. And just like Maradona, he is a soccer sensation!

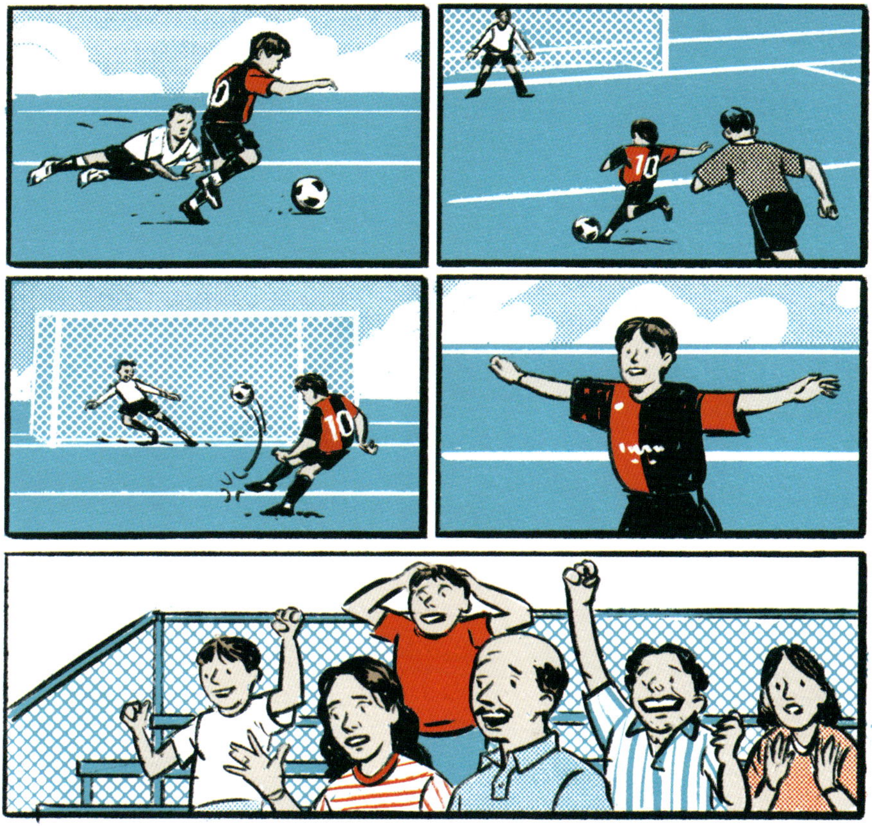

During halftimes, Leo would dazzle the fans with ball tricks.

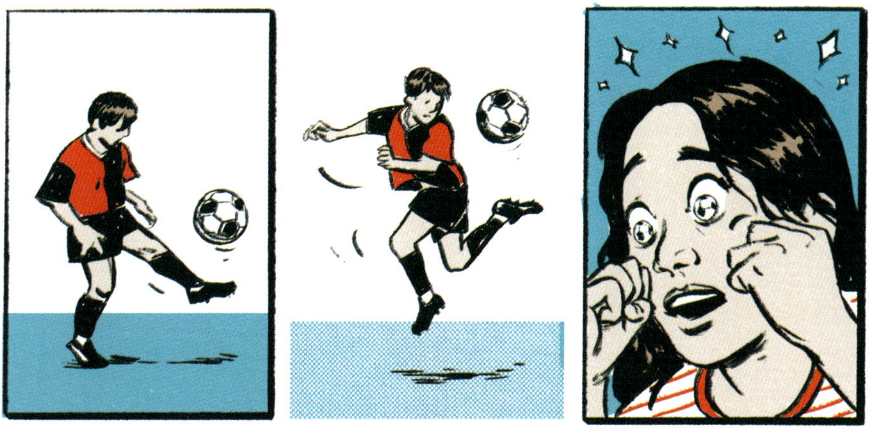

Young Messi leads his underage team to remarkable heights. The legendary squad is dubbed, "La Maquina del '87," or "The Machine of '87," named after the birth year of the young players. They are more than good. They are unbeatable.

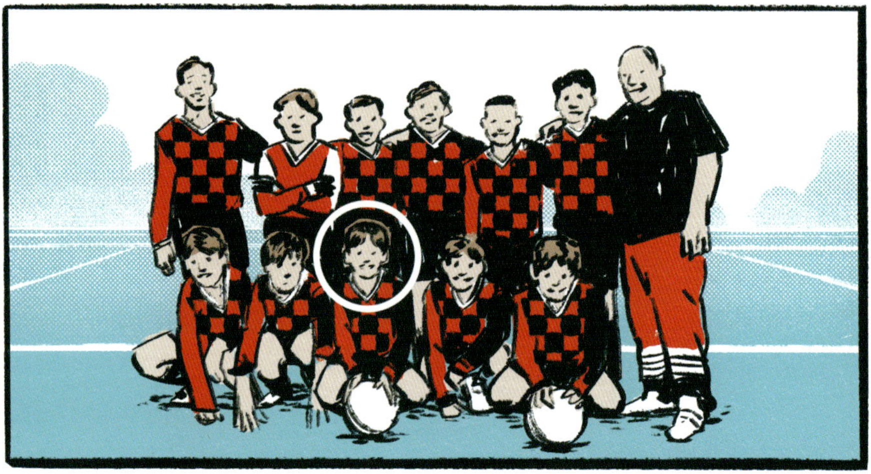

It is said that the Machine of '87 didn't lose a match in over three years. They defeated youth teams far and wide, all the way to Peru. And Lionel Messi, their soccer superhero, reportedly scored over five hundred goals!

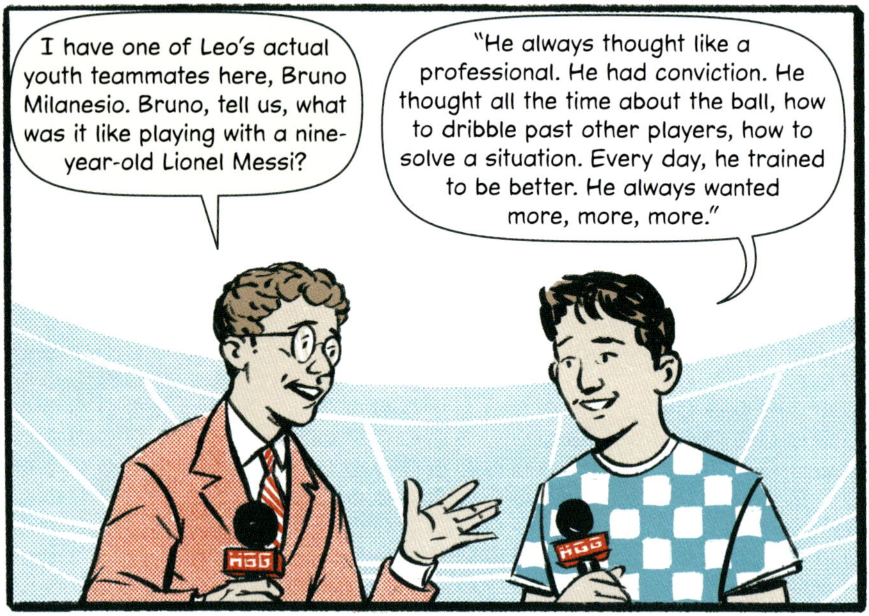
I have one of Leo's actual youth teammates here, Bruno Milanesio. Bruno, tell us, what was it like playing with a nine-year-old Lionel Messi?
"He always thought like a professional. He had conviction. He thought all the time about the ball, how to dribble past other players, how to solve a situation. Every day, he trained to be better. He always wanted more, more, more."
HGG
HGG

It seemed nothing could stop little Lionel from seizing his destiny... except his health.

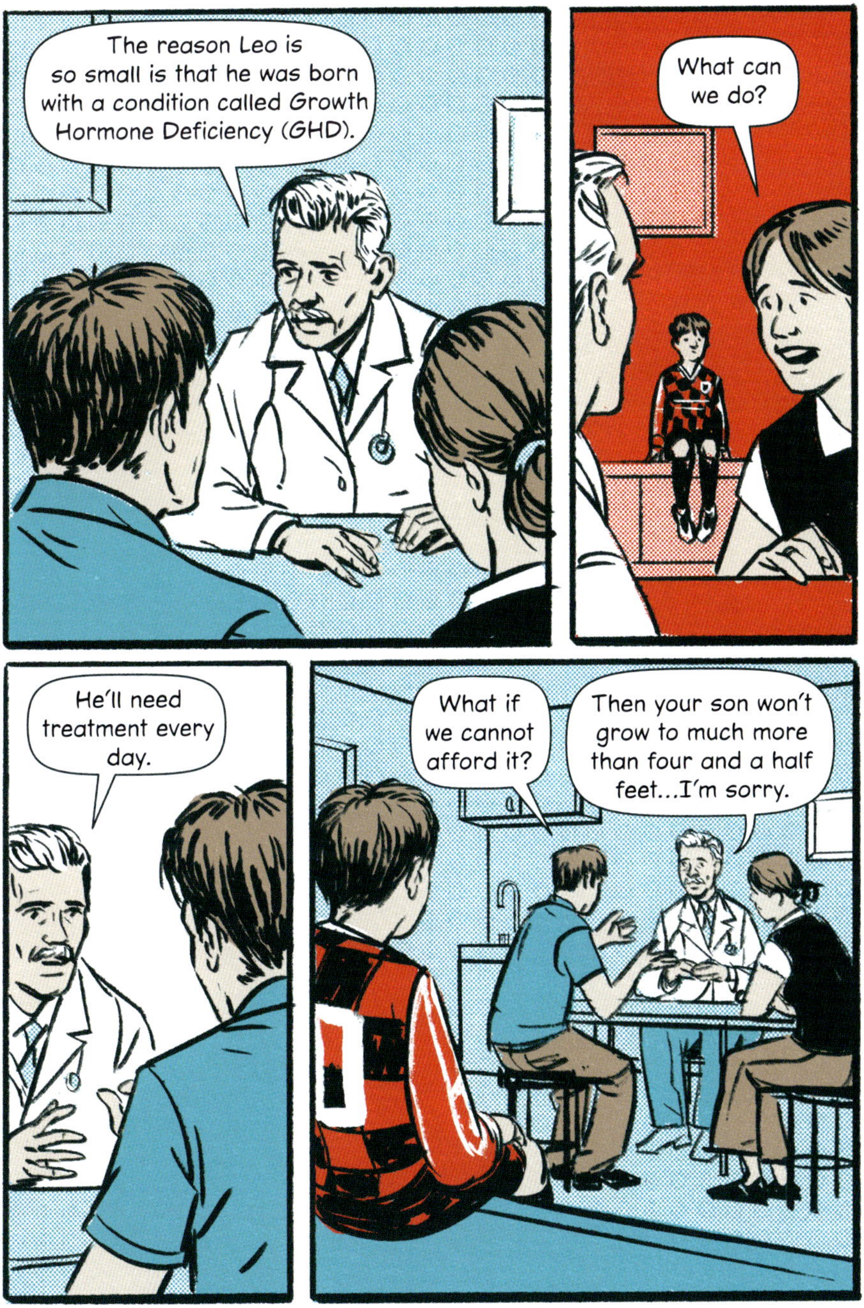
The reason Leo is so small is that he was born with a condition called Growth Hormone Deficiency (GHD).
What can we do?
He'll need treatment every day.
What if we cannot afford it?
Then your son won't grow to much more than four and a half feet...I'm sorry.

Even with his tiny stature, Messi continued his dominance in front of the local spectators. And one time, there was somebody else watching, too. A man who had come all the way from Europe.

It was an important agent representing the soccer club FC Barcelona, a member of the elite Spanish professional league, La Liga. After a two-week tryout in Spain, the club had made a decision. One that would change the course of soccer history.

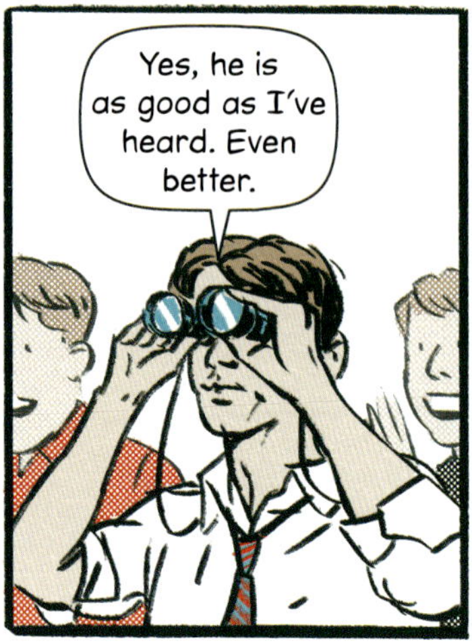
Yes, he is as good as I've heard. Even better.

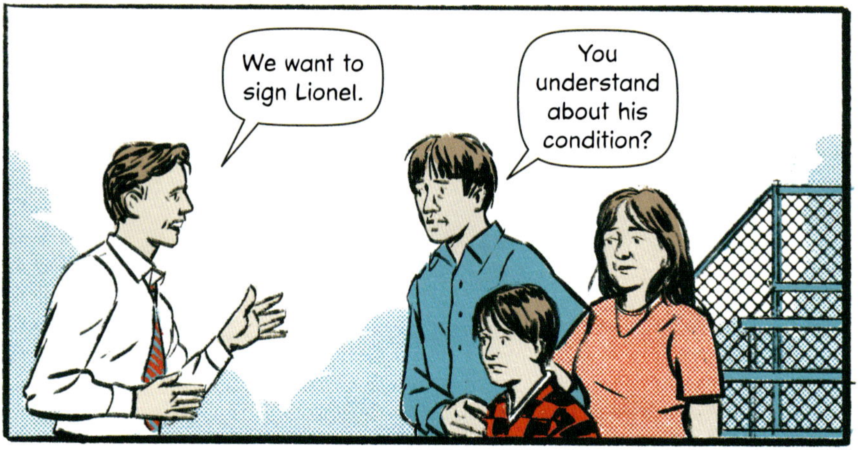
We want to sign Lionel.
You understand about his condition?

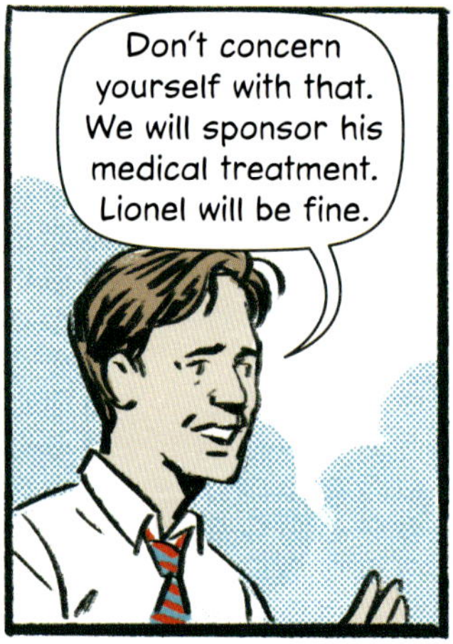
Don't concern yourself with that. We will sponsor his medical treatment. Lionel will be fine.

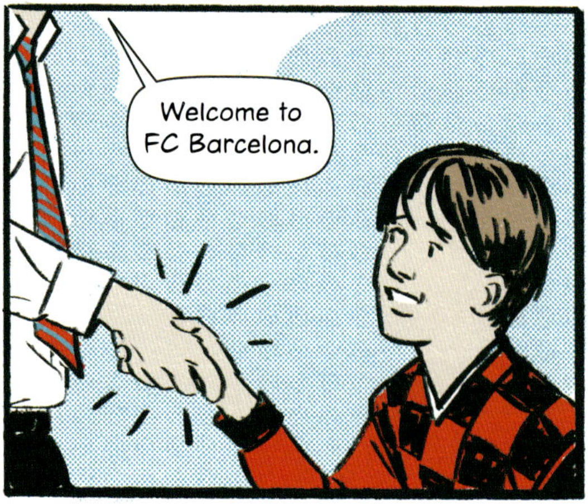
Welcome to FC Barcelona.

When Lionel was thirteen, the Messi family left their neighborhood in Argentina to embark on a new life in Barcelona, Spain. Though this opportunity was the best decision that Lionel and his family could have made, it didn't sit well with some of his countrymen.

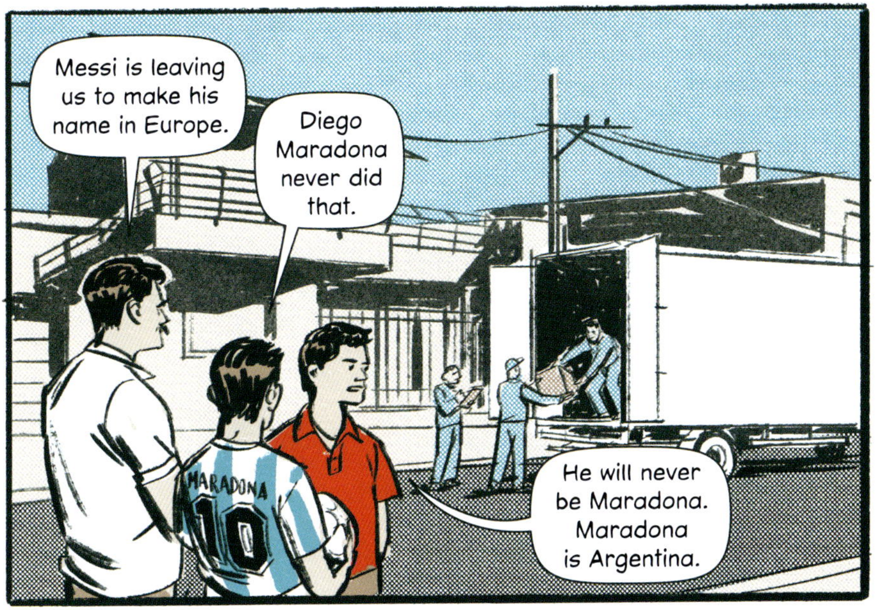
Messi is leaving us to make his name in Europe.
Diego Maradona never did that.
He will never be Maradona. Maradona is Argentina.
MARADONA
10

In Spain, Lionel began training at the Barca Youth Academy. He was so quiet and unassuming that at first some people believed he was mute.

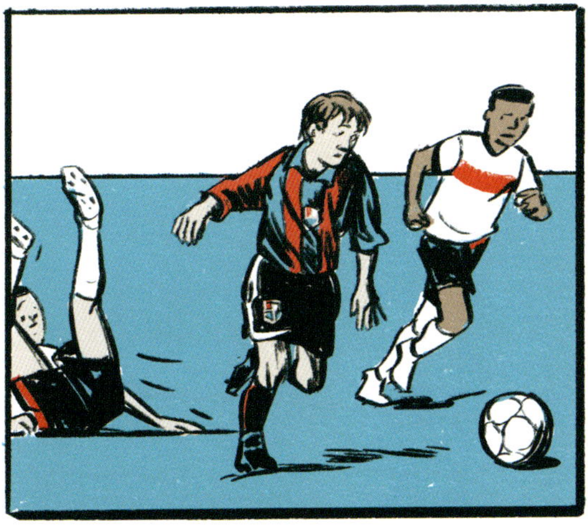

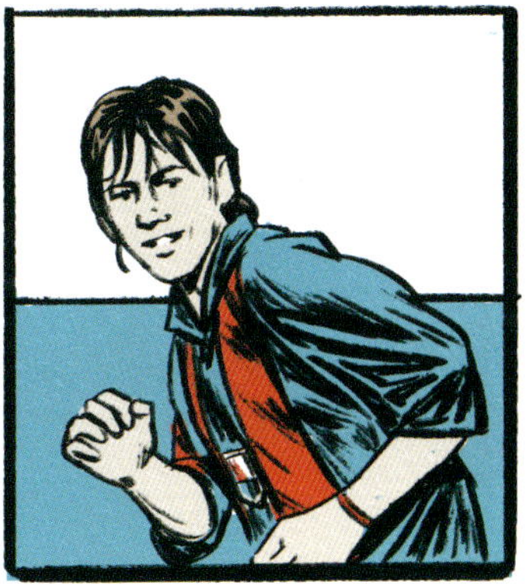

But he was just a little guarded at times. And as always, his play on the pitch spoke volumes. Almost immediately, Messi began to shine.

WATER BREAK!
YOUNG STAR ATHLETES

Lionel Messi was signed by FC Barcelona when he was barely a teenager. Check out these other athletic prodigies:

Dimitrios Loundras, 10
Gymnast, 1896 Olympics, bronze medal for Greece

Carlos Front, 11
Rower, 1992 Olympics, Spain

Jennifer Capriati, 13
Professional tennis player, USA, 1990

Joe Nuxhall, 15
Major league baseball player, USA, 1944

Wayne Gretzky, 17
Professional ice hockey player, Canada, 1978

Joey Logano, 16
Professional auto racer, USA, 2006

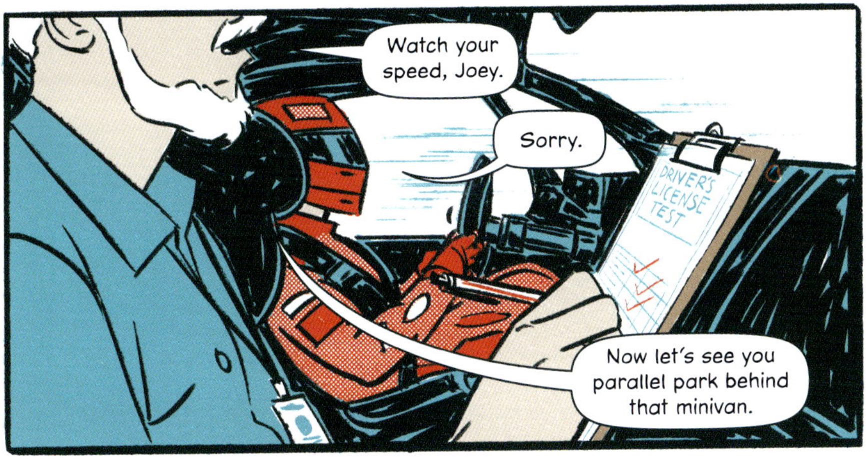

Watch your speed, Joey.
Sorry.
DRIVER'S LICENSE TEST
Now let's see you parallel park behind that minivan.

TRIVIA GOALS

Which fact is true about the first contract Messi signed with FC Barcelona?

A) The soccer club required him to shave his head.

B) It was written on a restaurant napkin.

C) It included a bonus of a soccer ball stuffed with money.

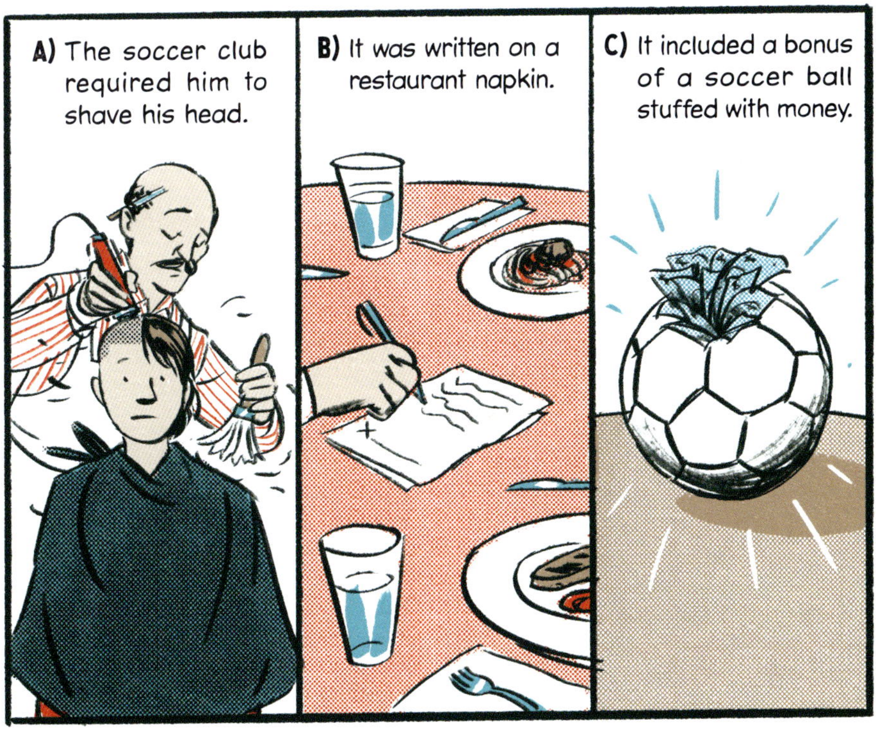

CHAPTER

4

REACHING NEW HEIGHTS

After three years of astounding play at the Barca Youth Academy, Lionel is promoted to the FC Barcelona professional squad. He is exceptionally young for the honor.

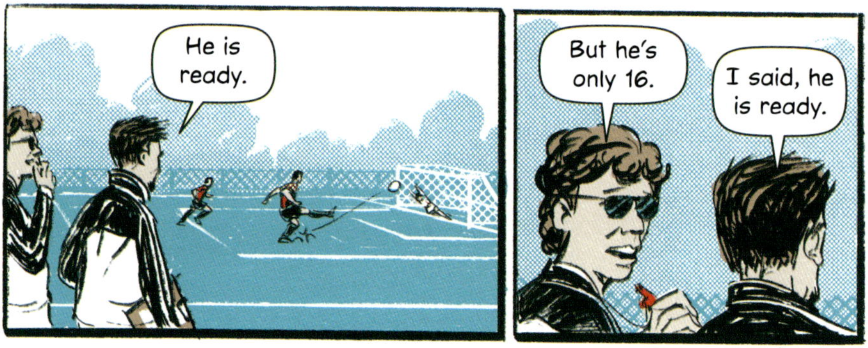
He is ready.
But he's only 16.
I said, he is ready.

Lionel's career with FC Barcelona quickly took off. He would lead his team to the 2004/2005 Liga championship, and the titles, records, and accolades would keep coming...

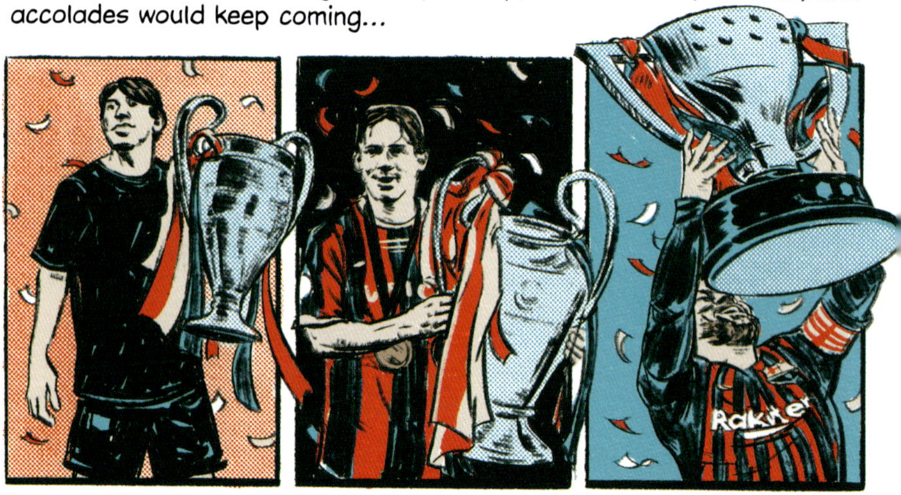

Lionel Messi became the most decorated player in soccer history. With talent so otherworldly, Argentinian fans gave him the moniker, the New Maradona. Yet in the hearts of many, there was one very big difference...

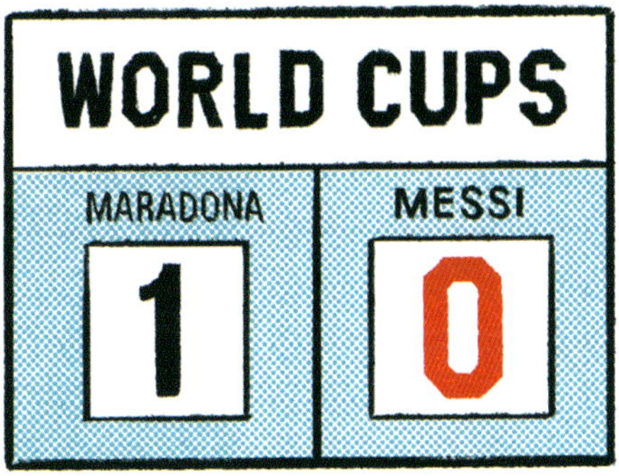
WORLD CUPS
MARADONA
1
MESSI
0

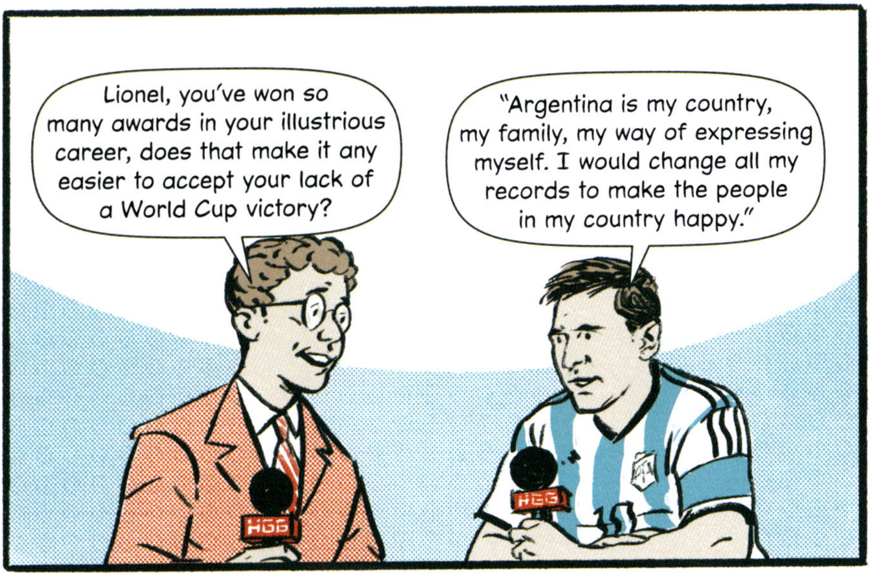
Lionel, you've won so many awards in your illustrious career, does that make it any easier to accept your lack of a World Cup victory?
"Argentina is my country, my family, my way of expressing myself. I would change all my records to make the people in my country happy."

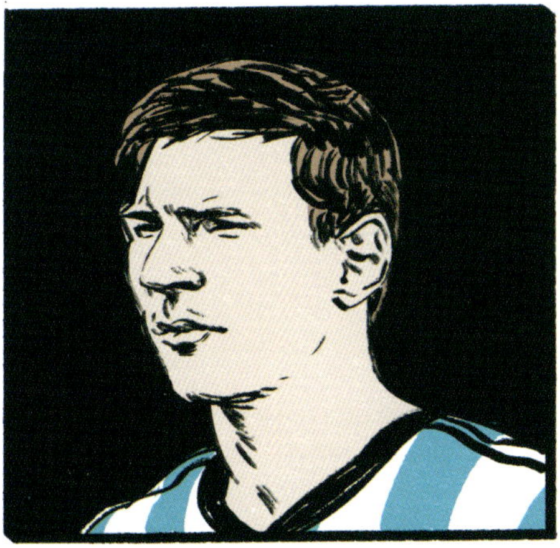

Lionel Messi had come up short twice already in his pursuit of the World Cup in 2006 and 2010.

But when the 2014 tournament came around, he had never been more determined to bring the treasured Cup back to his homeland. Could he pull it off?

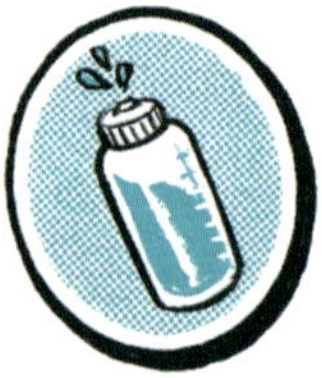

WATER BREAK!

LIONEL MESSI: SOCCER SUPERHUMAN

Lionel Messi is one of the most talented players in the history of the sport. It's almost as if he was manufactured in a lab by soccer scientists to create the ultimate soccer player!

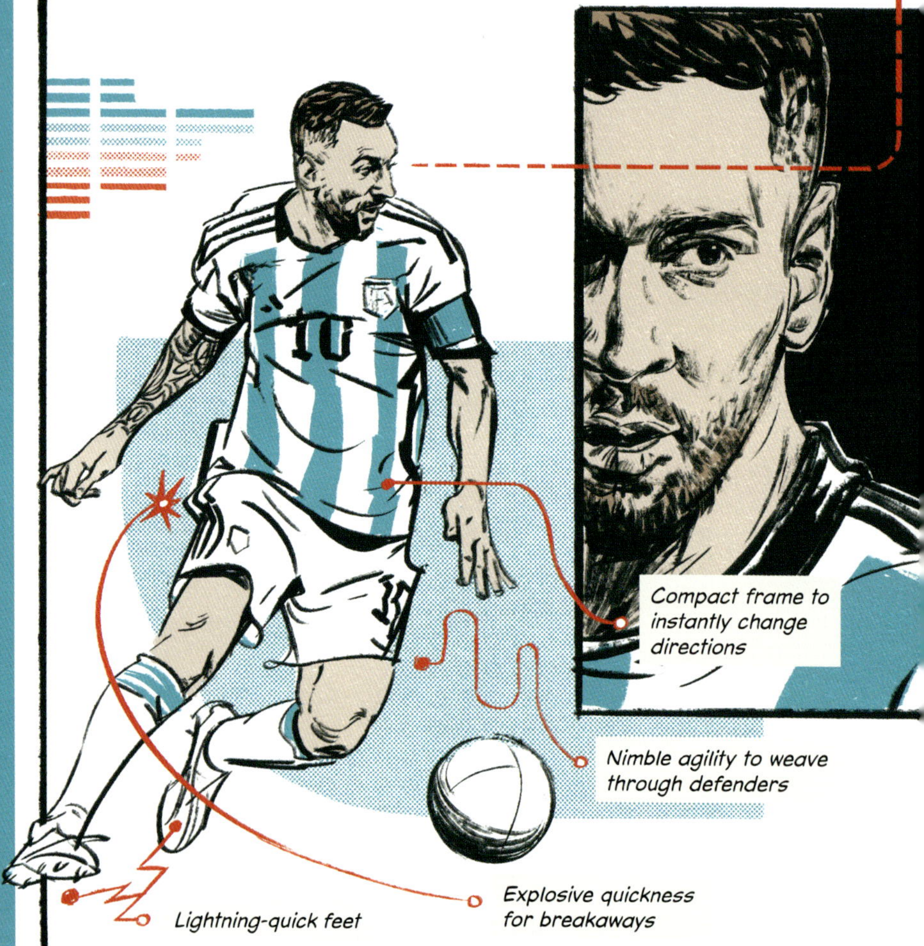

10
Compact frame to instantly change directions
Nimble agility to weave through defenders
Lightning-quick feet
Explosive quickness for breakaways

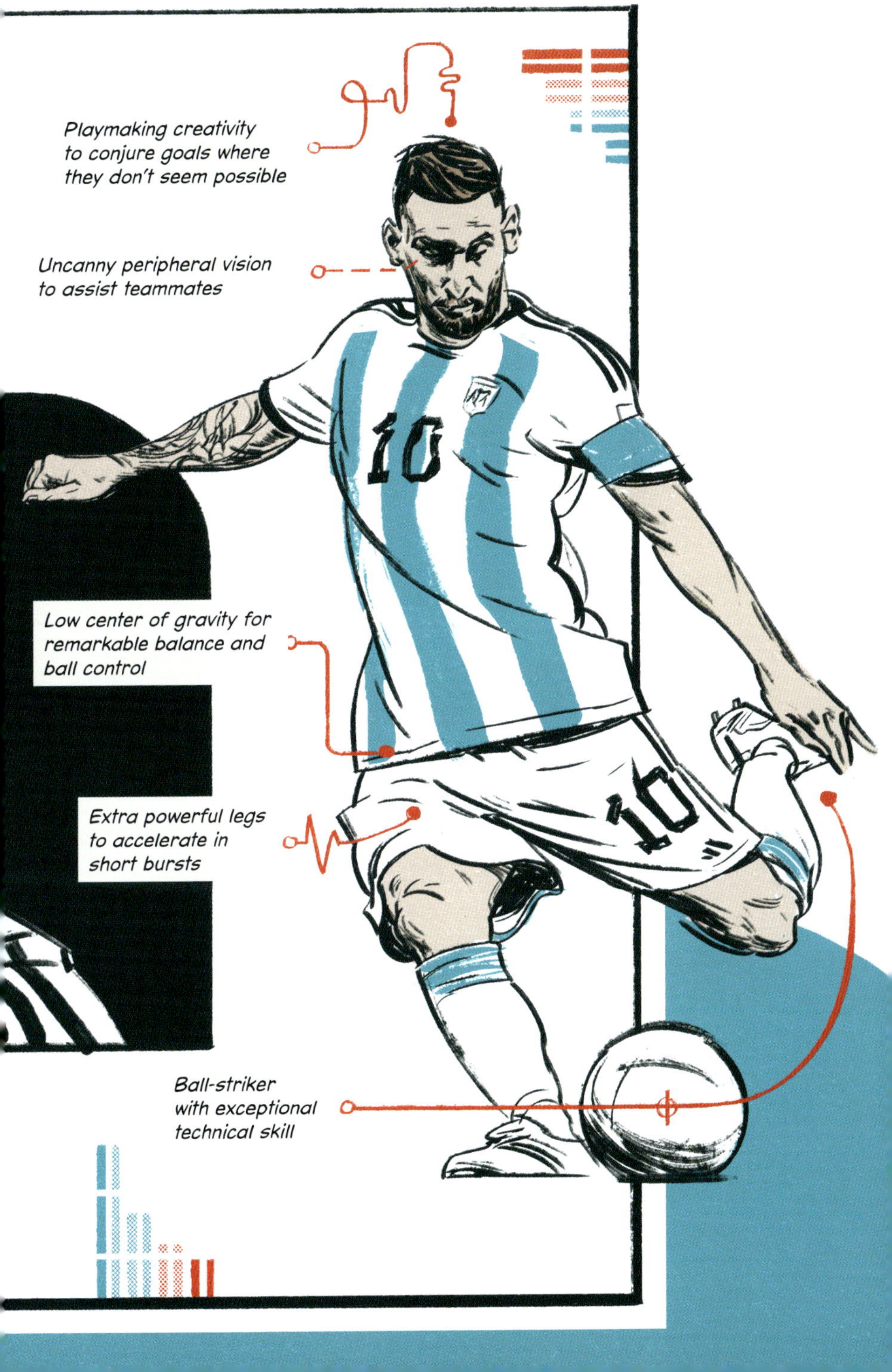
Playmaking creativity to conjure goals where they don't seem possible
Uncanny peripheral vision to assist teammates
Low center of gravity for remarkable balance and ball control
Extra powerful legs to accelerate in short bursts
Ball-striker with exceptional technical skill

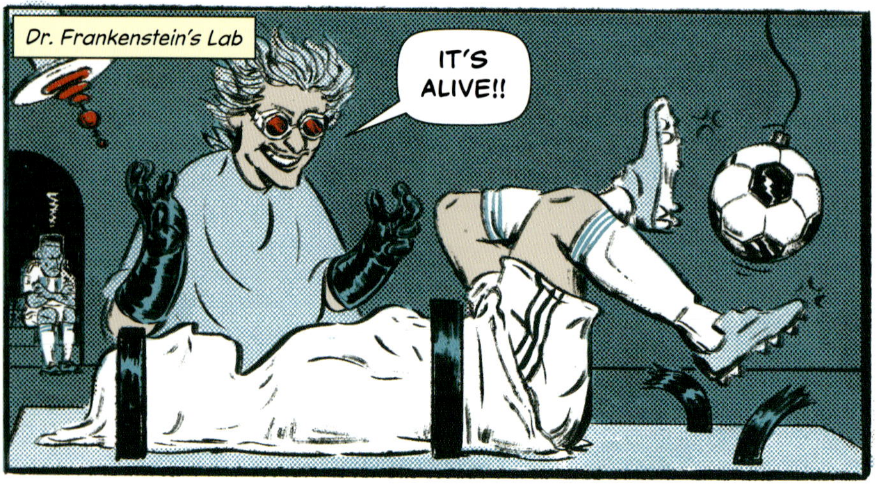
Dr. Frankenstein's Lab
IT'S ALIVE!!

TRIVIA GOALS

Starting in 1956, the French award, the Ballon d'Or, has been considered the most prestigious individual award given in soccer, recognizing the best player of the year. Which of the following is not true?

A) Only once has it been awarded to a goalkeeper.

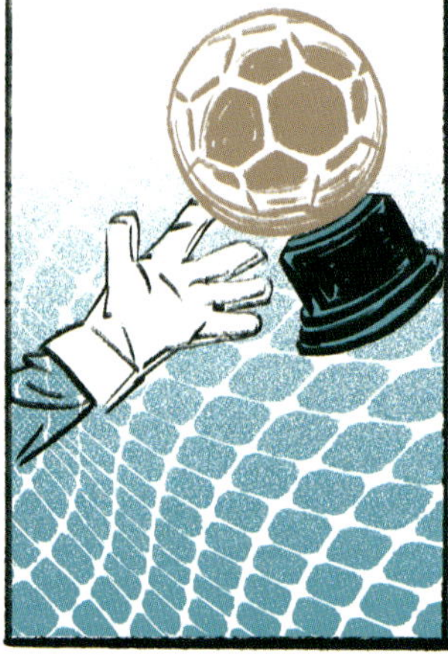

B) In French, the Ballon d'Or translates to "Golden Balloon."

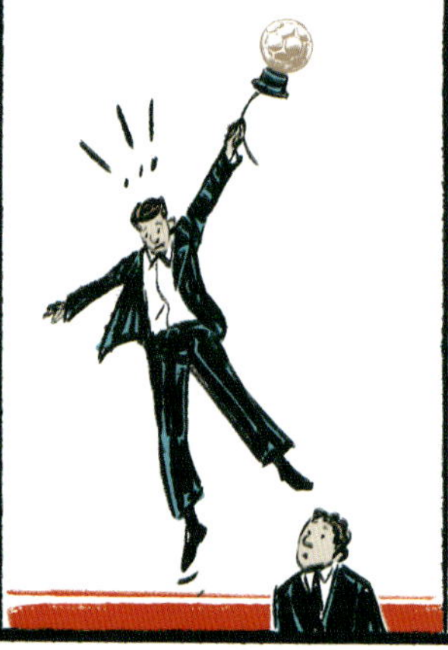

C) Lionel Messi has won it more than any other footballer in history.

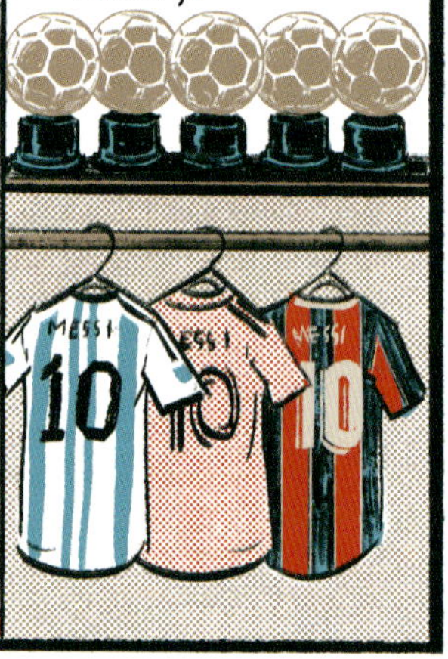
MESSI
10

CHAPTER 5

UNFINISHED BUSINESS

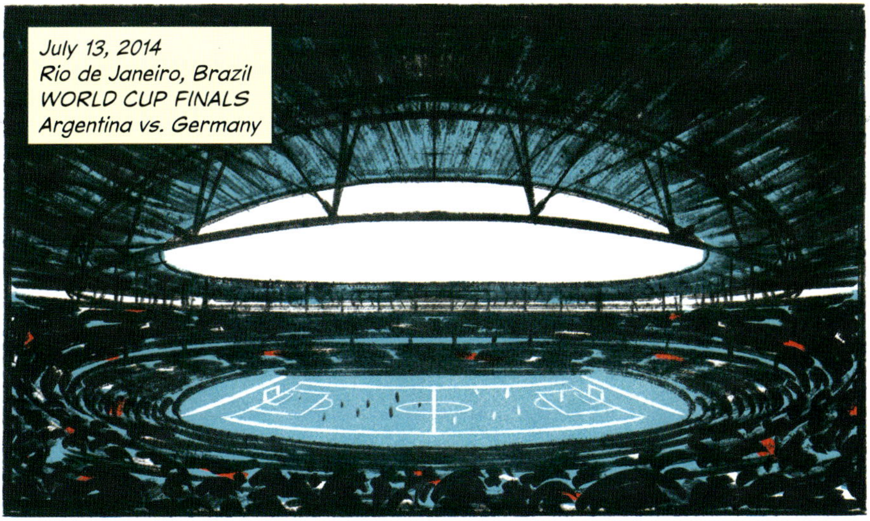
July 13, 2014
Rio de Janeiro, Brazil
WORLD CUP FINALS
Argentina vs. Germany

In the 2014 World Cup tournament, Messi performed at the peak of his powers and led his nation to the brink of the title against Germany.

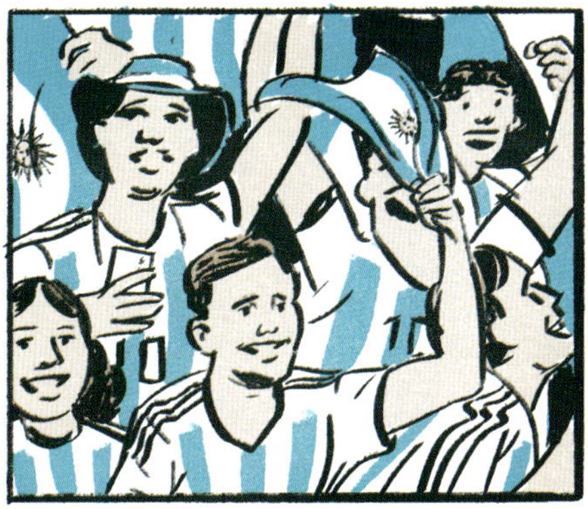

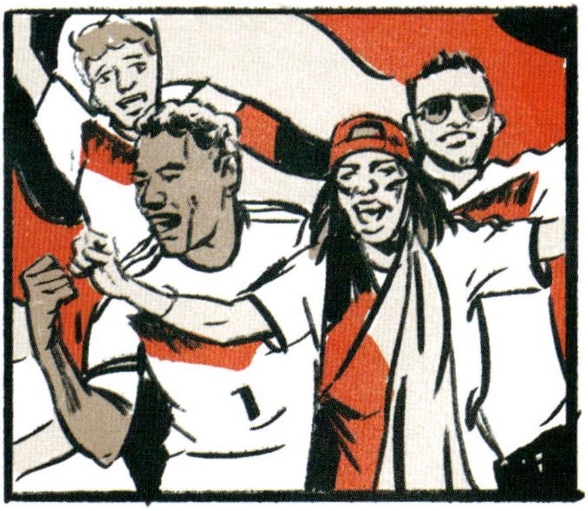

As fate would have it, the final game was a rematch of 1986 when Maradona had won for the sky blue and white against West Germany. Could Messi and his team close the deal? Would he cement his status as an icon in the class of Maradona?

Deep into the match, the game remained scoreless. As the joyous Argentine fans chanted fight songs, they could feel that Messi would finally realize his destiny.

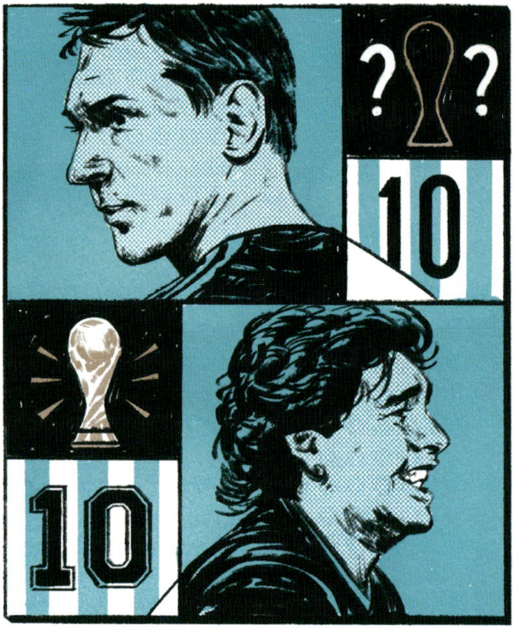
? ?
10
10

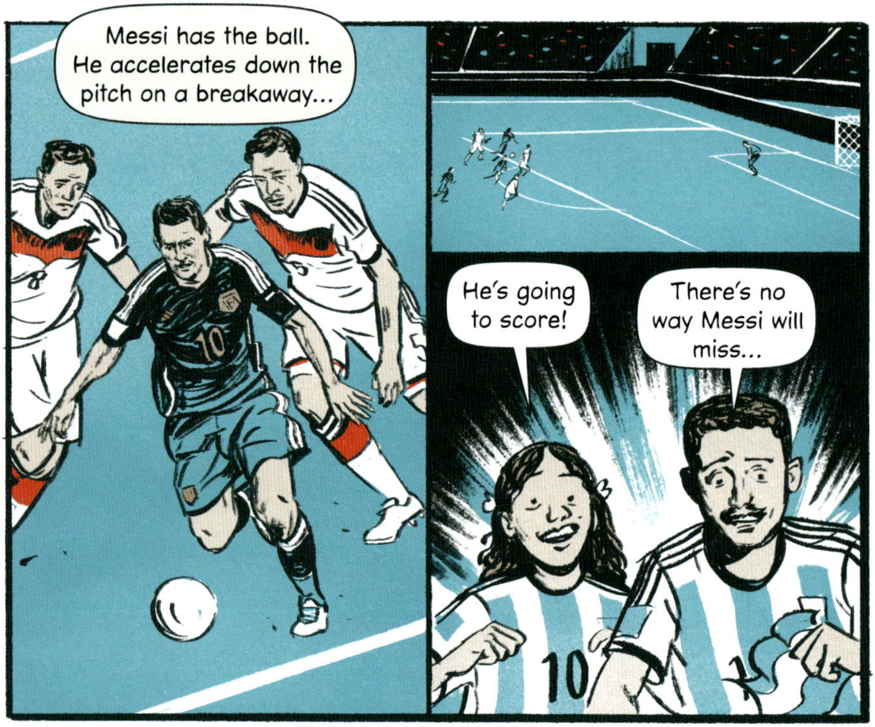
Messi has the ball. He accelerates down the pitch on a breakaway...
He's going to score!
There's no way Messi will miss...

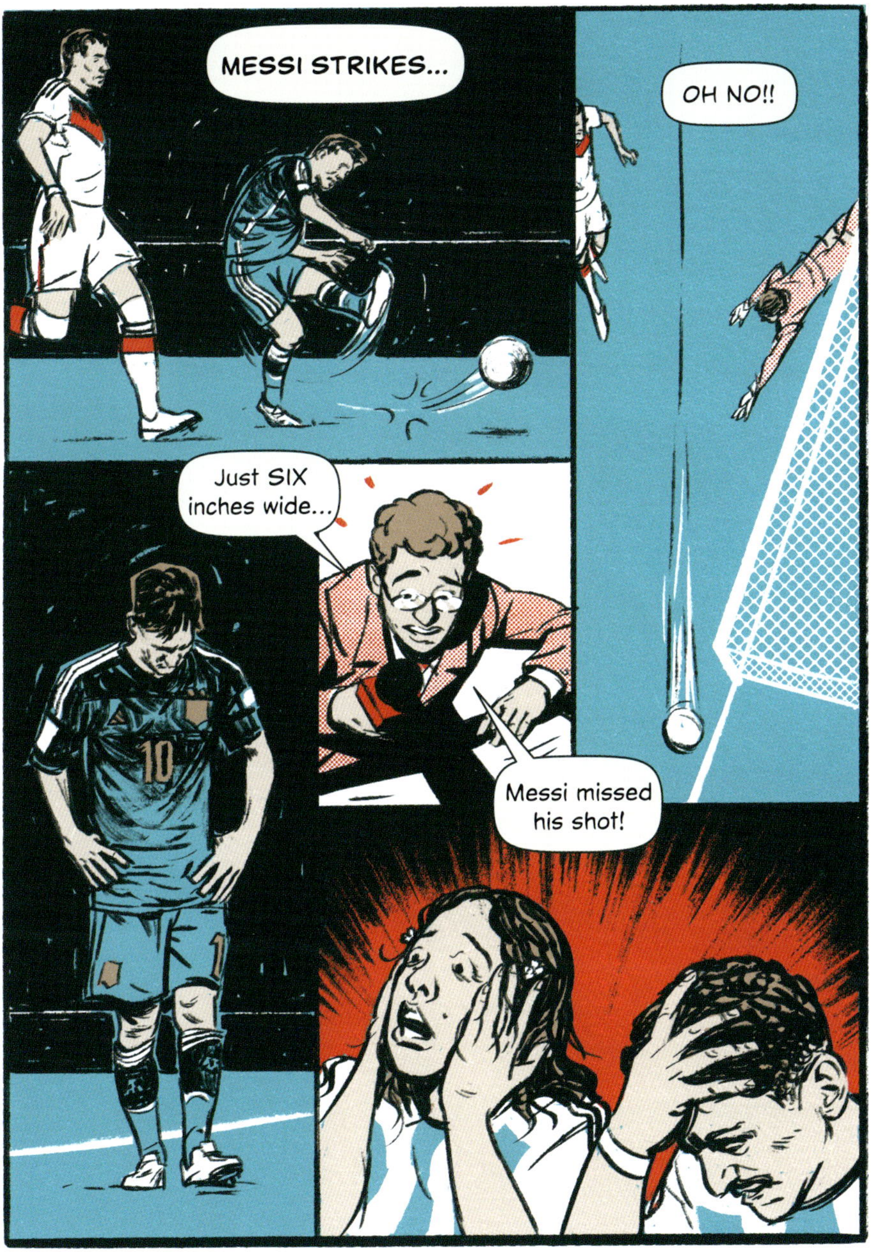
MESSI STRIKES...
OH NO!!
Just SIX inches wide...
Messi missed his shot!

The scoreless contest went into extra time. Finally, Germany scored the game-winner. Unlike 1986, when Maradona and Argentina were the victors, this time Germany claimed the World Cup.

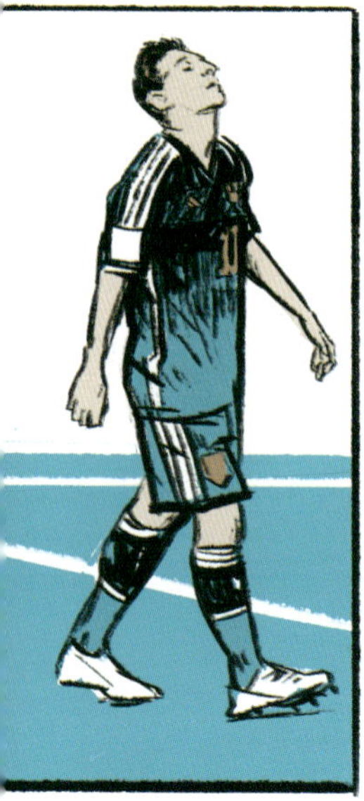

Some questioned whether Messi could win the biggest of games. But who hasn't missed a big shot at one time or another? It happens to all of us, even those who appear to be superhuman.

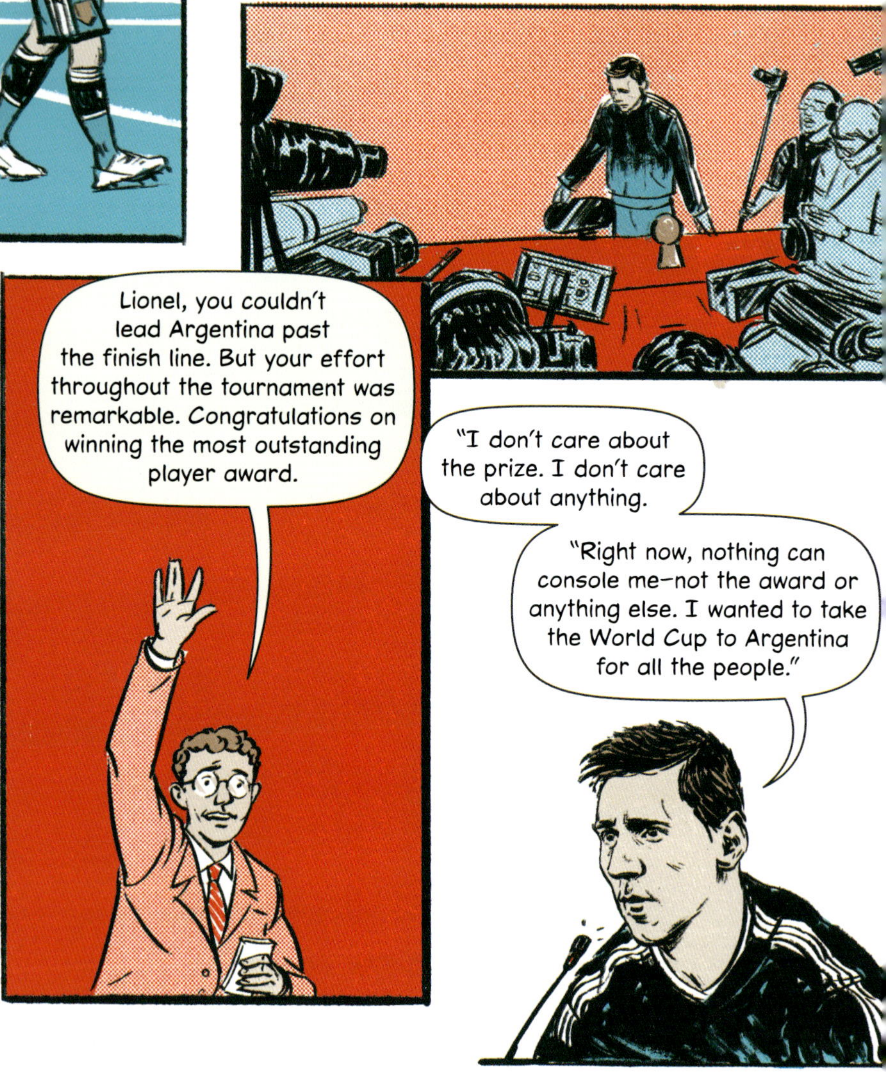

Lionel, you couldn't lead Argentina past the finish line. But your effort throughout the tournament was remarkable. Congratulations on winning the most outstanding player award.
"I don't care about the prize. I don't care about anything.
"Right now, nothing can console me—not the award or anything else. I wanted to take the World Cup to Argentina for all the people."

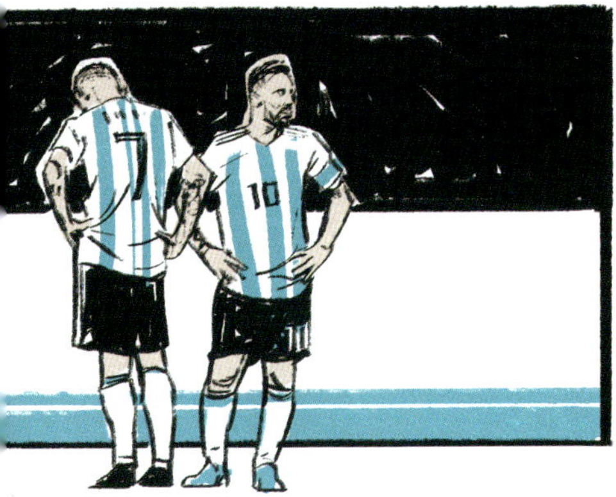

In 2018, Lionel Messi and Argentina would qualify again to play in the World Cup tournament, this time hosted by Russia. He had yet another opportunity to complete his lifelong quest.

For Argentina to advance, they had to get past France. But France was led by the world's next great prodigy, the flashy phenom Kylian Mbappé. He was just 19 years old, yet utterly calm and cool. He was an explosive player, skilled with both feet, and known for his speed, ball control, and eye for the goal.

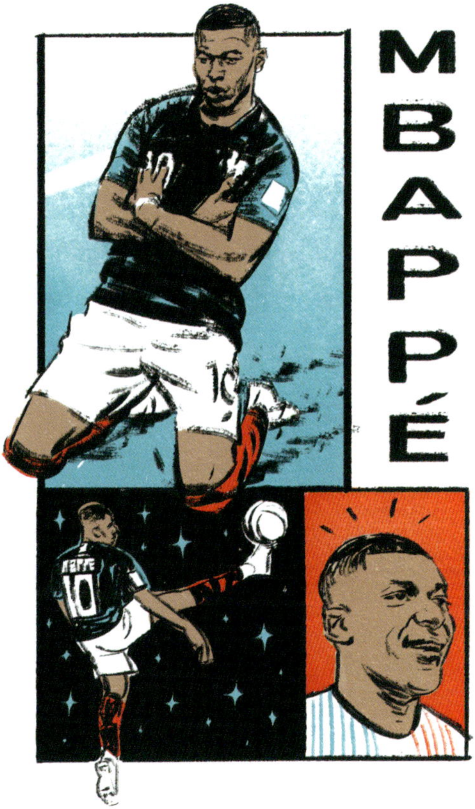
MBAPPÉ

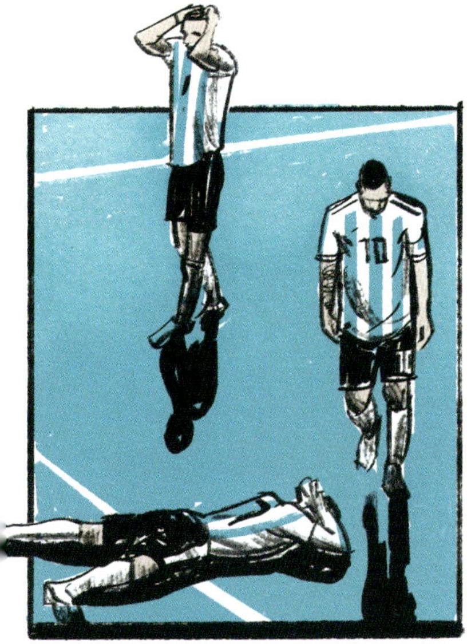

Then Argentina's tourney came to a sudden, crashing end. Early in the knockout stage, France took them down. Yet again, Messi's fairy tale was not meant to be.

France and their rising star Kylian Mbappé continued in the tournament and ultimately captured the 2018 World Cup. In one of the matches, Mbappé became only the second teenager to score two goals in one World Cup game. The other? The legendary Brazilian player, Pelé.

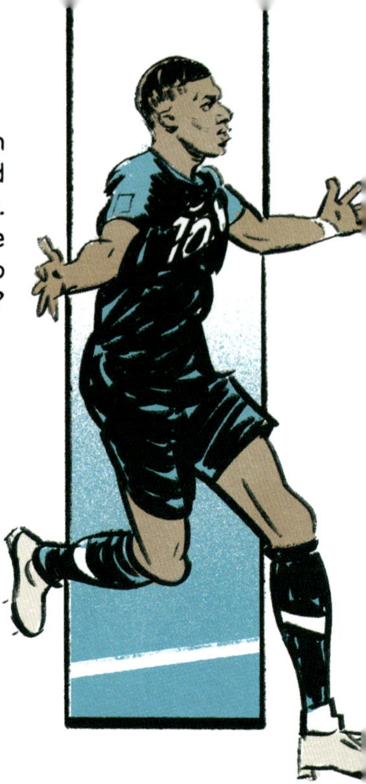

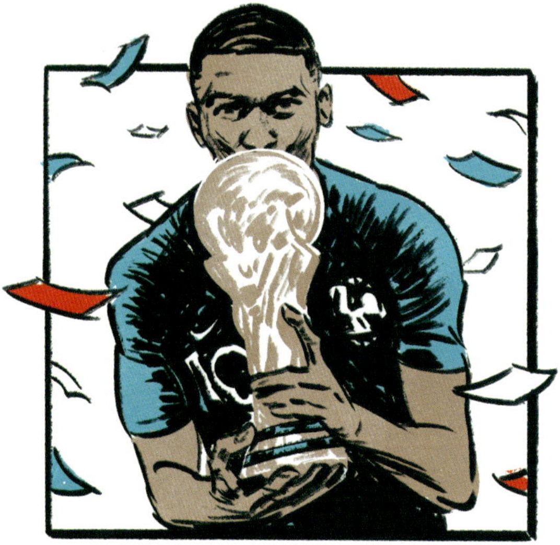

By now, the entire world was feeling Messi's anguish. Did his last chance to win a World Cup just slip away?

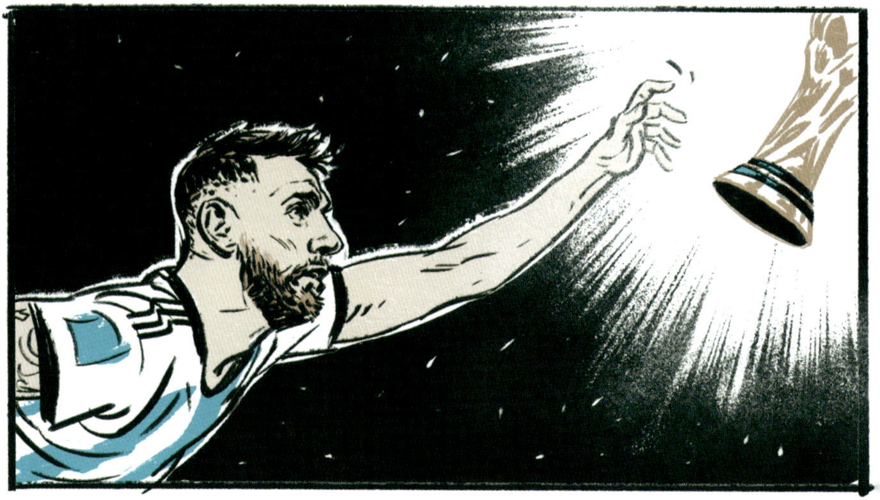

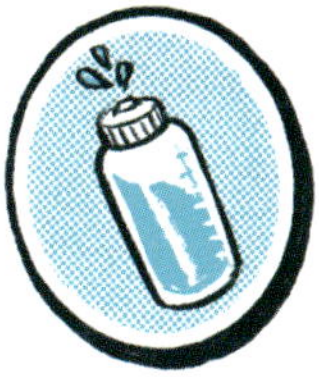

WATER BREAK!

PELÉ SCORES ONE FOR PEACE

Lionel Messi, Diego Maradona, and Kylian Mbappé have all been compared to Pelé, the Brazilian superstar considered by many to be the finest player of all time. He was also a player for peace.

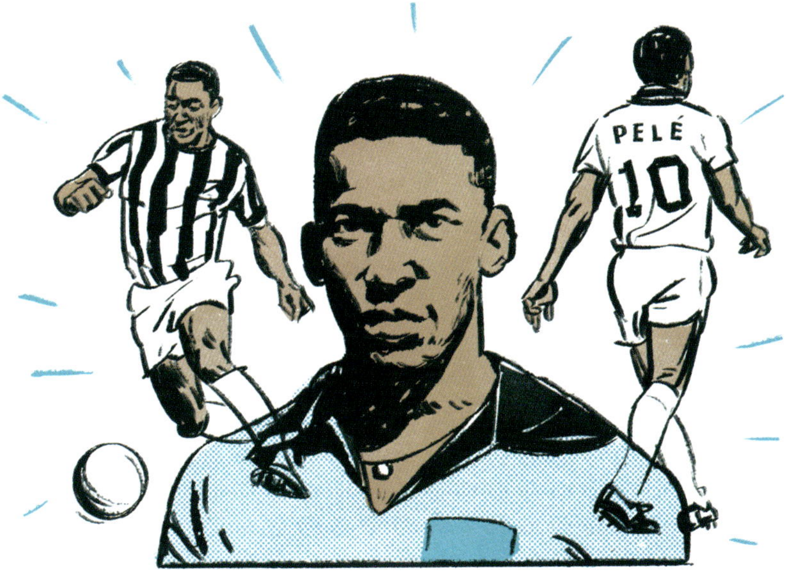
PELÉ
10

In 1969, as Nigeria was engaged in a bloody civil conflict known as the Biafra War, word got out that Pelé was interested in playing an exhibition game for the people of Nigeria. The general on one side of the battle and the king on the other declared a national holiday. Then they opened the bridge that connected their regions.

Twenty-five thousand spectators came to the peaceful celebration of soccer, what Pelé called "The Beautiful Game," and watched the legendary player and his team score a victory.

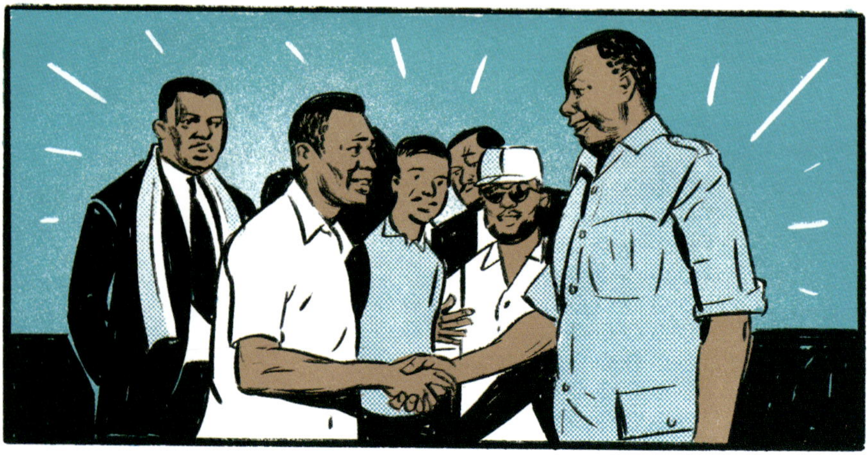

TRIVIA GOALS

What did Kylian Mbappé do with the large amount of money he earned from his World Cup victory in 2018?

A) He purchased 365 pairs of new sneakers so that he could wear a different set every day of the year.

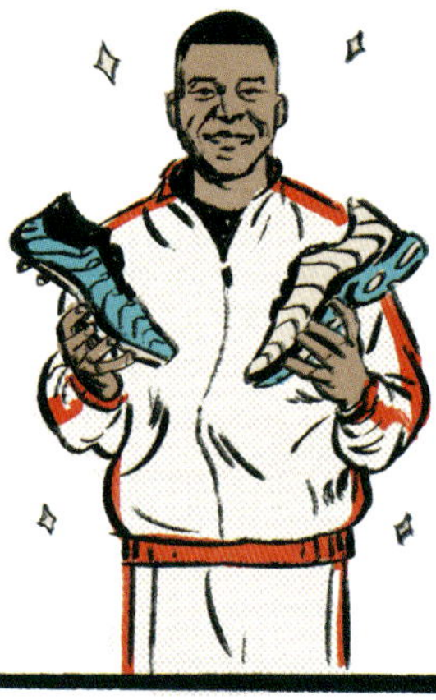

B) He helped renovate a broken elevator on the Eiffel Tower.

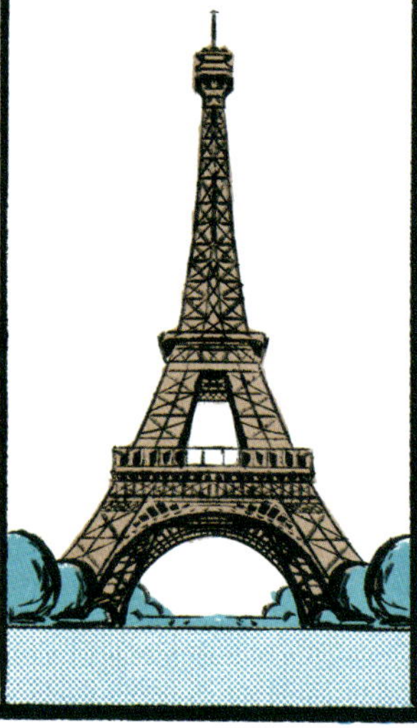

C) He donated the entire sum to a children's charity.

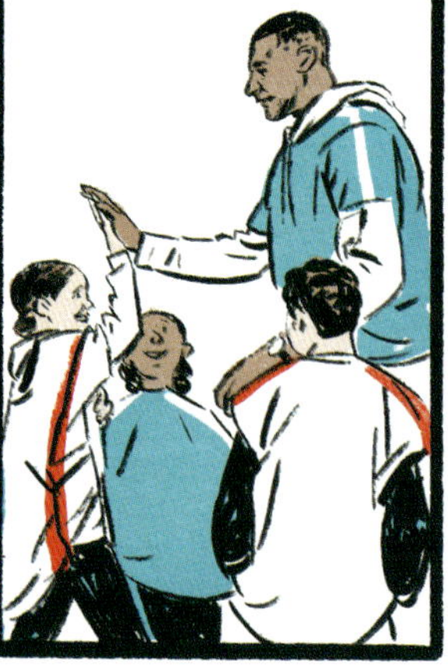

CHAPTER 6
QATAR: A MOST HISTORIC HOST

On the southern tip of the Arabian Peninsula sits the country of Qatar, the host of the 2022 World Cup. The choice of Qatar was not universally embraced. There were a handful of concerns, such as the mistreatment of the laborers who helped build the stadiums, the harsh laws that could punish visitors who publicly criticized the government, even the banning of beer, a favorite of many World Cup fans. But the choice was also historic for many reasons...

FIRST ARABIC COUNTRY
Qatar was the first-ever Arabic-speaking host of a World Cup tournament. Following Jules Rimet's vision that the event would truly represent the world, finally having it on Middle Eastern soil was a breakthrough for global soccer. Now the people of Qatar would have a front-row seat to soccer history, while making some of their own.

Then, in an exhilarating twist, the Arabic nation of Morocco went on an astounding run, going all the way to the semifinals. In the history of the World Cup, no other Arabic country had gone further.

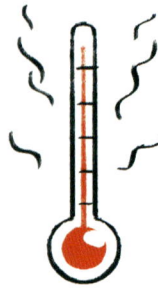

HELD IN THE WINTER

Up until 2022, the World Cup had always been hosted during the summer. But Qatar is sizzling hot during that time of year, with temperatures soaring above 110 degrees Fahrenheit. So, for the first time ever, the World Cup took place in November and December, when the weather was much more comfortable.

SMALLEST NATION

Based on its square mileage, Qatar was the tiniest nation ever to host the World Cup, similar in size to the island of Jamaica or the US state of Connecticut. Some of the tournament's planners were concerned that the country would be too small to host an event so mammoth in popularity, yet it all came together.

FIRST FEMALE REFEREE

When Costa Rica and Germany squared off on December 1, 2022—for the first time ever, at a men's World Cup match—the head referee was a woman, Stéphanie Frappart of France. Her assistants for that game were also women: Neuza Back from Brazil and Karen Diaz of Mexico.

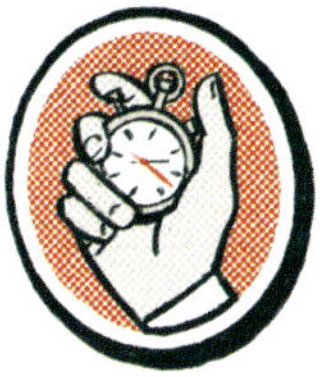

TIME-OUT FOR HISTORY

POLITICS ON THE PITCH

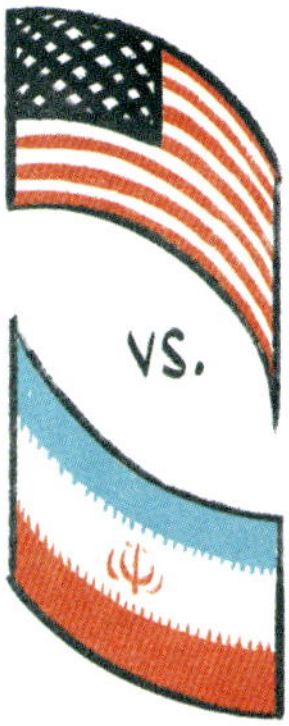
VS.

International politics can be fragile. There have been times when the fraught relations between countries have come to a head at the World Cup. Yet time and again, soccer has been a great unifier, helping bring nations together when other methods fail.

In the Qatari 2022 World Cup, one of the storylines was that the United States and Iran would be facing off in a much-anticipated rematch decades in the making. Neither team was expected to be a finalist, so why was this game so talked about? Because it was the first time the nations would face each other at the World Cup since a very heated contest in 1998.

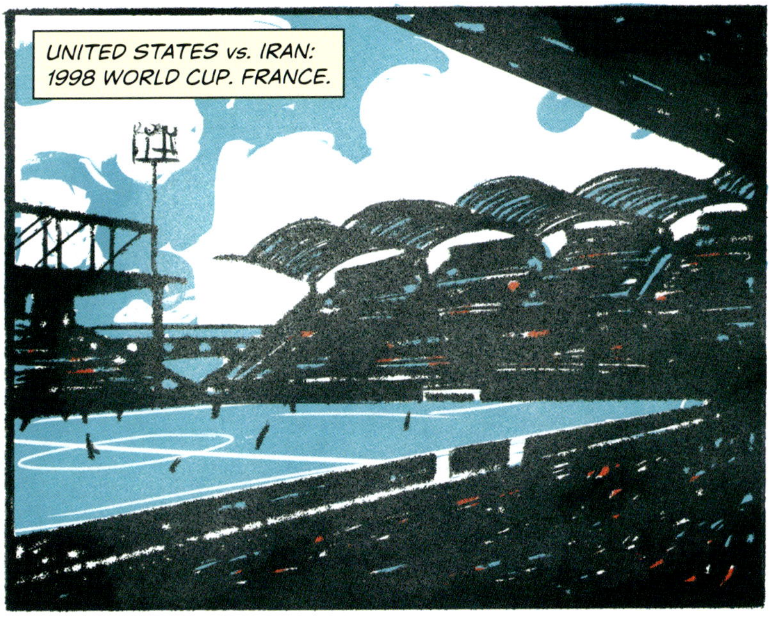
UNITED STATES vs. IRAN:
1998 WORLD CUP. FRANCE.

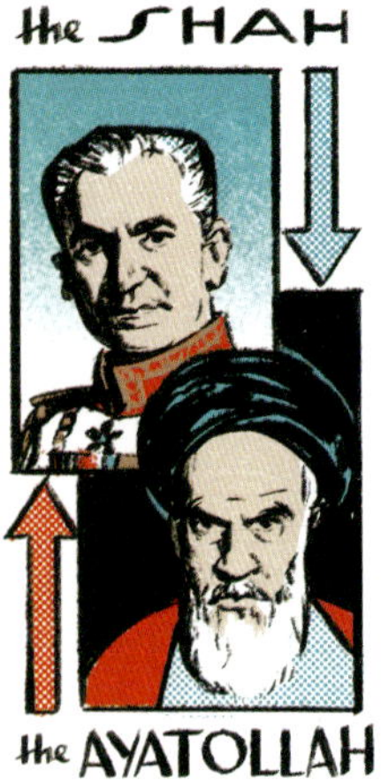
the SHAH
the AYATOLLAH

The story of the USA versus Iran matchup from 1998 went back even decades before that. In the 1970s, tensions between the rival nations heated up quickly.

When Iranians toppled the US-approved leader called the shah, the Iranian government installed a new regime led by the ayatollah, whom the US believed to be more dangerous to American interests. Soon after, Iranian militants stormed the United States embassy in their capital city of Tehran.

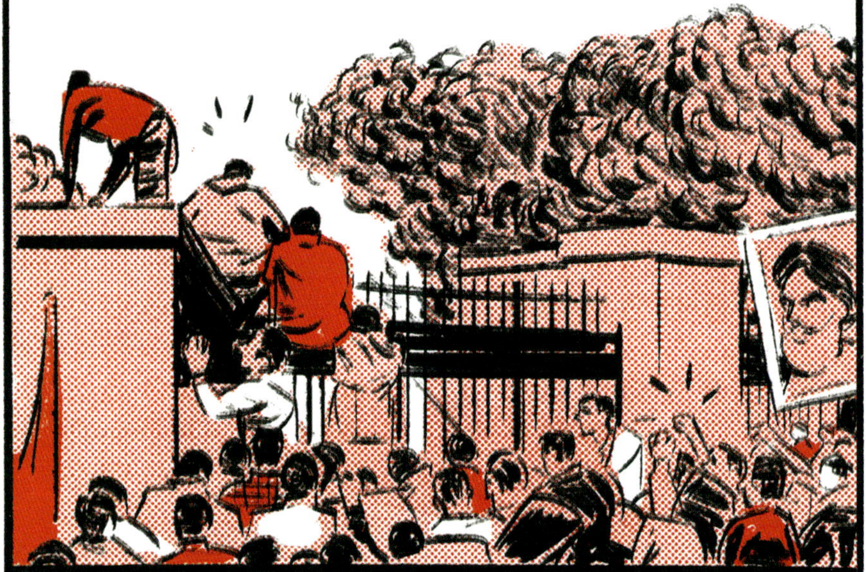

They took US citizens as hostages and held them in captivity for well over a year. Eventually, the hostages were released back to the United States.

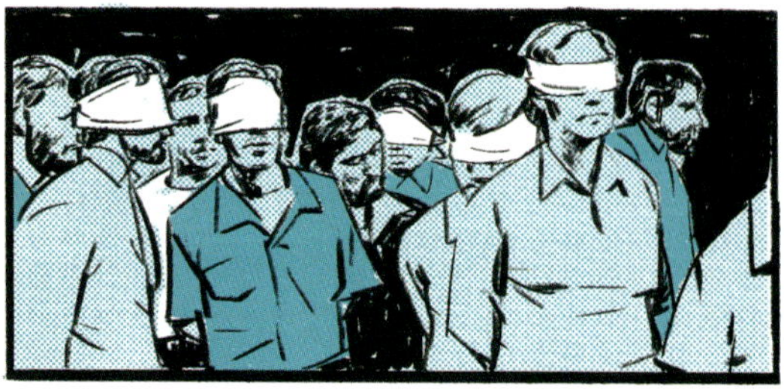

When the 1998 World Cup came around, the United States and Iran were scheduled to play one another. Though many years had passed, the rival nations still hadn't patched up their differences. In fact, it seemed time had only made matters more hostile. One month before the 1998 World Cup kickoff in France, the US State Department named Iran the number one terrorist state in the world.

In a pregame meeting with officials, representatives from the Iranian regime said they would not be shaking the hands of the American team prior to the match, even though it was protocol.

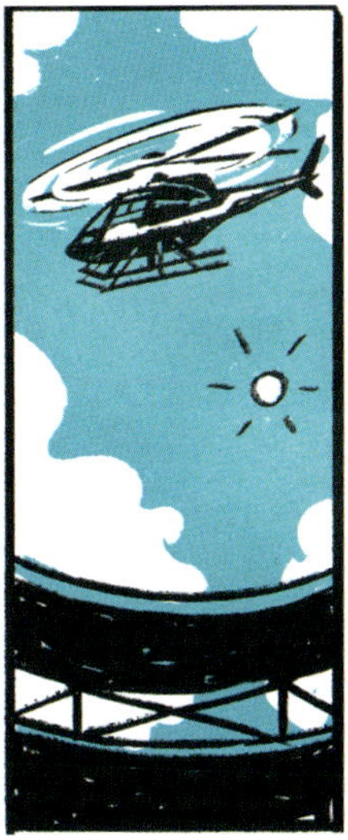

As the opening kickoff approached, the tension was rising. For added protection, there were heavily armed SWAT teams on hand and sharpshooting snipers on the roof of the stadium. A large military helicopter hovered above the pitch to alert players and fans that security would be a top priority.

However, the Iranian players and coaches had made a surprising decision. The head coach of Iran, Jalal Talebi, said, "We decided to make something special. Let us go and give them nice flowers to say that we are here for peace."

And so, the Iranian team presented the Americans with bouquets of white flowers.

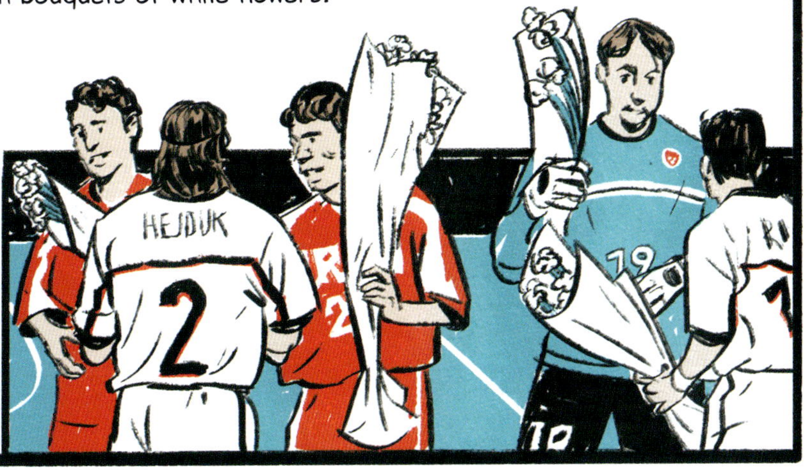
HEJDUK
2

The USA team responded in kind by gifting the Iranian team US Soccer Federation pennants. The players from both squads then posed together for a pregame team picture.

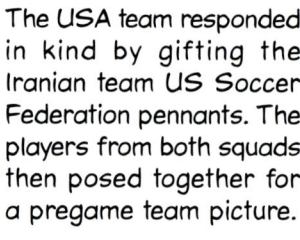

Though the governments of these two nations have had many problems with each other, the athletes respected one another and realized that they were much more similar than different.

As for the game, the Iranian team scored a major upset and defeated the United States. It was a brutal loss for the Americans, but the Iranians were euphoric.

American player Eric Wynalda recalled, "We didn't know how much the game meant to Iran until it was over. They were crying. We knew we were out, so we were dealing with our own demons, but to watch them celebrate—there was something beautiful about it. And they deserved it."

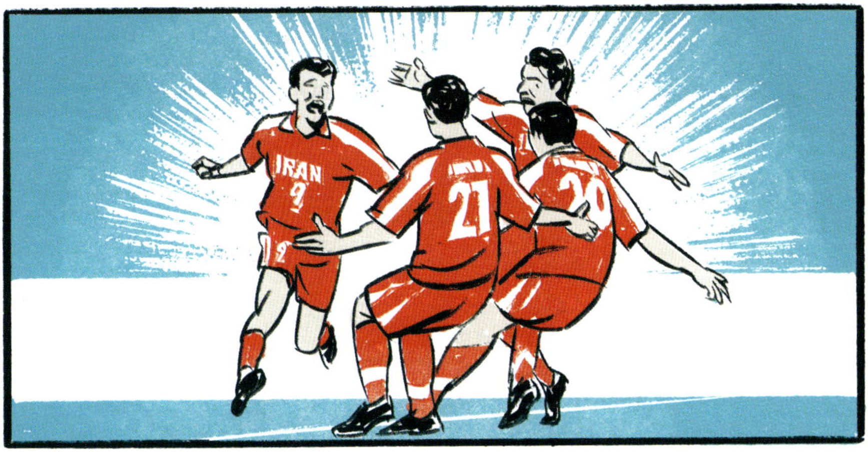
IRAN

TRIVIA GOALS

Soccer is a popular sport in Qatar. Which other sporting activity also takes place in the deserts of Qatar?

A) Glass-blowing contests

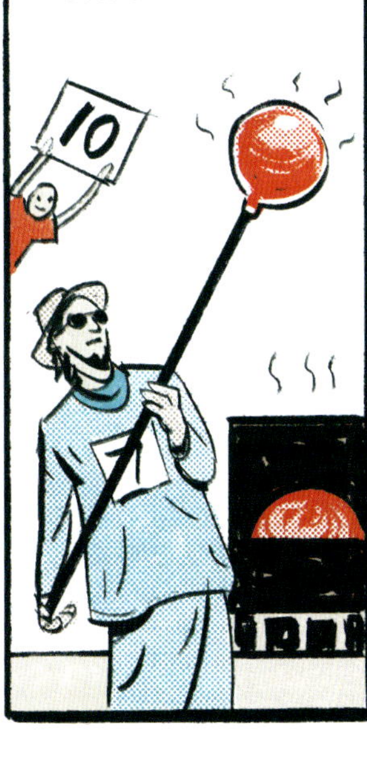
10

B) Robot camel racing

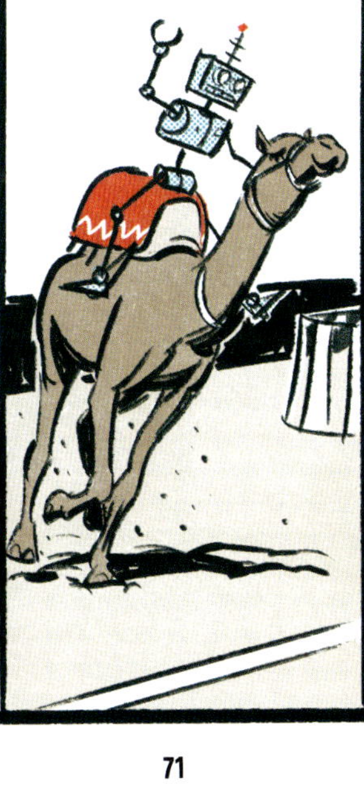

C) The sand dune Olympics

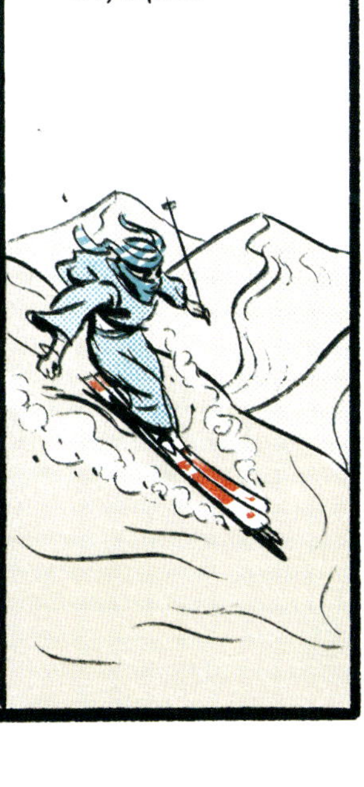

CHAPTER

7
STARS COLLIDE

In 2022, Messi was now thirty-five years old and on a mission. Months earlier, in a World Cup qualifier match, Messi scored a hat trick–3 goals!–and Argentina won 3-0. Then, as the tournament unfolded in Qatar, Messi and Argentina appeared unstoppable, earning a spot in the 2022 World Cup Finals. Once again, they would be competing for the championship.

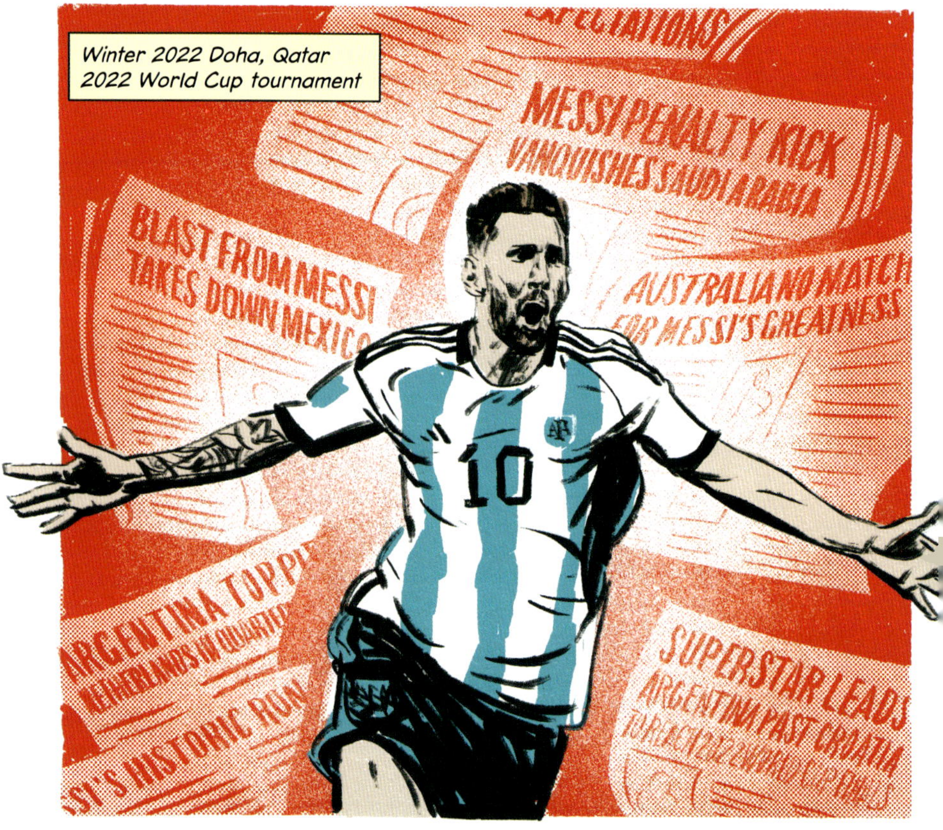
Winter 2022 Doha, Qatar
2022 World Cup tournament
MESSI PENALTY KICK
VANQUISHES SAUDI ARABIA
BLAST FROM MESSI
TAKES DOWN
AUSTRALIA NO
FOR MESSI'S GREATNESS
SUPERSTAR LEADS
ARGENTINA PAST CROATIA
10

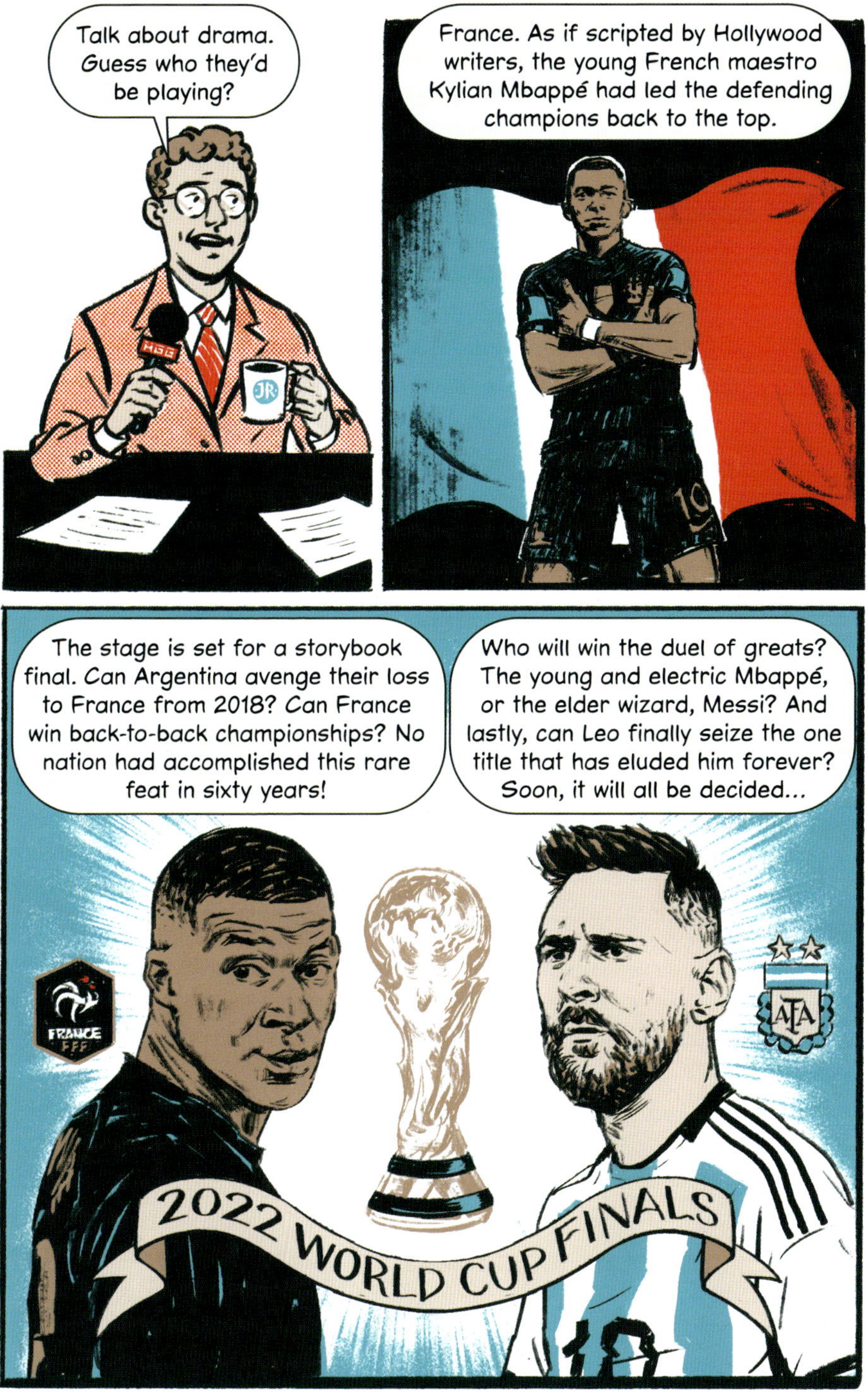
Talk about drama. Guess who they'd be playing?
France. As if scripted by Hollywood writers, the young French maestro Kylian Mbappé had led the defending champions back to the top.
The stage is set for a storybook final. Can Argentina avenge their loss to France from 2018? Can France win back-to-back championships? No nation had accomplished this rare feat in sixty years!
Who will win the duel of greats? The young and electric Mbappé, or the elder wizard, Messi? And lastly, can Leo finally seize the one title that has eluded him forever? Soon, it will all be decided...
FRANCE
FFF
AFA
2022 WORLD CUP FINALS

CHAPTER

8

2022 WORLD CUP FINAL

ONE FOR THE AGES

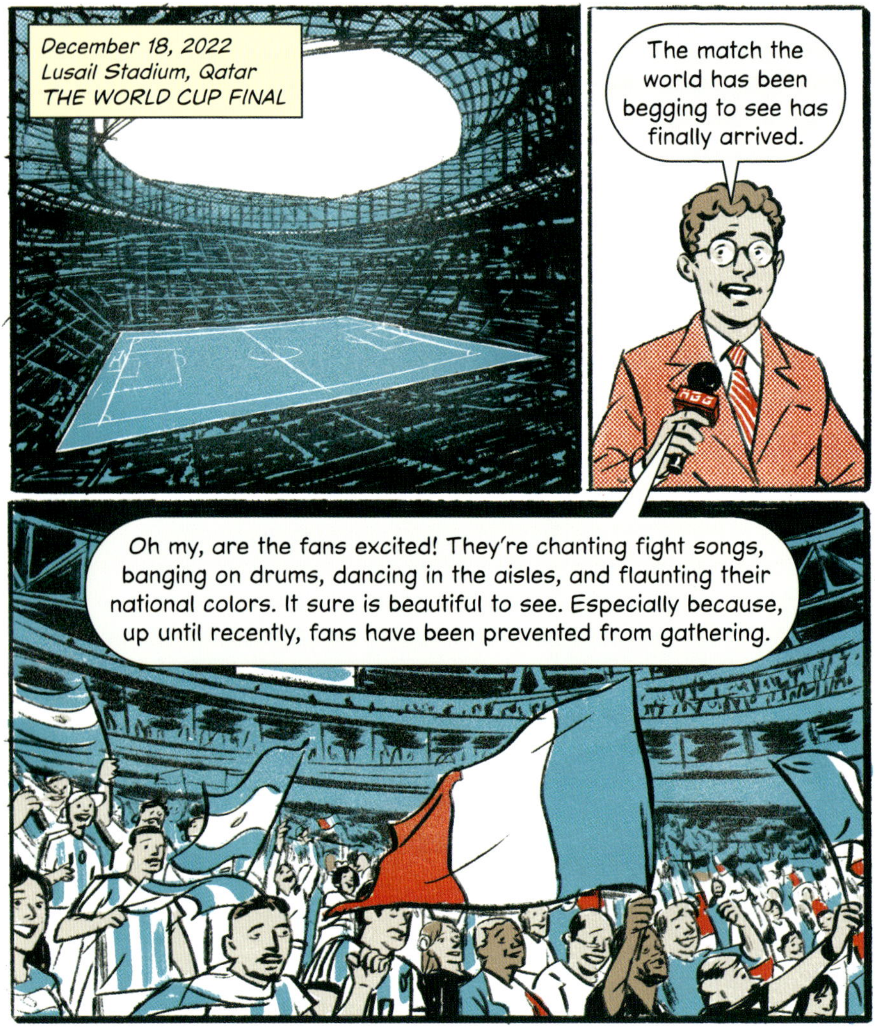

December 18, 2022
Lusail Stadium, Qatar
THE WORLD CUP FINAL
The match the world has been begging to see has finally arrived.
Oh my, are the fans excited! They're chanting fight songs, banging on drums, dancing in the aisles, and flaunting their national colors. It sure is beautiful to see. Especially because, up until recently, fans have been prevented from gathering.

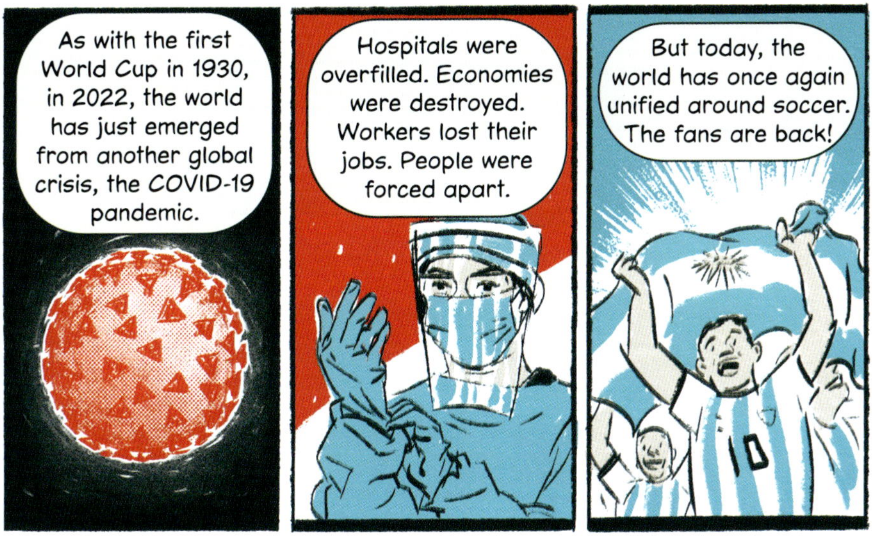
As with the first World Cup in 1930, in 2022, the world has just emerged from another global crisis, the COVID-19 pandemic.
Hospitals were overfilled. Economies were destroyed. Workers lost their jobs. People were forced apart.
But today, the world has once again unified around soccer. The fans are back!
10

And here's the starting lineup...

WORLD CUP FINAL

ARGENTINA VS. FRANCE

ARG

23	MARTÍNEZ
26	MOLINA
13	ROMERO
19	OTAMENDI
8	ACUÑA
11	DI MARÍA
7	DE PAUL
24	FERNÁNDEZ
20	MAC ALLISTER
10	MESSI
9	ÁLVAREZ

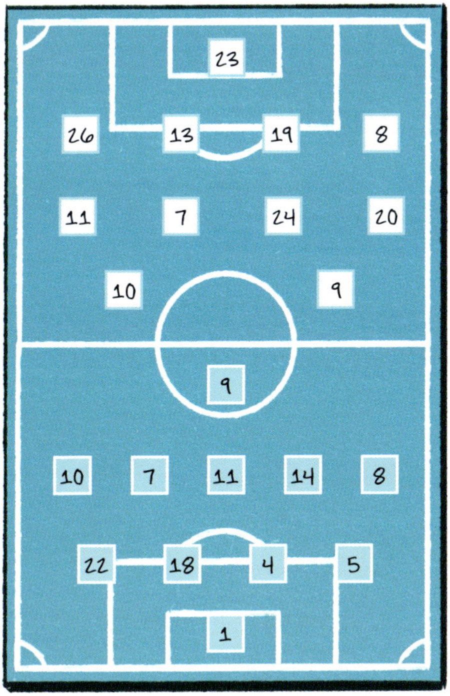
23
26
13
19
8
11
7
24
20
10
9
9
10
7
11
14
8
22
18
4
5
1

FRA

1	LLORIS
5	KOUNDE
4	VARANE
18	UPAMECANO
22	HERNANDEZ
8	TCHOUAMENI
14	RABIOT
11	DEMBELE
7	GRIEZMANN
10	MBAPPÉ
9	GIROUD

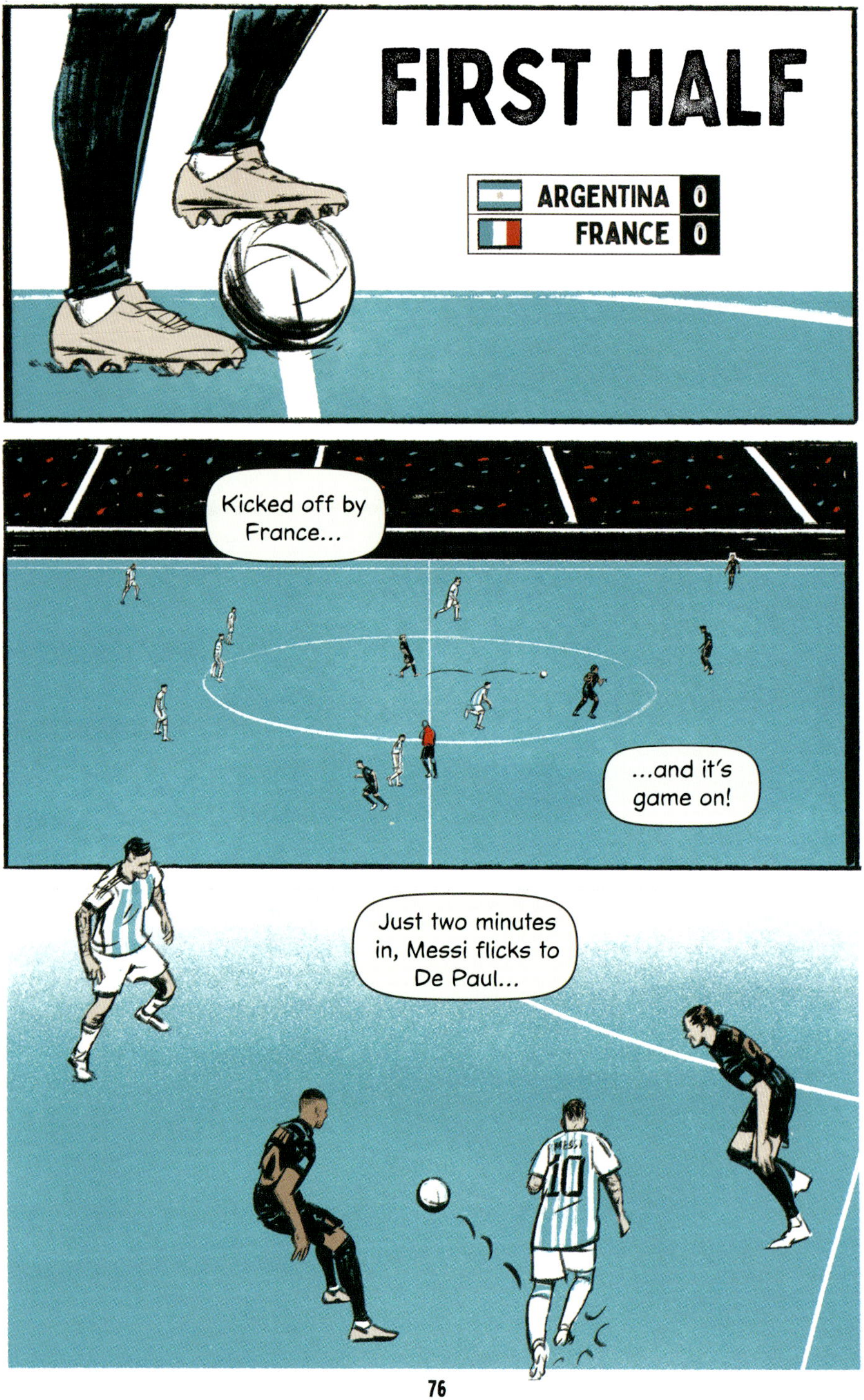
FIRST HALF
ARGENTINA 0
FRANCE 0
Kicked off by France...
...and it's game on!
Just two minutes in, Messi flicks to De Paul...

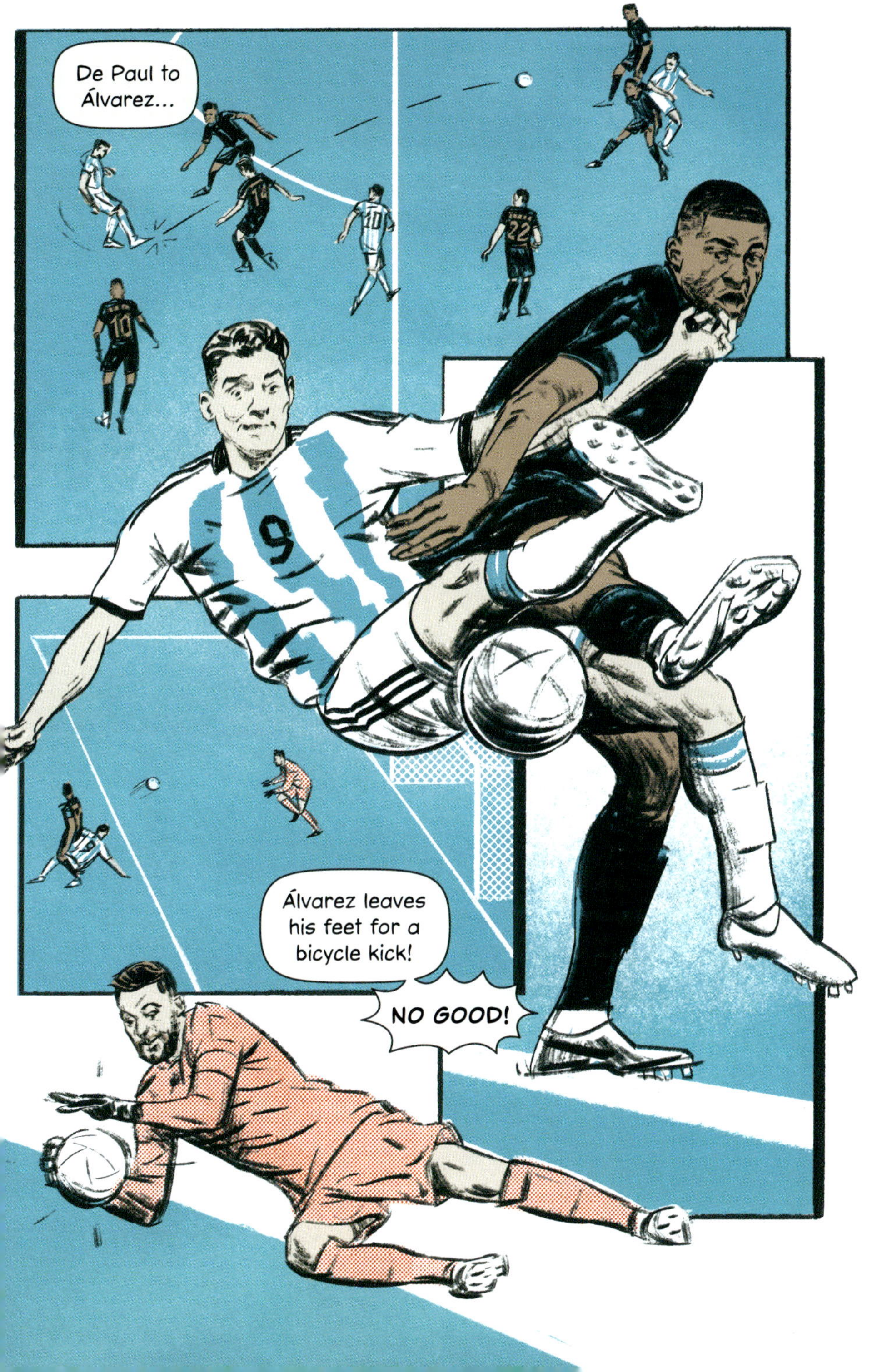
De Paul to Álvarez...
Álvarez leaves his feet for a bicycle kick!
NO GOOD!

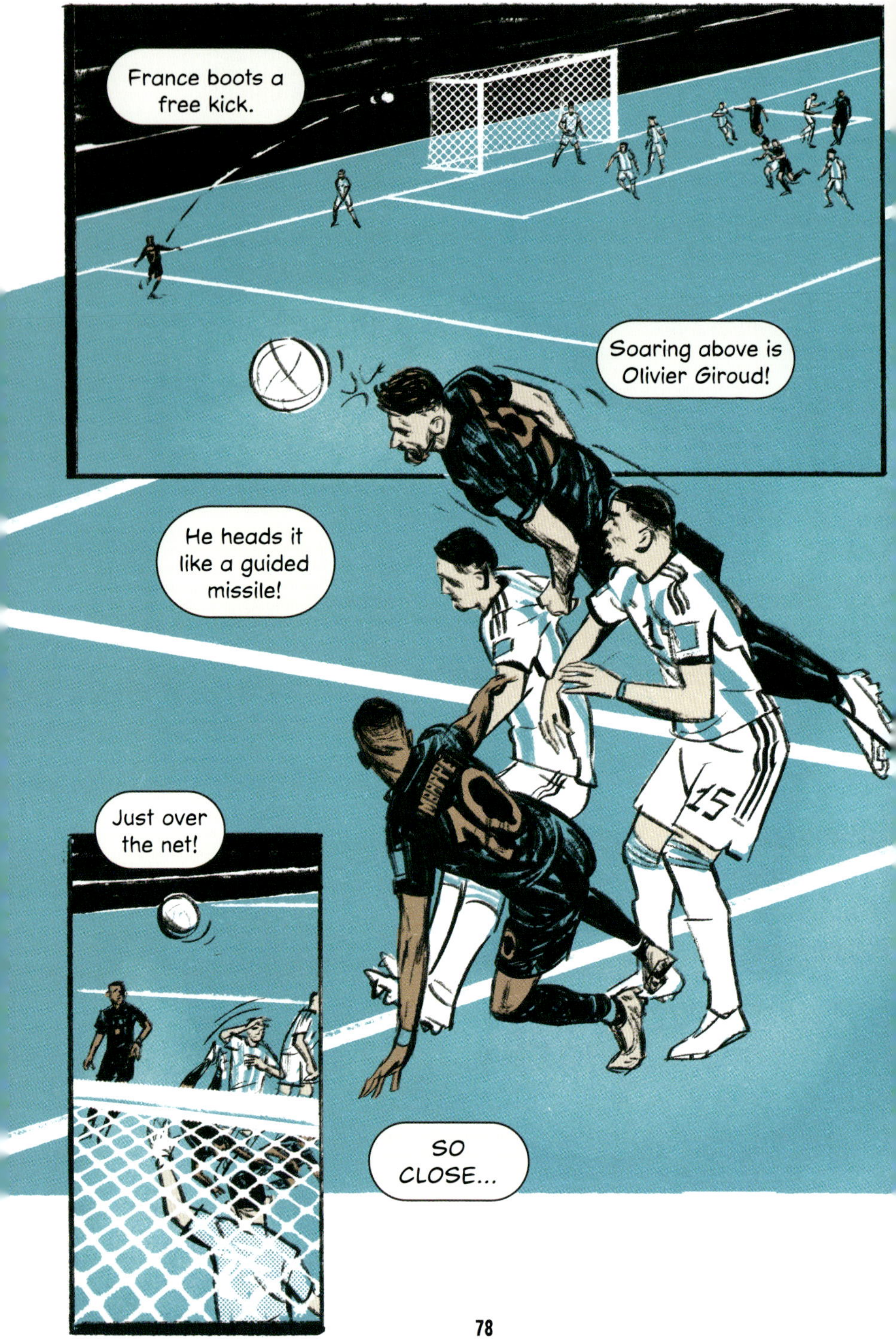
France boots a free kick.
Soaring above is Olivier Giroud!
He heads it like a guided missile!
Just over the net!
SO CLOSE...
MBAPPE
10
15

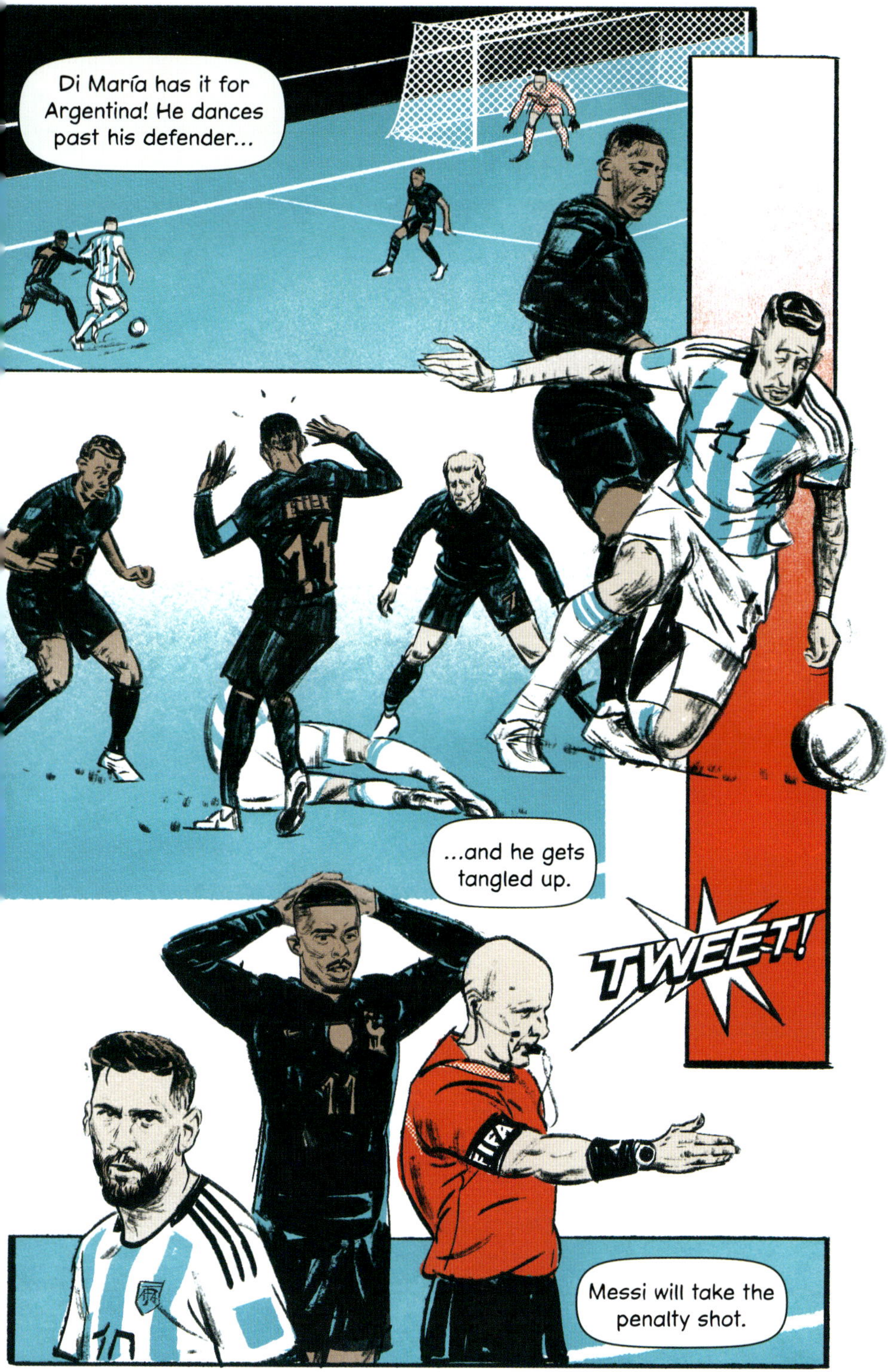
Di María has it for Argentina! He dances past his defender...
...and he gets tangled up.
TWEET!
Messi will take the penalty shot.

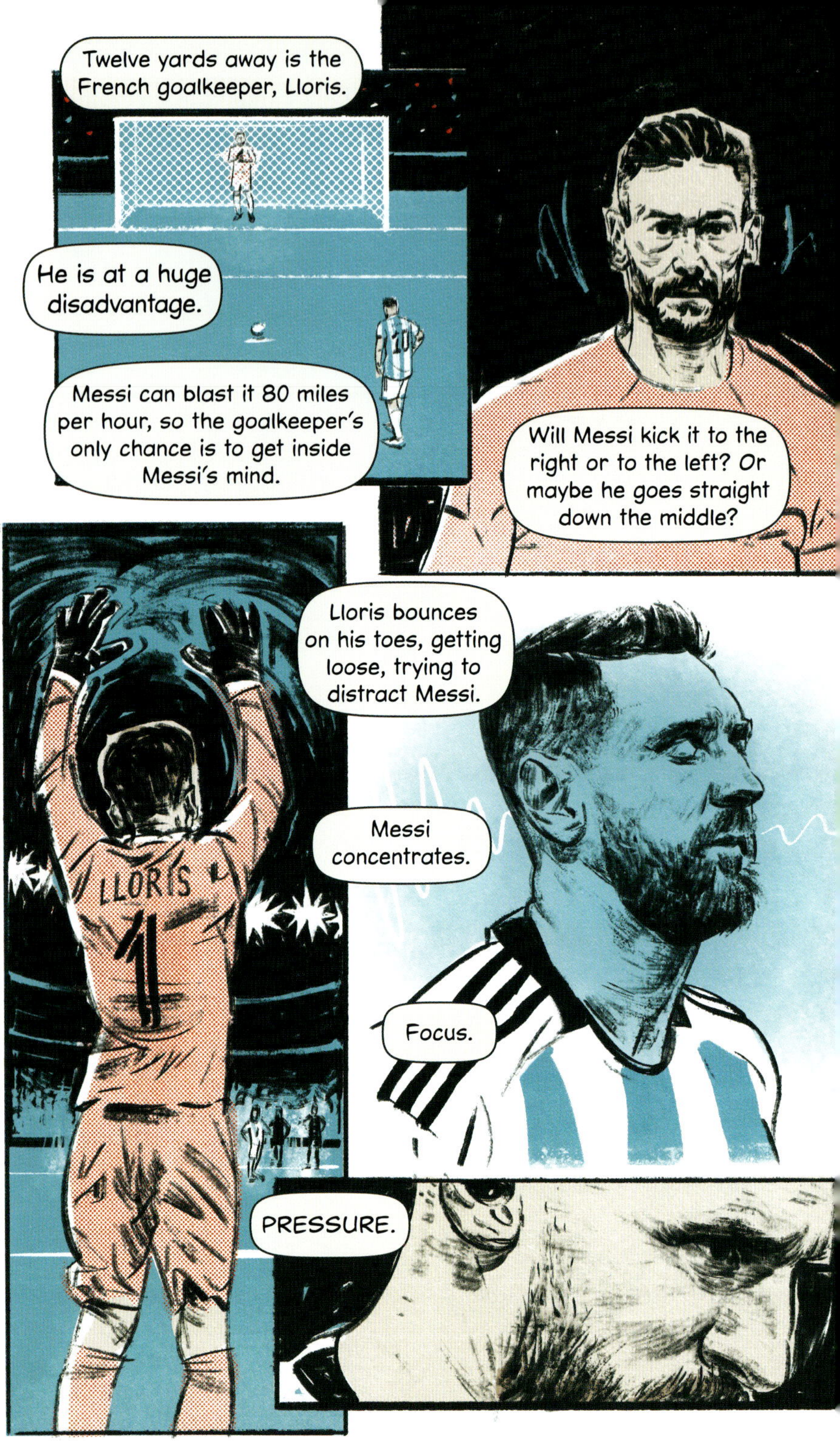

Twelve yards away is the French goalkeeper, Lloris.
He is at a huge disadvantage.
Messi can blast it 80 miles per hour, so the goalkeeper's only chance is to get inside Messi's mind.
Will Messi kick it to the right or to the left? Or maybe he goes straight down the middle?
LLORIS
1
Lloris bounces on his toes, getting loose, trying to distract Messi.
Messi concentrates.
Focus.
PRESSURE.

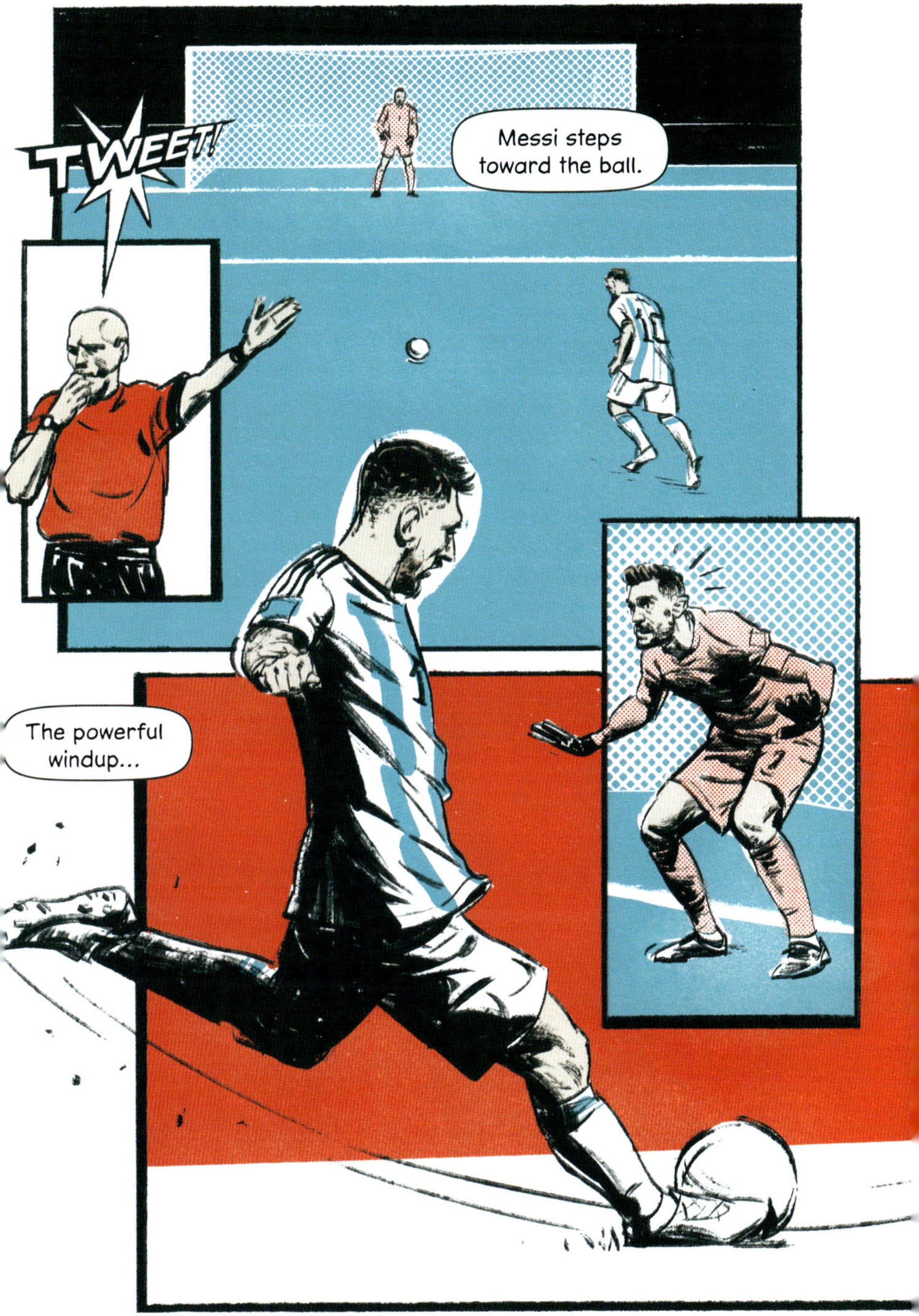
TWEET!
Messi steps toward the ball.
The powerful windup...

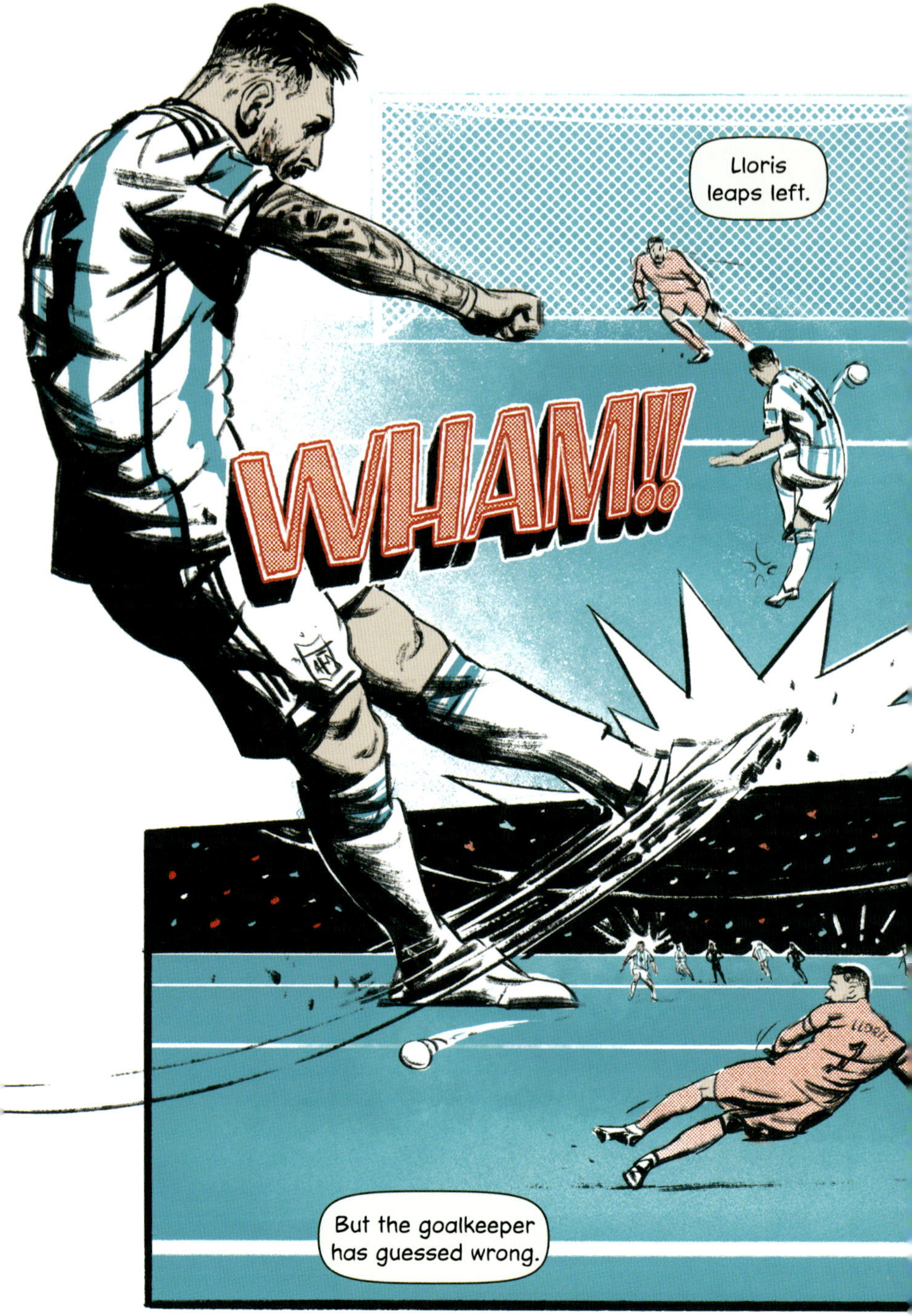
Lloris leaps left.
WHAM!!
LLORIS
But the goalkeeper has guessed wrong.

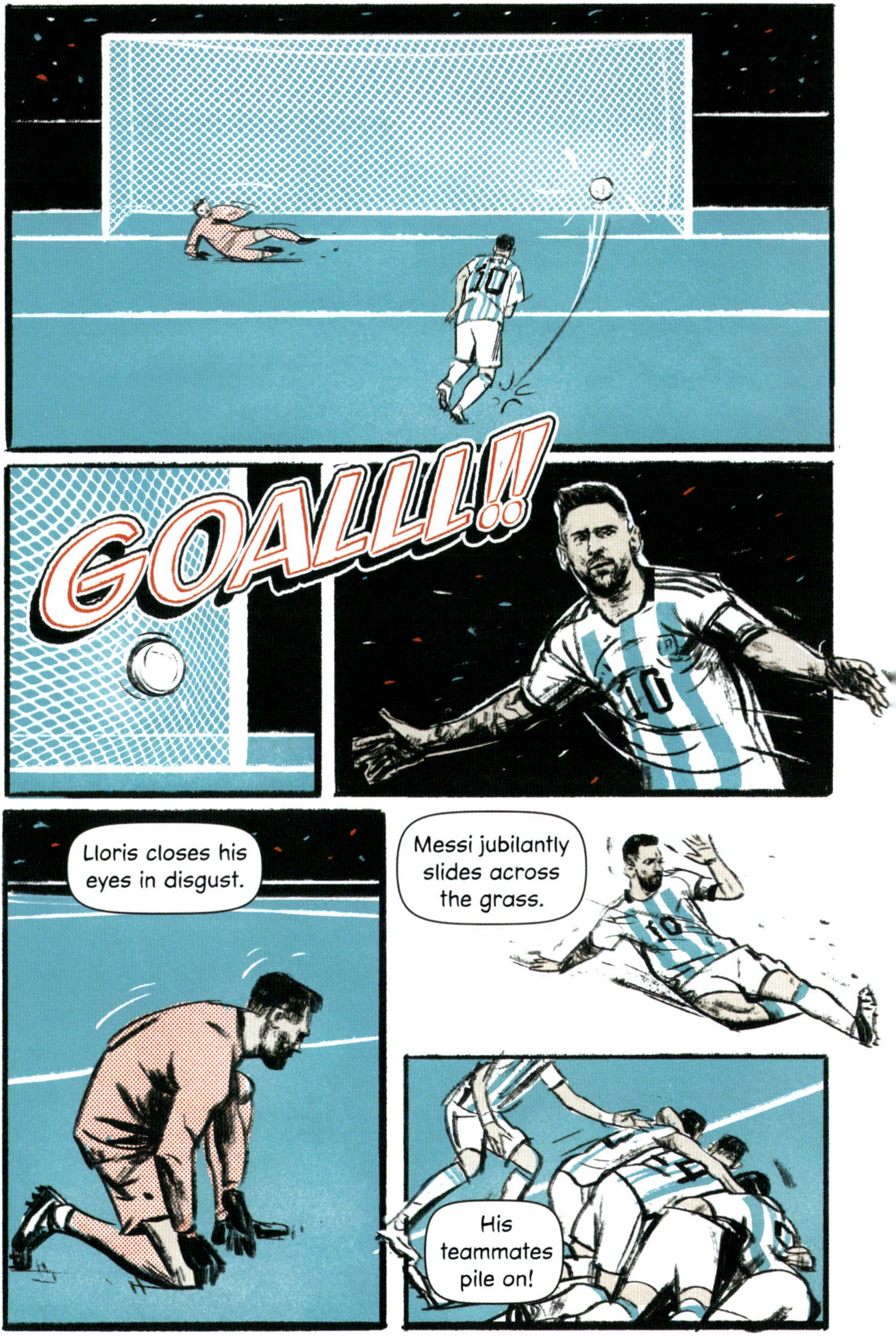
GOALLL!!
Lloris closes his eyes in disgust.
Messi jubilantly slides across the grass.
His teammates pile on!

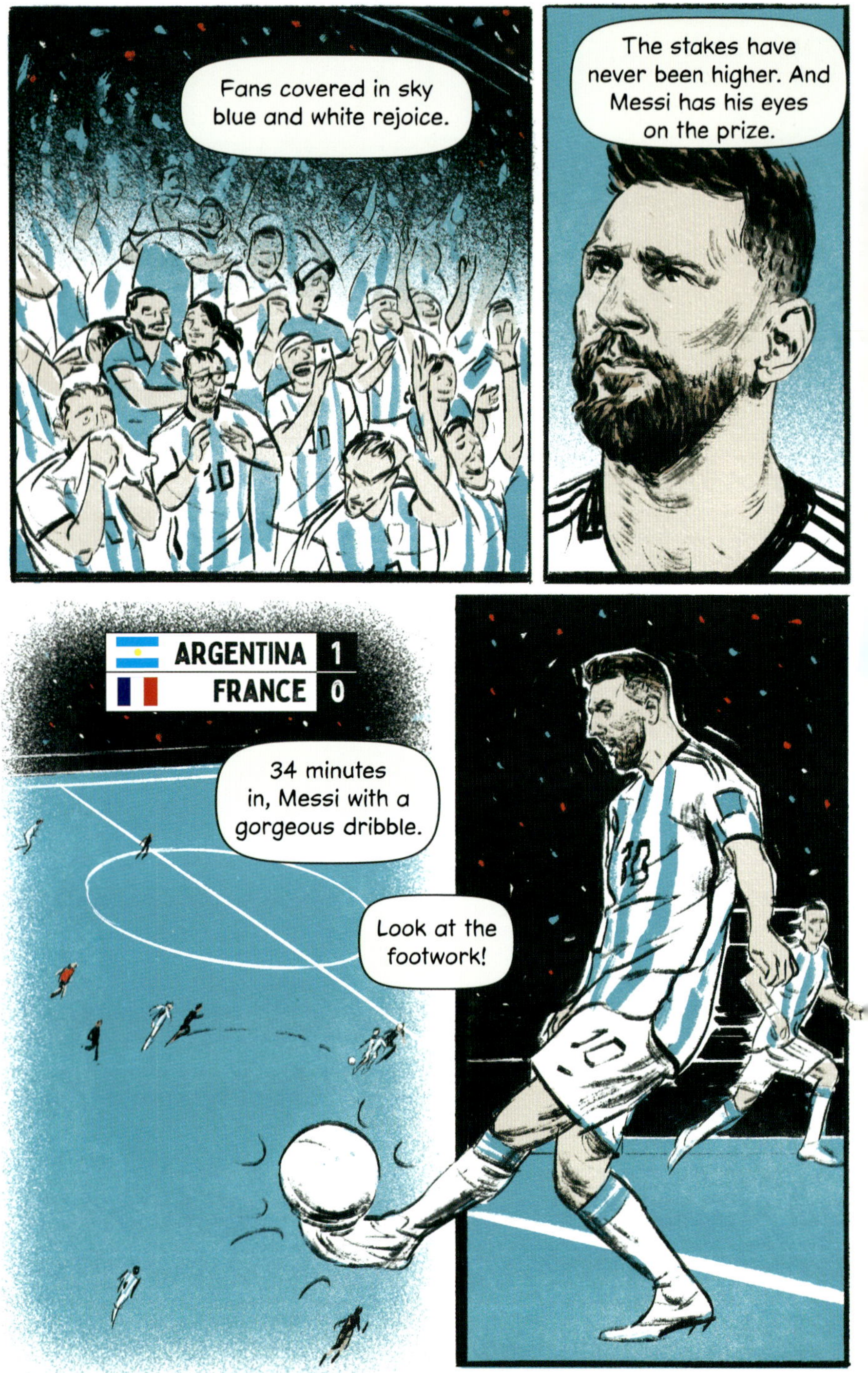
Fans covered in sky blue and white rejoice.
The stakes have never been higher. And Messi has his eyes on the prize.
ARGENTINA 1
FRANCE 0
34 minutes in, Messi with a gorgeous dribble.
Look at the footwork!

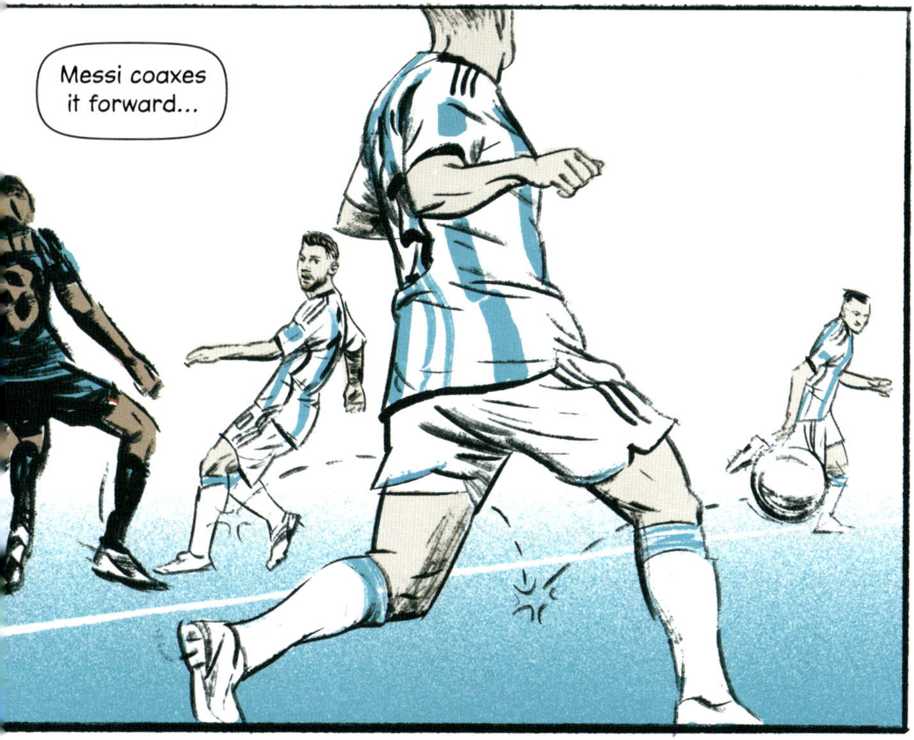
Messi coaxes it forward...

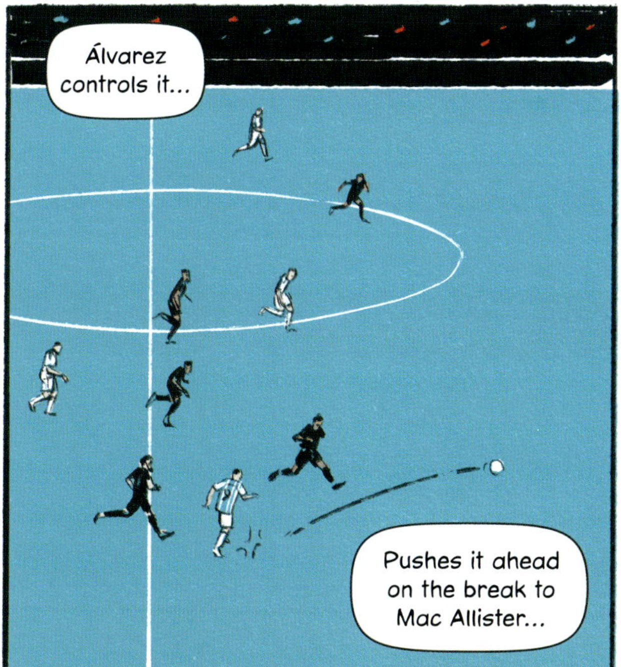
Álvarez controls it...
Pushes it ahead on the break to Mac Allister...

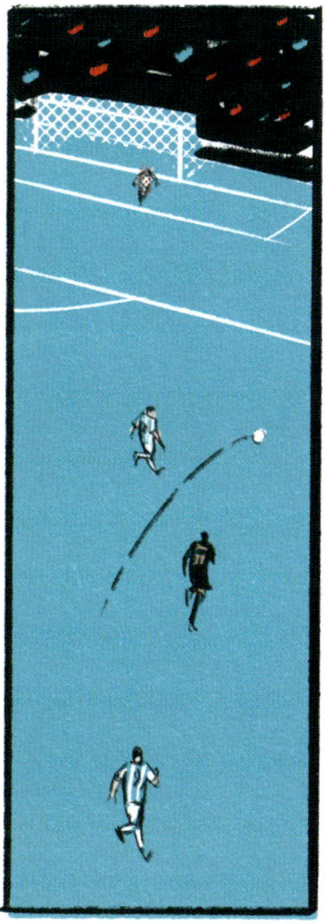

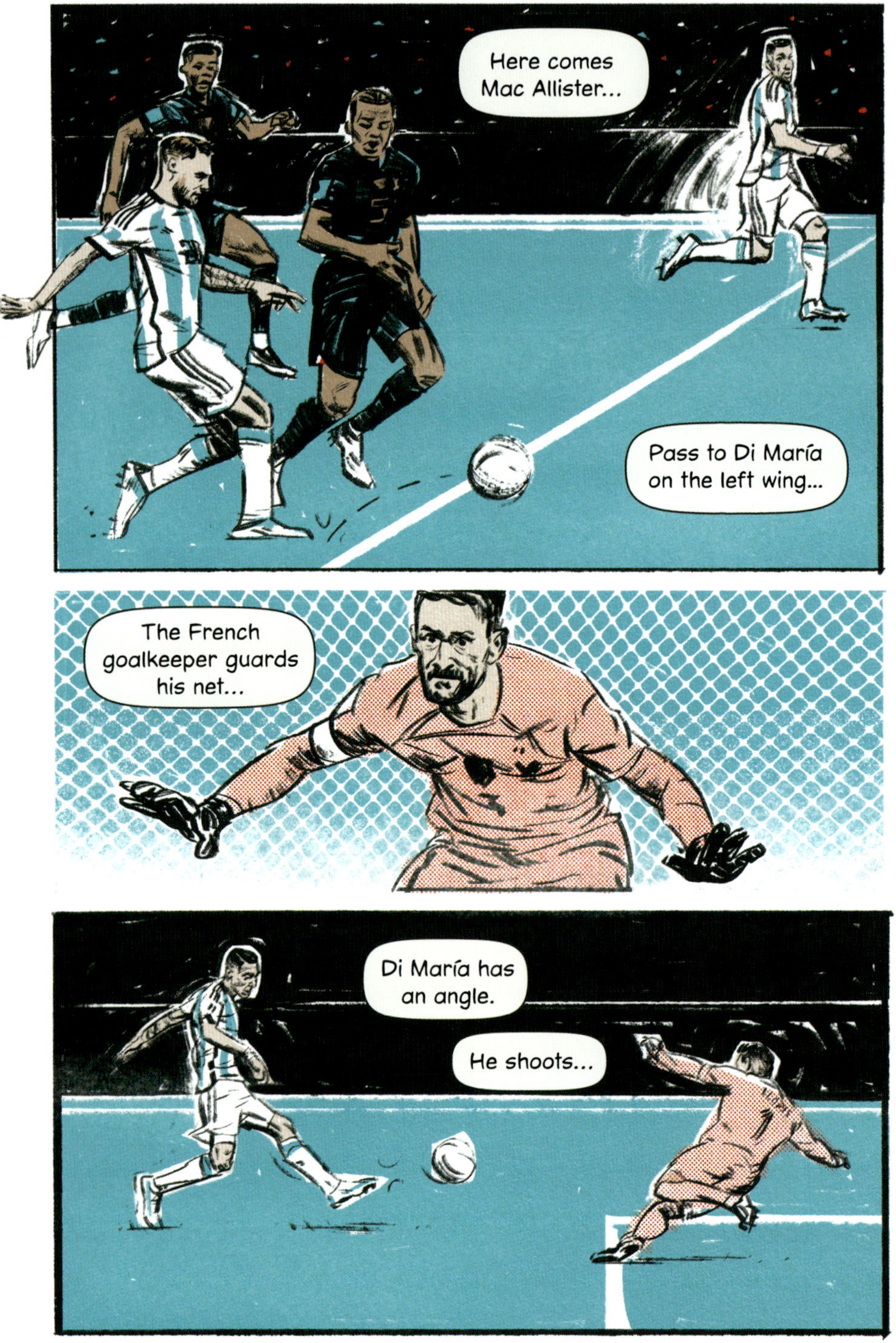
Here comes Mac Allister...
Pass to Di María on the left wing...
The French goalkeeper guards his net...
Di María has an angle.
He shoots...

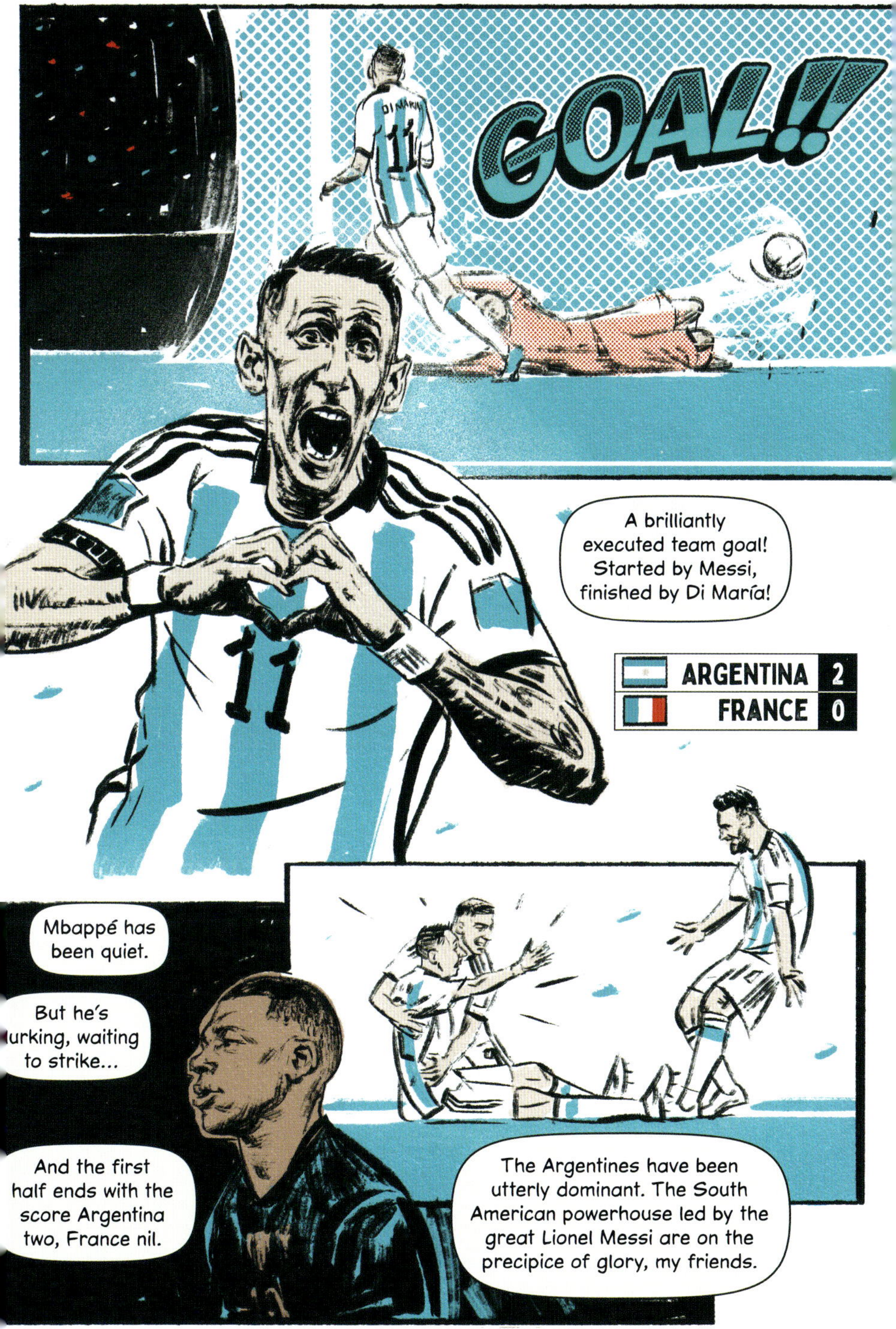
GOAL!!
A brilliantly executed team goal! Started by Messi, finished by Di María!
ARGENTINA 2
FRANCE 0
Mbappé has been quiet.
But he's lurking, waiting to strike...
And the first half ends with the score Argentina two, France nil.
The Argentines have been utterly dominant. The South American powerhouse led by the great Lionel Messi are on the precipice of glory, my friends.

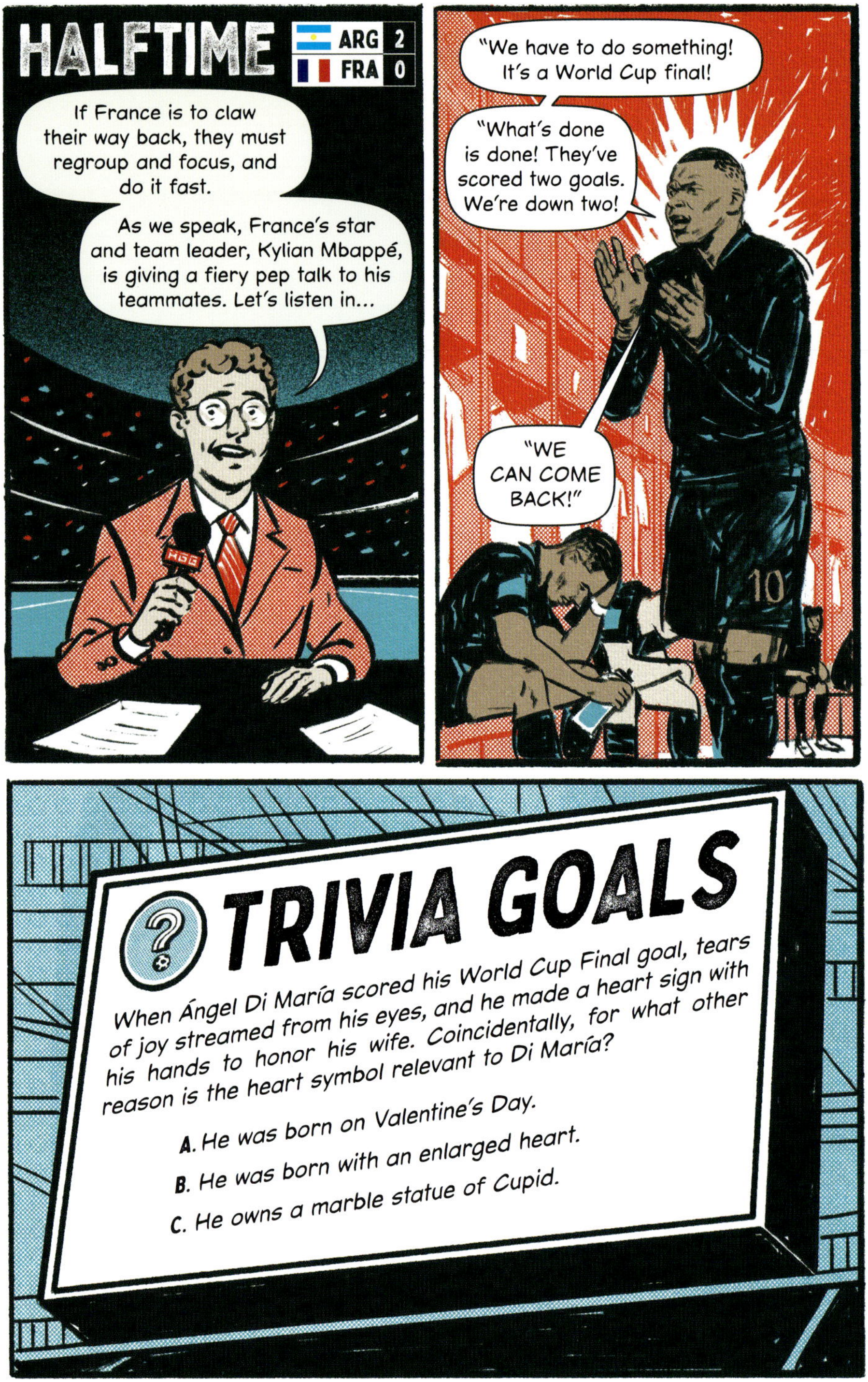
HALFTIME
ARG 2
FRA 0
If France is to claw their way back, they must regroup and focus, and do it fast.
As we speak, France's star and team leader, Kylian Mbappé, is giving a fiery pep talk to his teammates. Let's listen in...
"We have to do something! It's a World Cup final!
"What's done is done! They've scored two goals. We're down two!
"WE CAN COME BACK!"
10
TRIVIA GOALS
When Ángel Di María scored his World Cup Final goal, tears of joy streamed from his eyes, and he made a heart sign with his hands to honor his wife. Coincidentally, for what other reason is the heart symbol relevant to Di María?
A. He was born on Valentine's Day.
B. He was born with an enlarged heart.
C. He owns a marble statue of Cupid.

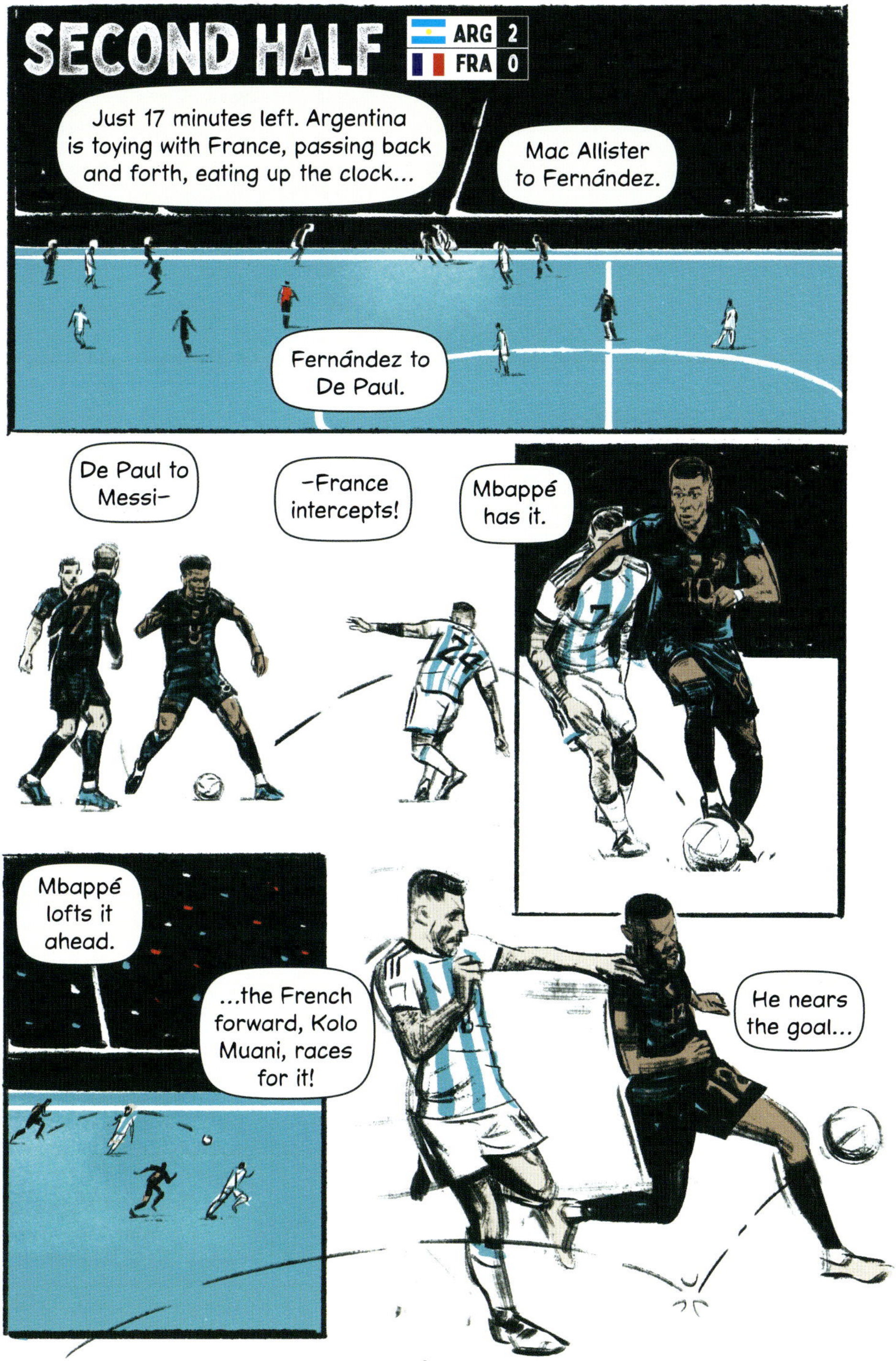
SECOND HALF
ARG 2
FRA 0
Just 17 minutes left. Argentina is toying with France, passing back and forth, eating up the clock...
Mac Allister to Fernández.
Fernández to De Paul.
De Paul to Messi–
–France intercepts!
Mbappé has it.
Mbappé lofts it ahead.
...the French forward, Kolo Muani, races for it!
He nears the goal...

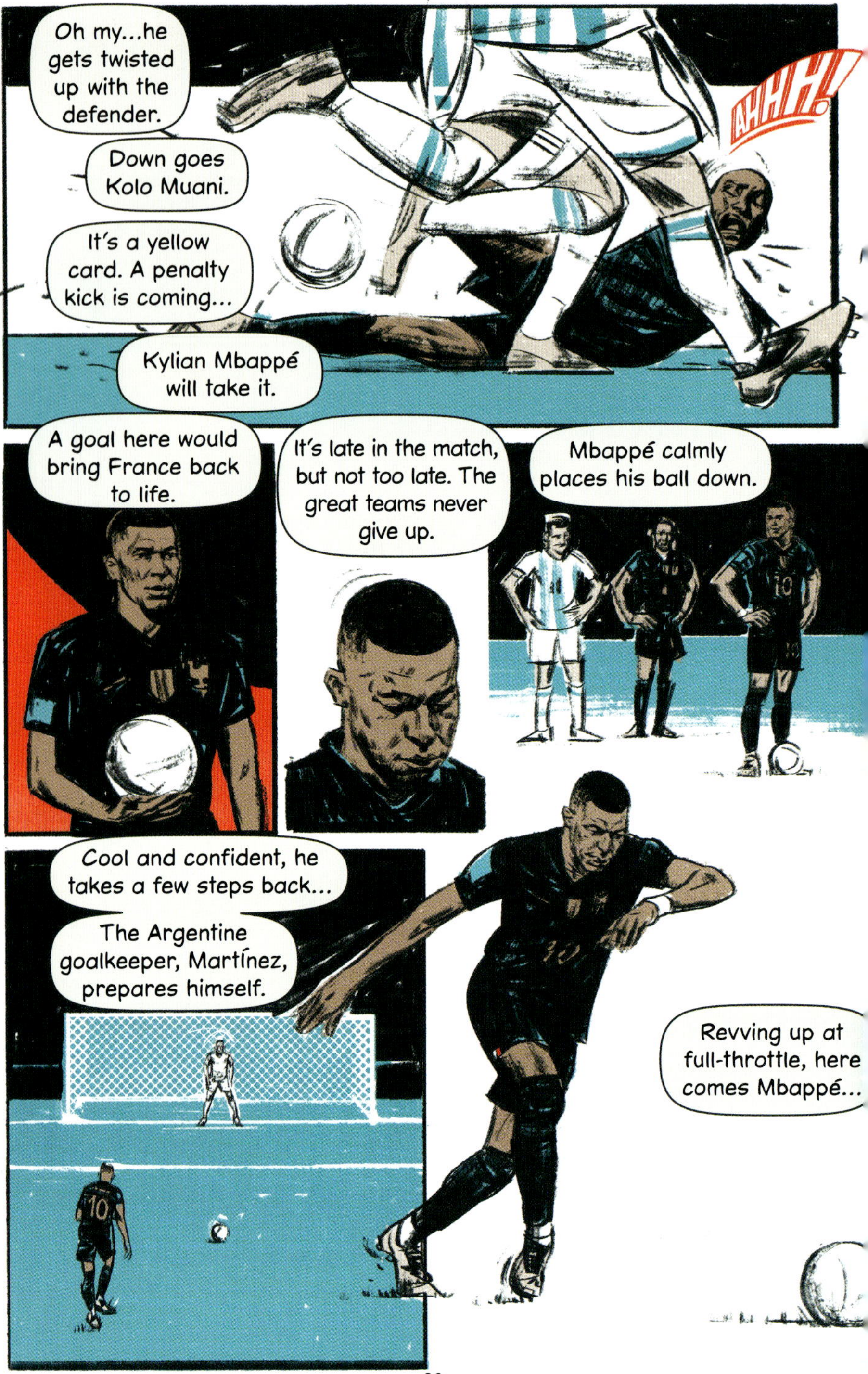
Oh my...he gets twisted up with the defender.
AHHH!
Down goes Kolo Muani.
It's a yellow card. A penalty kick is coming...
Kylian Mbappé will take it.
A goal here would bring France back to life.
It's late in the match, but not too late. The great teams never give up.
Mbappé calmly places his ball down.
Cool and confident, he takes a few steps back...
The Argentine goalkeeper, Martínez, prepares himself.
Revving up at full-throttle, here comes Mbappé...

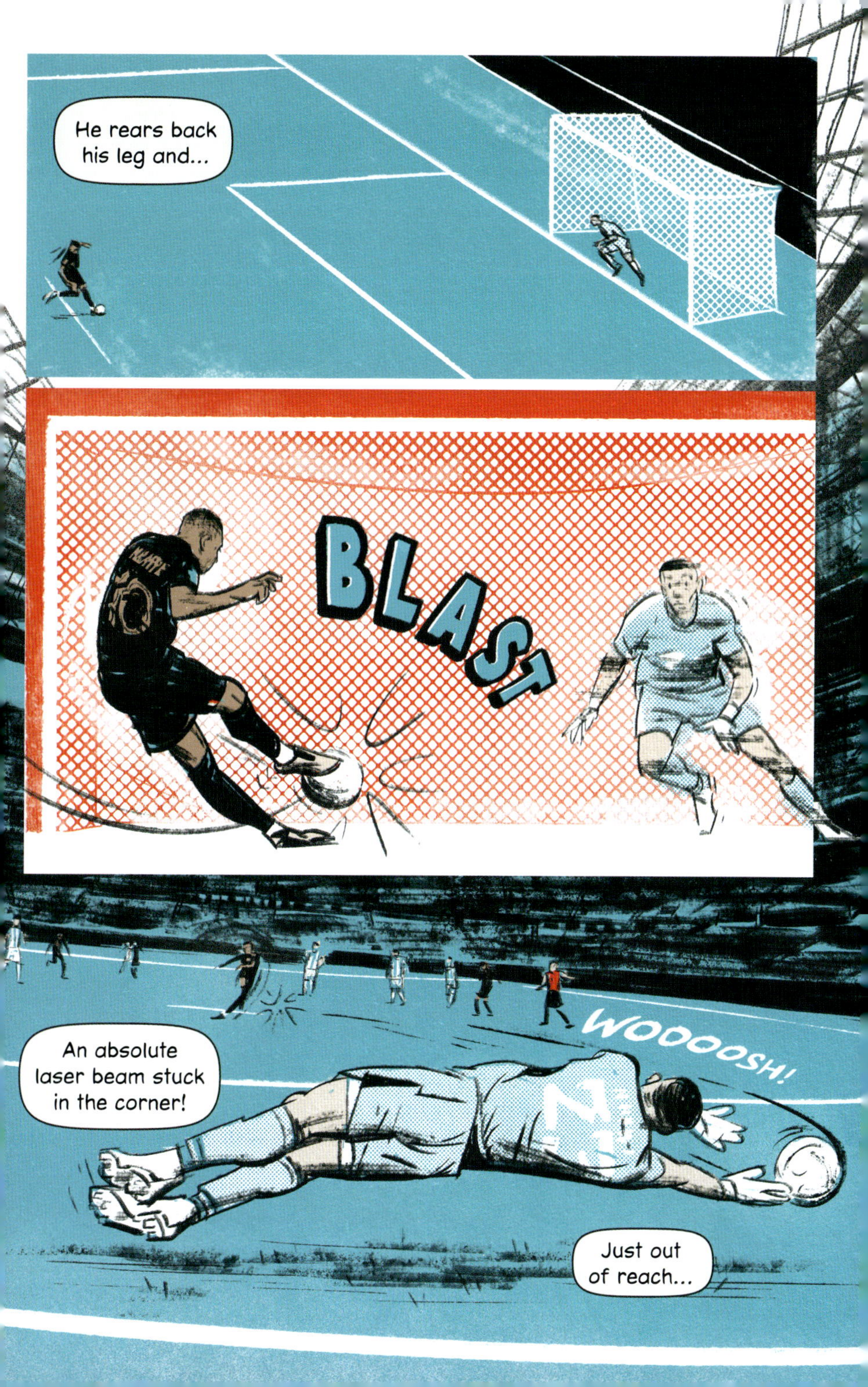
He rears back his leg and...
BLAST
An absolute laser beam stuck in the corner!
WOOOOSH!
Just out of reach...

GOAL!

Mbappé delivers!

The goalkeeper slaps his hands in frustration. A game of inches.

🇦🇷	ARGENTINA	2
🇫🇷	FRANCE	1

Mbappé is mobbed by his teammates.

The French fans roar.

French president, Emmanuel Macron, pumps his fist! Today he's not a politician. He is a fan.

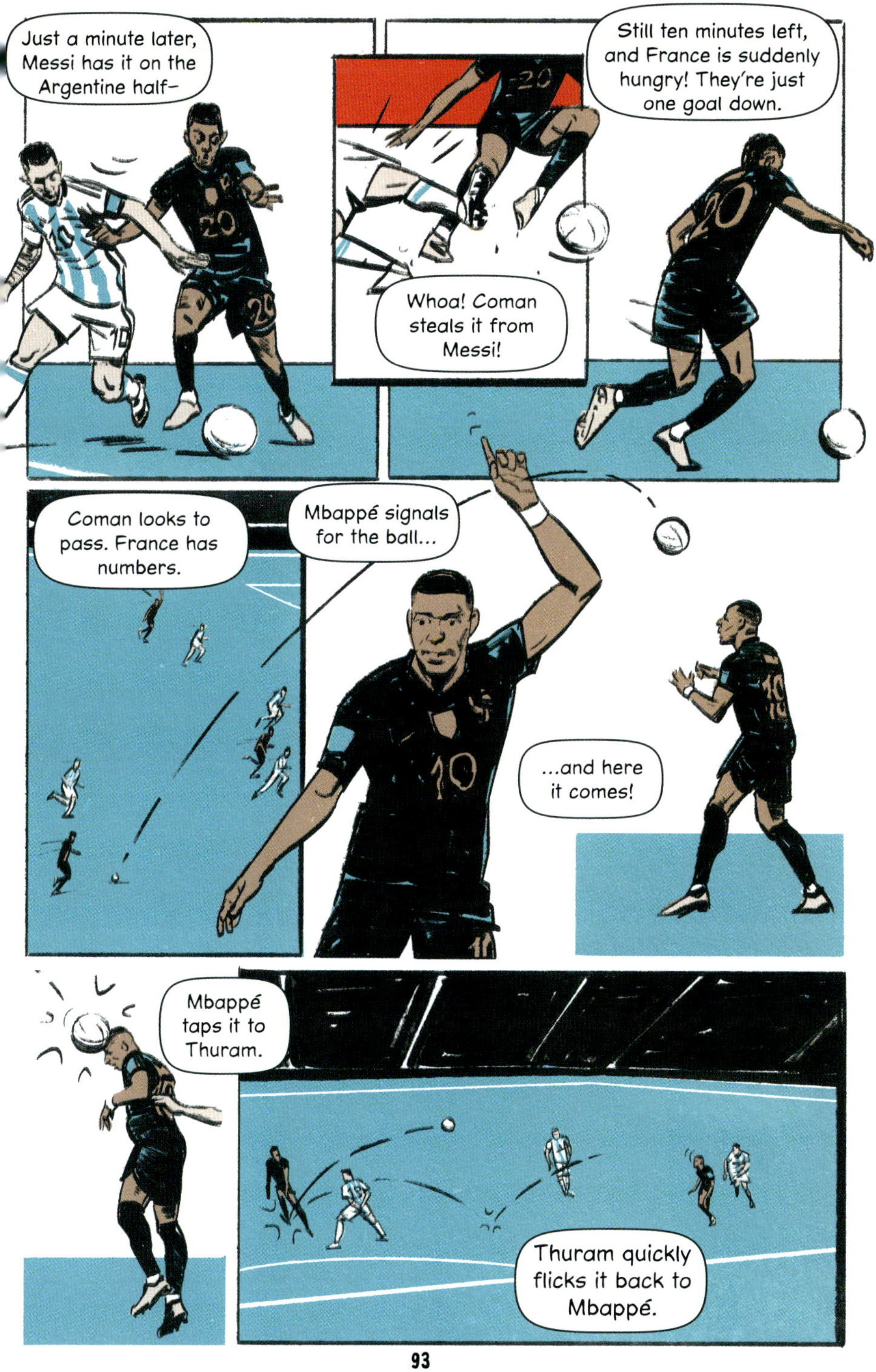
Just a minute later, Messi has it on the Argentine half–
Whoa! Coman steals it from Messi!
Still ten minutes left, and France is suddenly hungry! They're just one goal down.
Coman looks to pass. France has numbers.
Mbappé signals for the ball...
...and here it comes!
Mbappé taps it to Thuram.
Thuram quickly flicks it back to Mbappé.

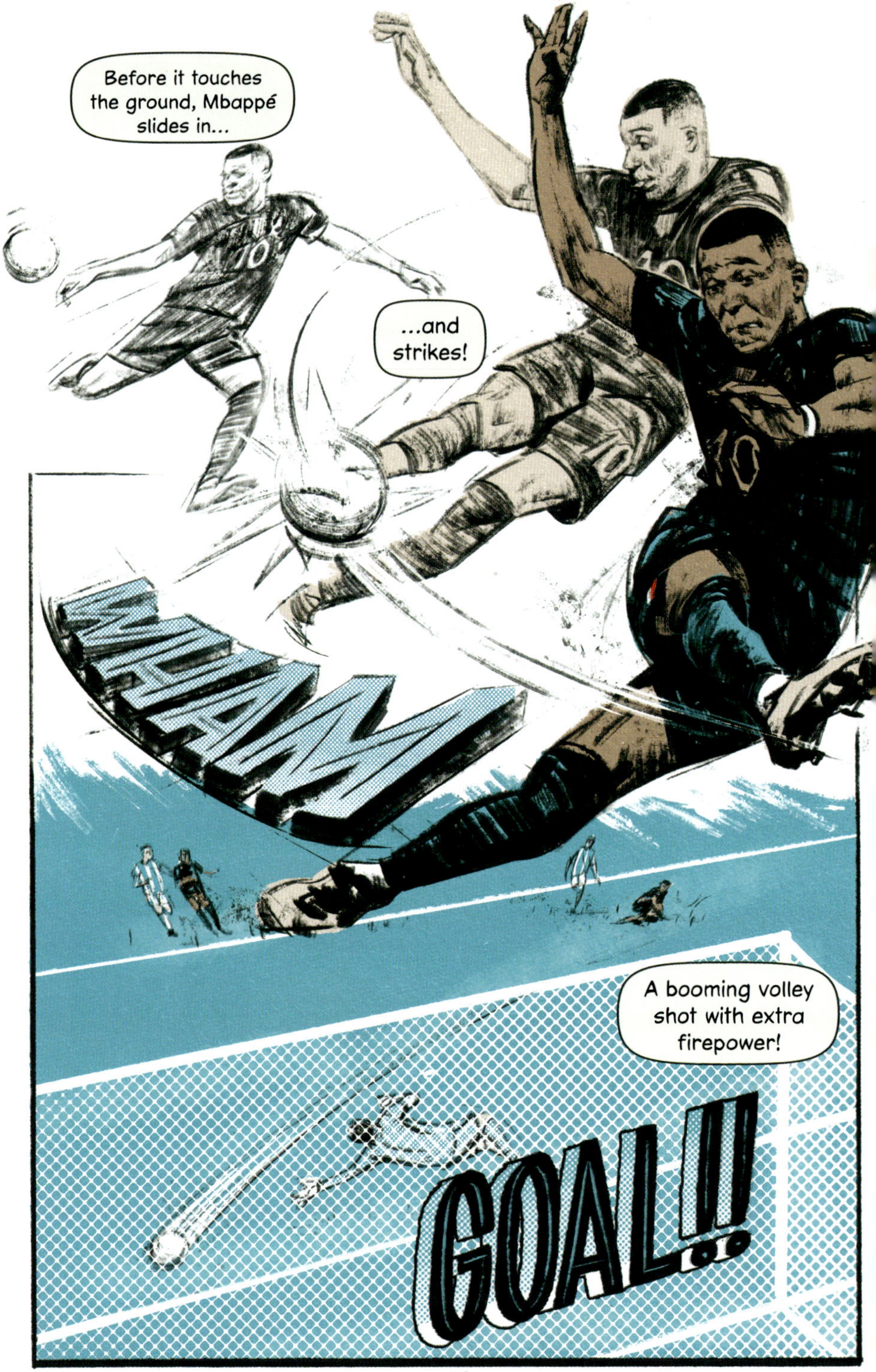
Before it touches the ground, Mbappé slides in...
...and strikes!
WHAM
A booming volley shot with extra firepower!
GOAL!!!

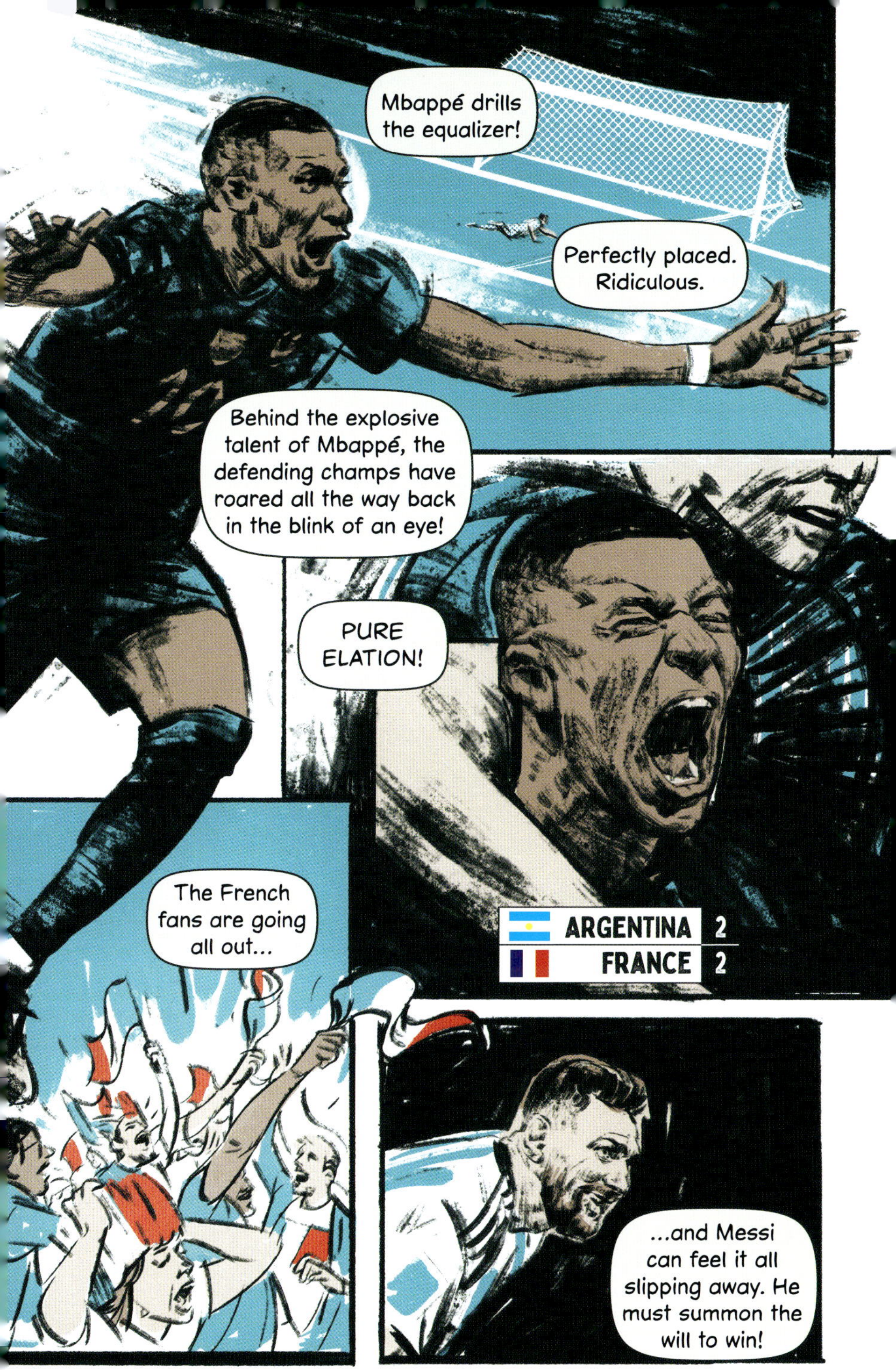
Mbappé drills the equalizer!
Perfectly placed. Ridiculous.
Behind the explosive talent of Mbappé, the defending champs have roared all the way back in the blink of an eye!
PURE ELATION!
ARGENTINA 2
FRANCE 2
The French fans are going all out...
...and Messi can feel it all slipping away. He must summon the will to win!

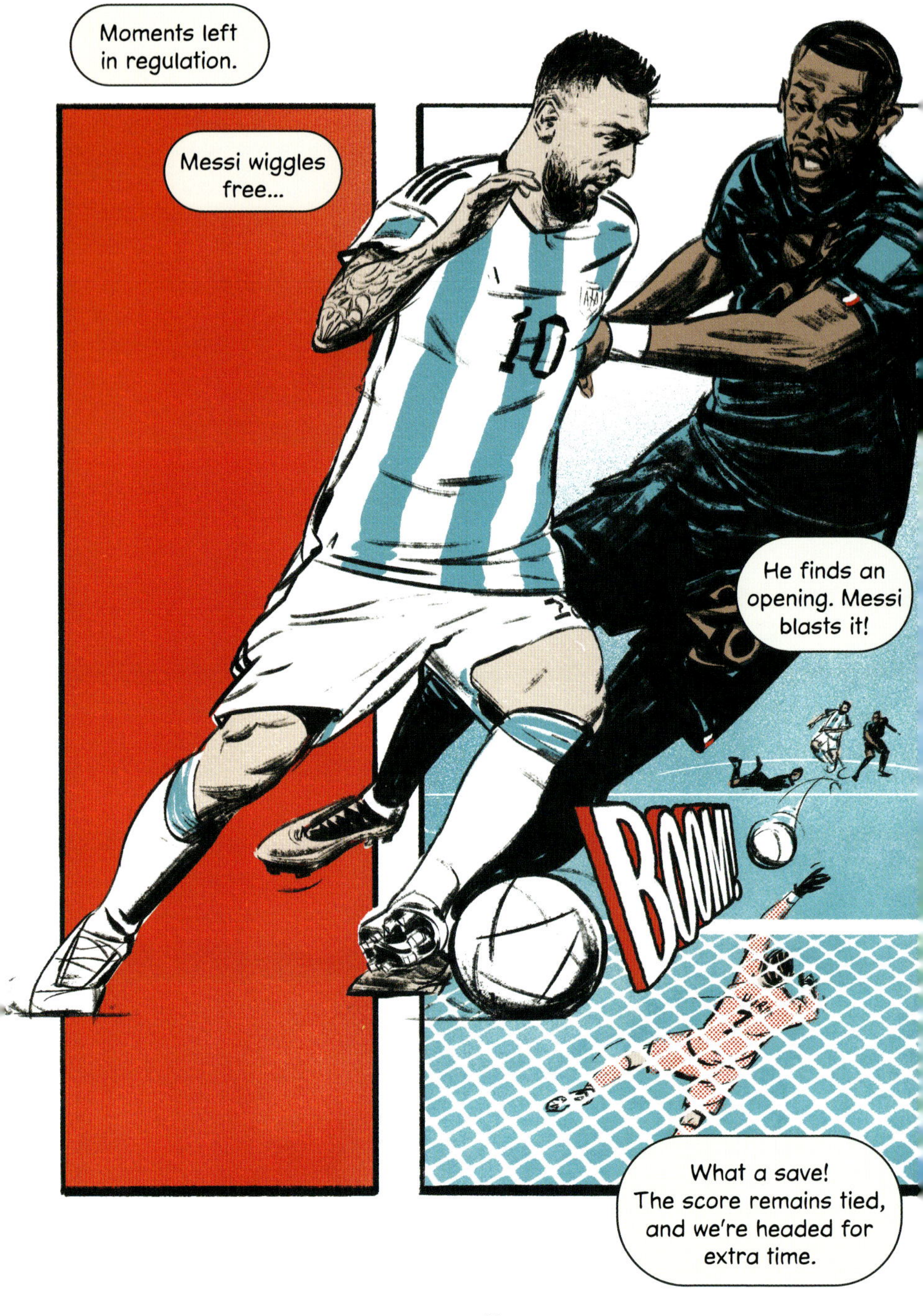
Moments left in regulation.
Messi wiggles free...
He finds an opening. Messi blasts it!
BOOM!
What a save! The score remains tied, and we're headed for extra time.

END OF REGULATION TIME

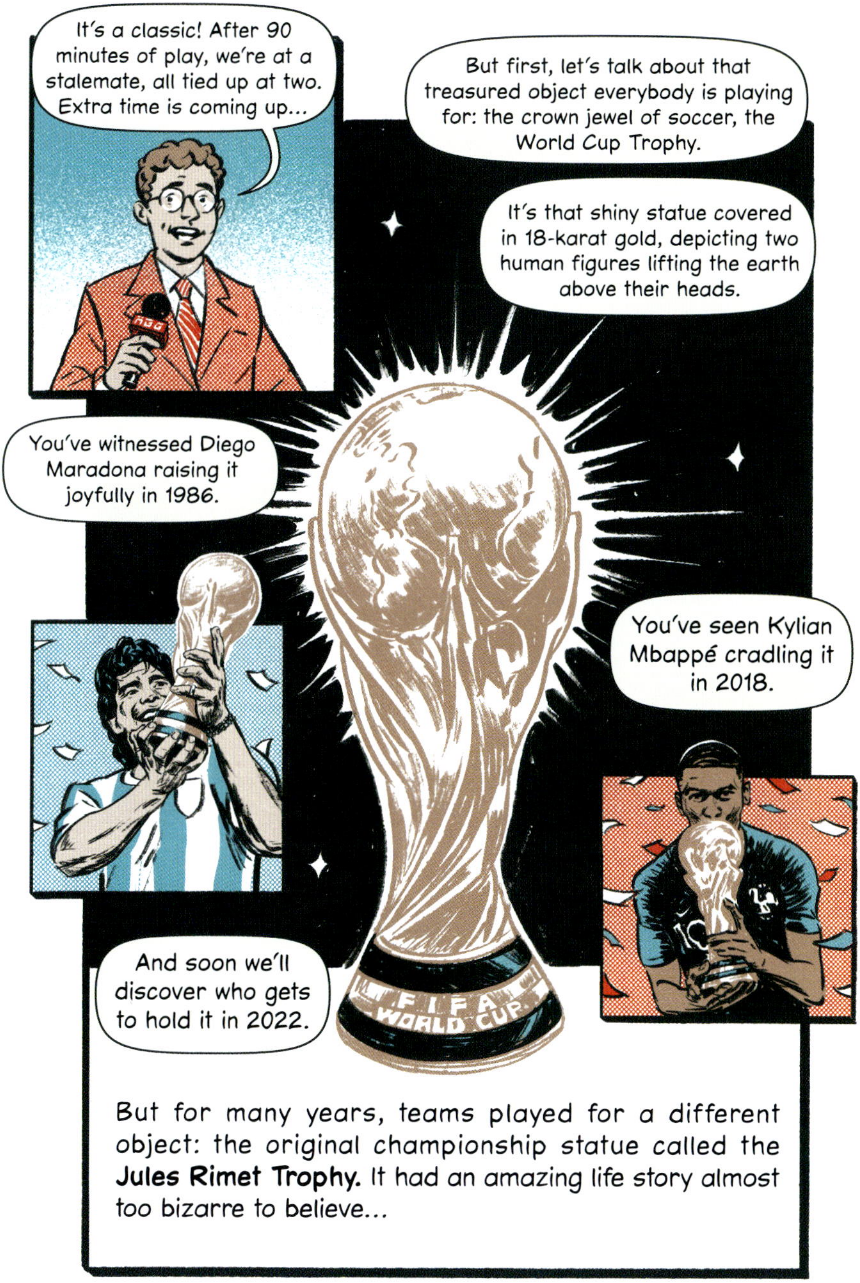
It's a classic! After 90 minutes of play, we're at a stalemate, all tied up at two. Extra time is coming up...
But first, let's talk about that treasured object everybody is playing for: the crown jewel of soccer, the World Cup Trophy.
It's that shiny statue covered in 18-karat gold, depicting two human figures lifting the earth above their heads.
You've witnessed Diego Maradona raising it joyfully in 1986.
You've seen Kylian Mbappé cradling it in 2018.
FIFA WORLD CUP
And soon we'll discover who gets to hold it in 2022.
But for many years, teams played for a different object: the original championship statue called the **Jules Rimet Trophy.** It had an amazing life story almost too bizarre to believe...

TIME-OUT FOR HISTORY

THE TWISTED TALE OF THE WORLD CUP TROPHY

From the first World Cup in 1930 up until 1970, the ultimate prize in soccer was the Jules Rimet Trophy. It was crafted by a famous French sculptor in the image of the Greek goddess of triumph, Nike.

The trophy's first curious plot twist occurred in 1938 during the onset of World War II. Italy had just won its second World Cup in a row, and for safekeeping, the trophy was being held in an Italian bank in Rome.

Yet the president of Italian soccer, Ottorino Barassi, had a strange feeling that even under lock and key, the Jules Rimet Trophy was not well protected. According to reports, Barassi secretly arranged for the treasured keepsake to be moved to his apartment. Sure enough, the Nazis came looking for it.

They searched his home inside and out but couldn't find it. That's because the trophy was hidden in a shoebox beneath Barassi's bed, and it was safe...for the time being.

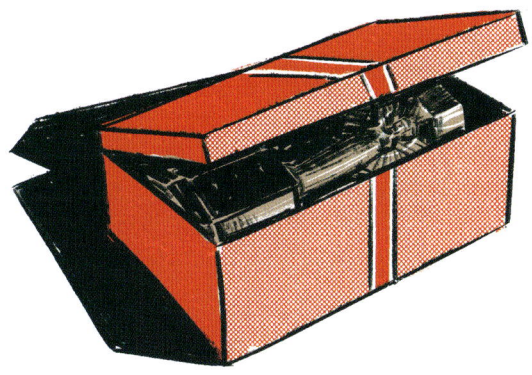

Next, the saga of the Jules Rimet Trophy took an even stranger turn. We fast forward to the World Cup of 1966 hosted by England. Just a few months prior to opening kickoff, the trophy was put on display in a prominent London hall for all the public to admire. But a few days later, British guards came to check on it, and their worst fears had come true: the Jules Rimet Trophy was gone!

Who had taken it and why? The authorities didn't know. A week later, a hero recovered our holy grail. But the savior wasn't a human; it was a dog named Pickles. The canine was strutting down a street in London when it began sniffing around a package covered in newspaper in somebody's front garden.

The Jules Rimet Trophy had been found!
But not for long...

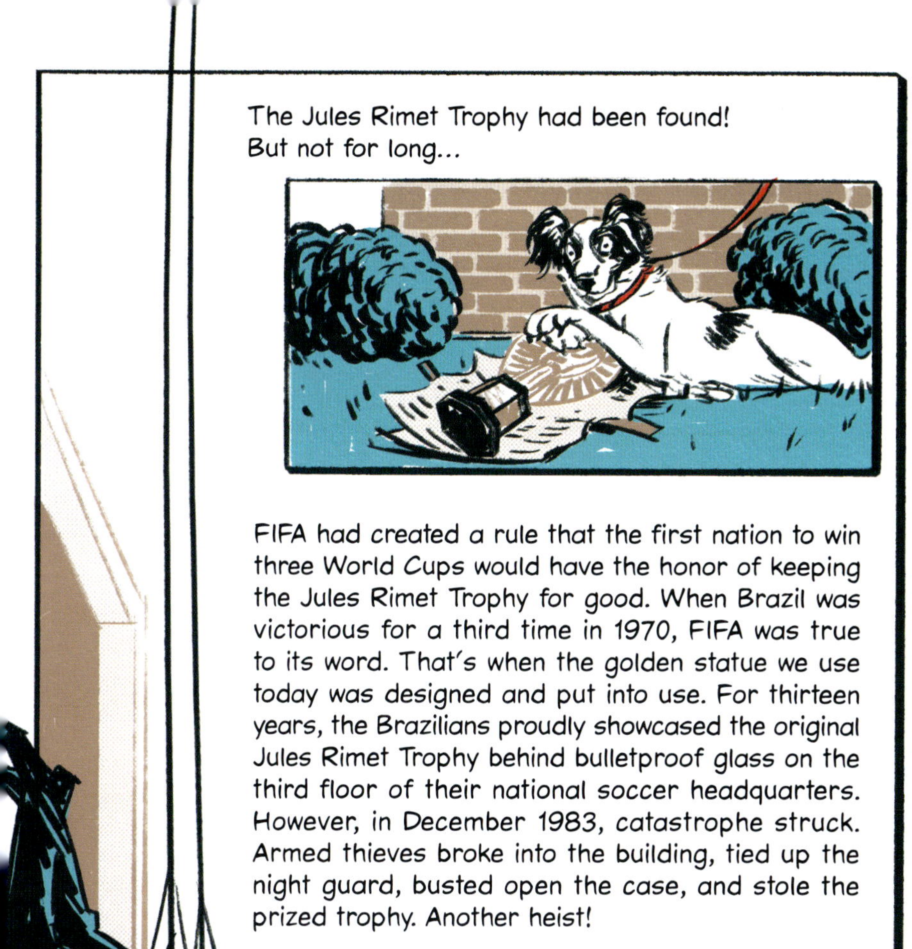

FIFA had created a rule that the first nation to win three World Cups would have the honor of keeping the Jules Rimet Trophy for good. When Brazil was victorious for a third time in 1970, FIFA was true to its word. That's when the golden statue we use today was designed and put into use. For thirteen years, the Brazilians proudly showcased the original Jules Rimet Trophy behind bulletproof glass on the third floor of their national soccer headquarters. However, in December 1983, catastrophe struck. Armed thieves broke into the building, tied up the night guard, busted open the case, and stole the prized trophy. Another heist!

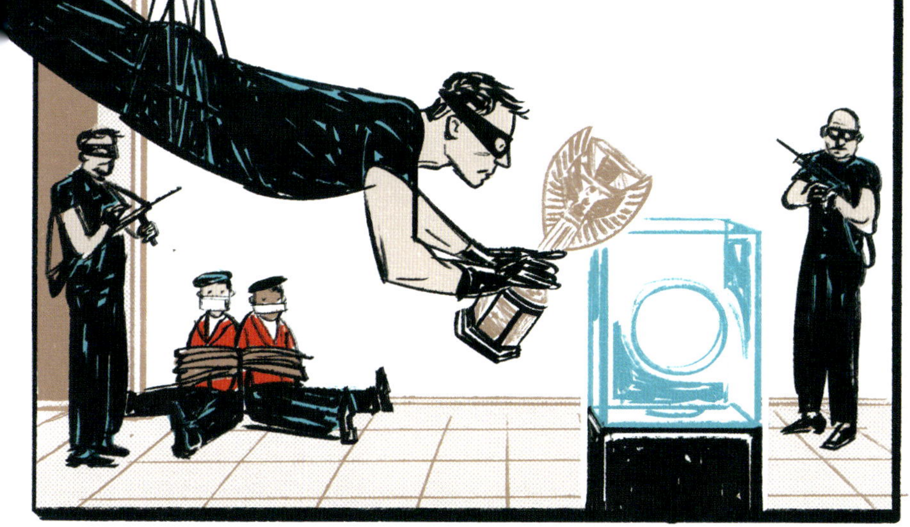

The Brazilian government was horrified. The Jules Rimet Trophy was priceless to Brazilians. The government announced that there would be a substantial reward to anybody who could help return the trophy.

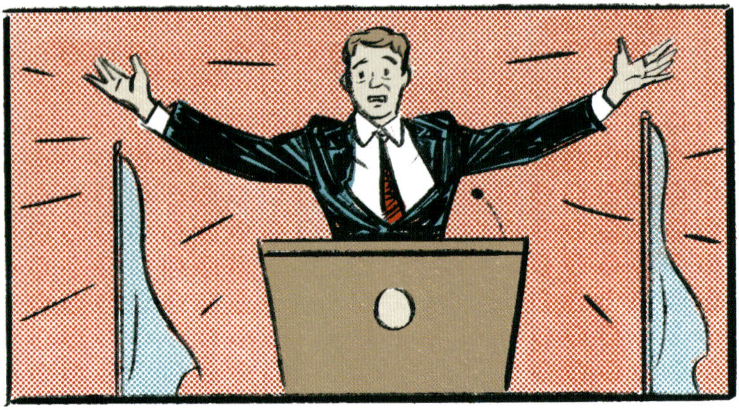

But it has never been found.

So where is the Jules Rimet Trophy today? Nobody knows.

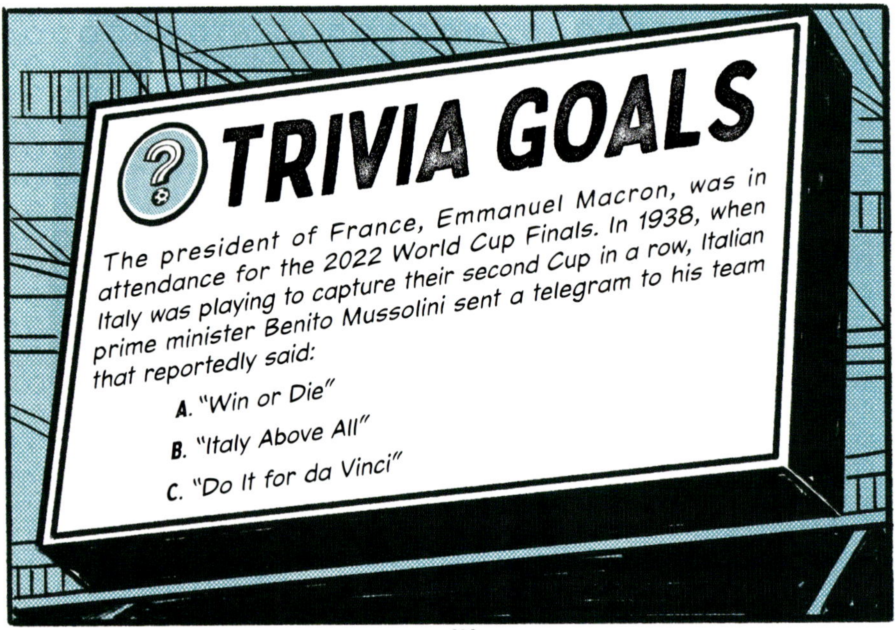
TRIVIA GOALS
The president of France, Emmanuel Macron, was in attendance for the 2022 World Cup Finals. In 1938, when Italy was playing to capture their second Cup in a row, Italian prime minister Benito Mussolini sent a telegram to his team that reportedly said:
A. "Win or Die"
B. "Italy Above All"
C. "Do It for da Vinci"

EXTRA TIME

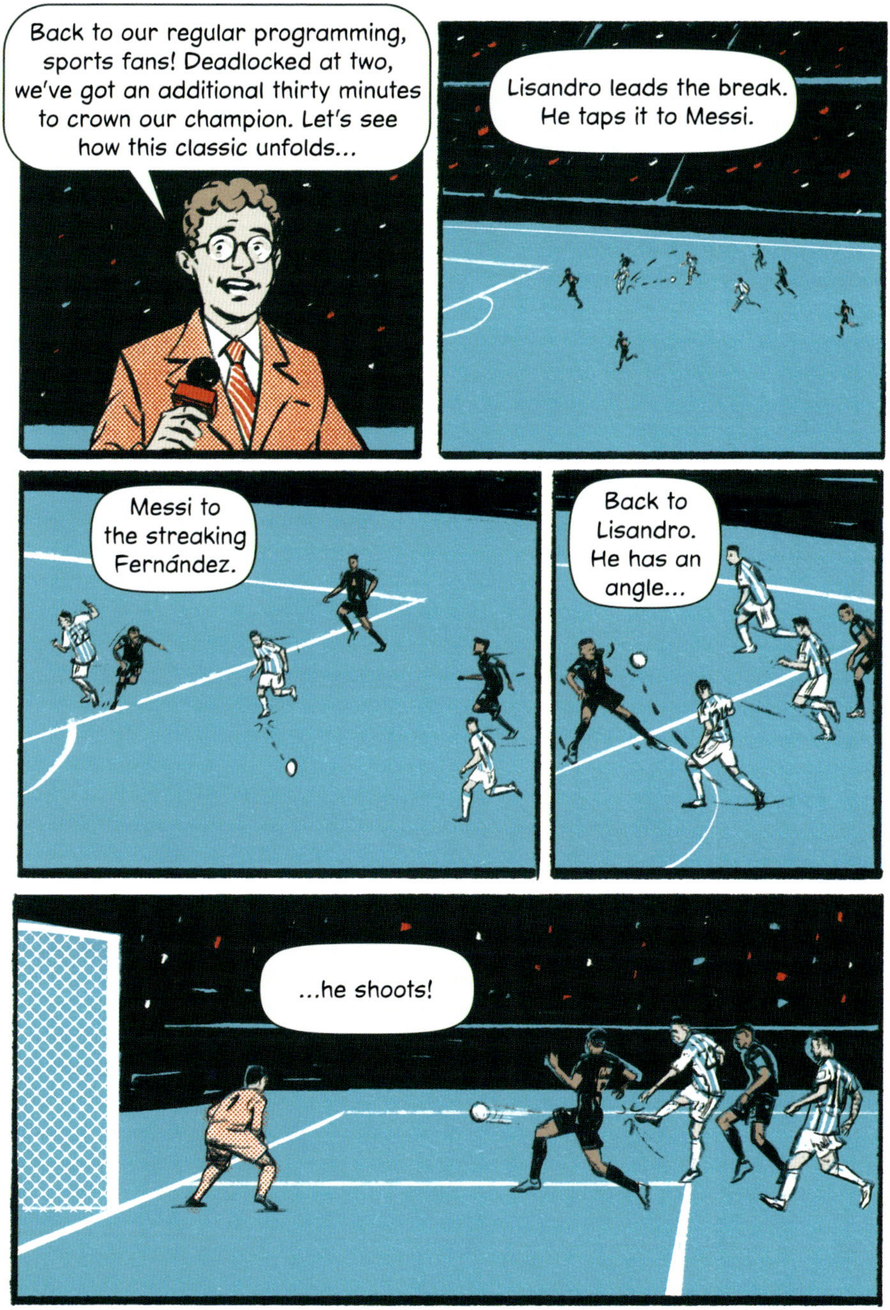
Back to our regular programming, sports fans! Deadlocked at two, we've got an additional thirty minutes to crown our champion. Let's see how this classic unfolds...
Lisandro leads the break. He taps it to Messi.
Messi to the streaking Fernández.
Back to Lisandro. He has an angle...
...he shoots!

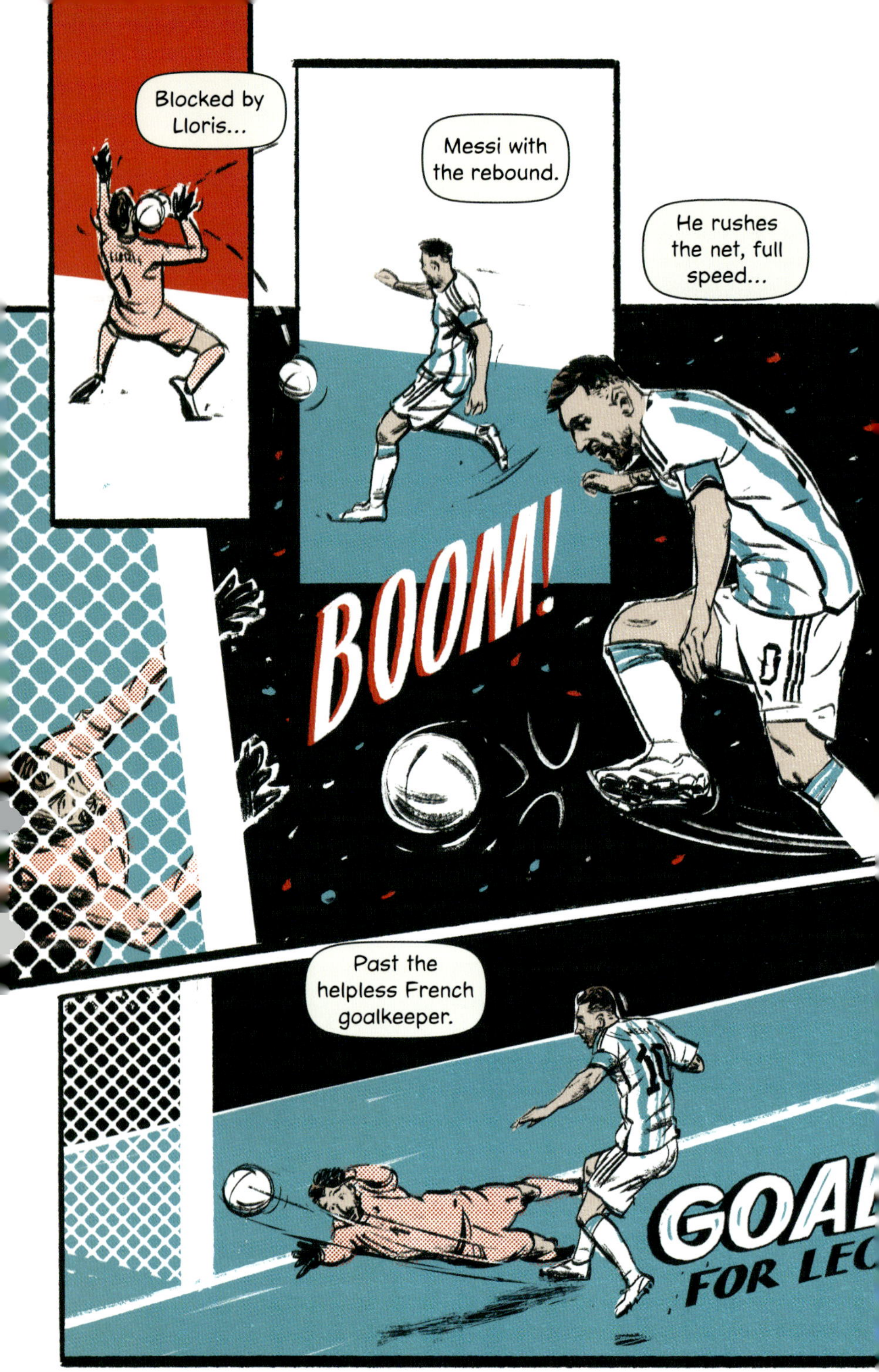
Blocked by Lloris...
Messi with the rebound.
He rushes the net, full speed...
BOOM!
Past the helpless French goalkeeper.
GOA
FOR LE

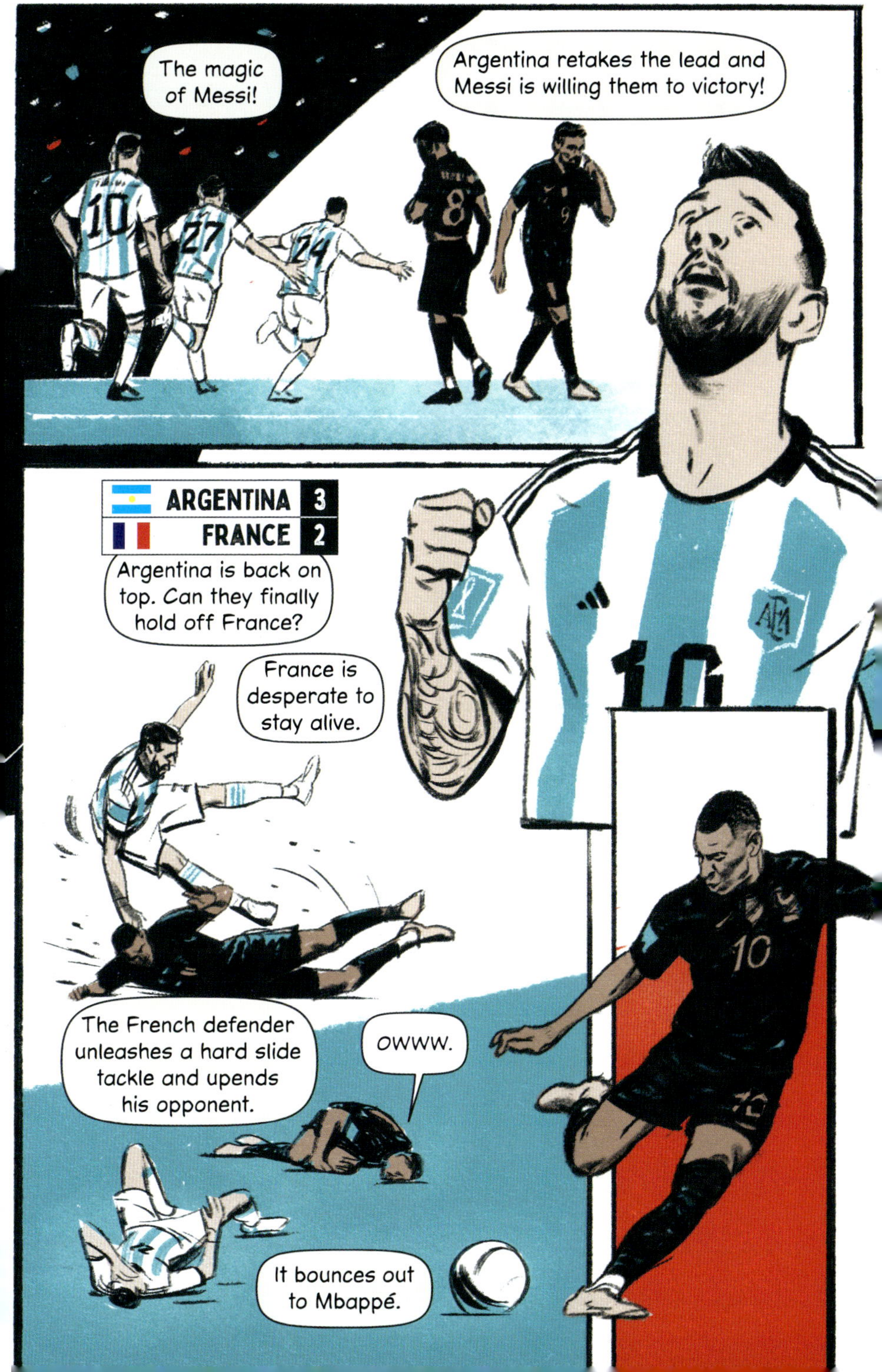

The magic of Messi!
Argentina retakes the lead and Messi is willing them to victory!
ARGENTINA 3
FRANCE 2
Argentina is back on top. Can they finally hold off France?
France is desperate to stay alive.
The French defender unleashes a hard slide tackle and upends his opponent.
OWWW.
It bounces out to Mbappé.

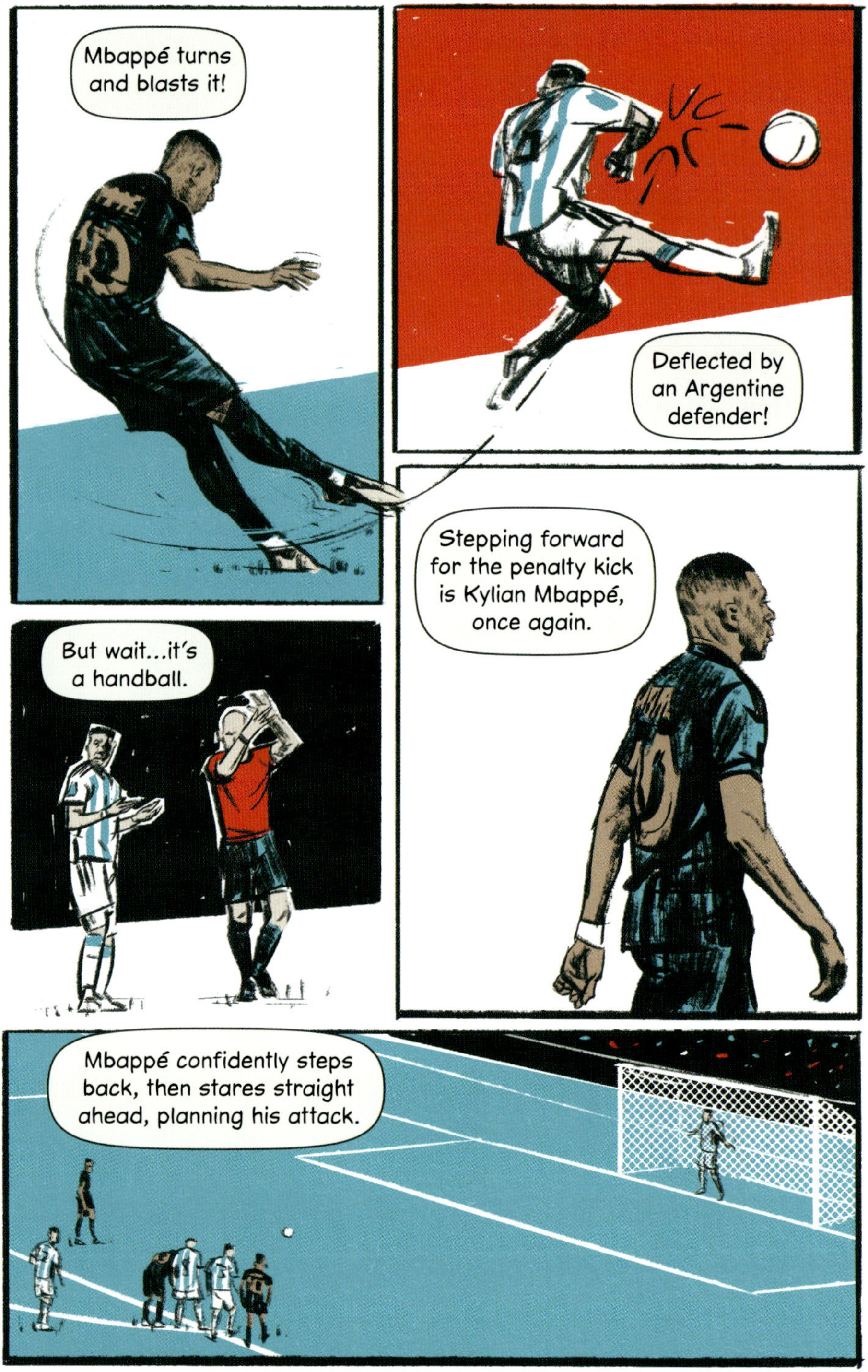
Mbappé turns and blasts it!
Deflected by an Argentine defender!
But wait...it's a handball.
Stepping forward for the penalty kick is Kylian Mbappé, once again.
Mbappé confidently steps back, then stares straight ahead, planning his attack.

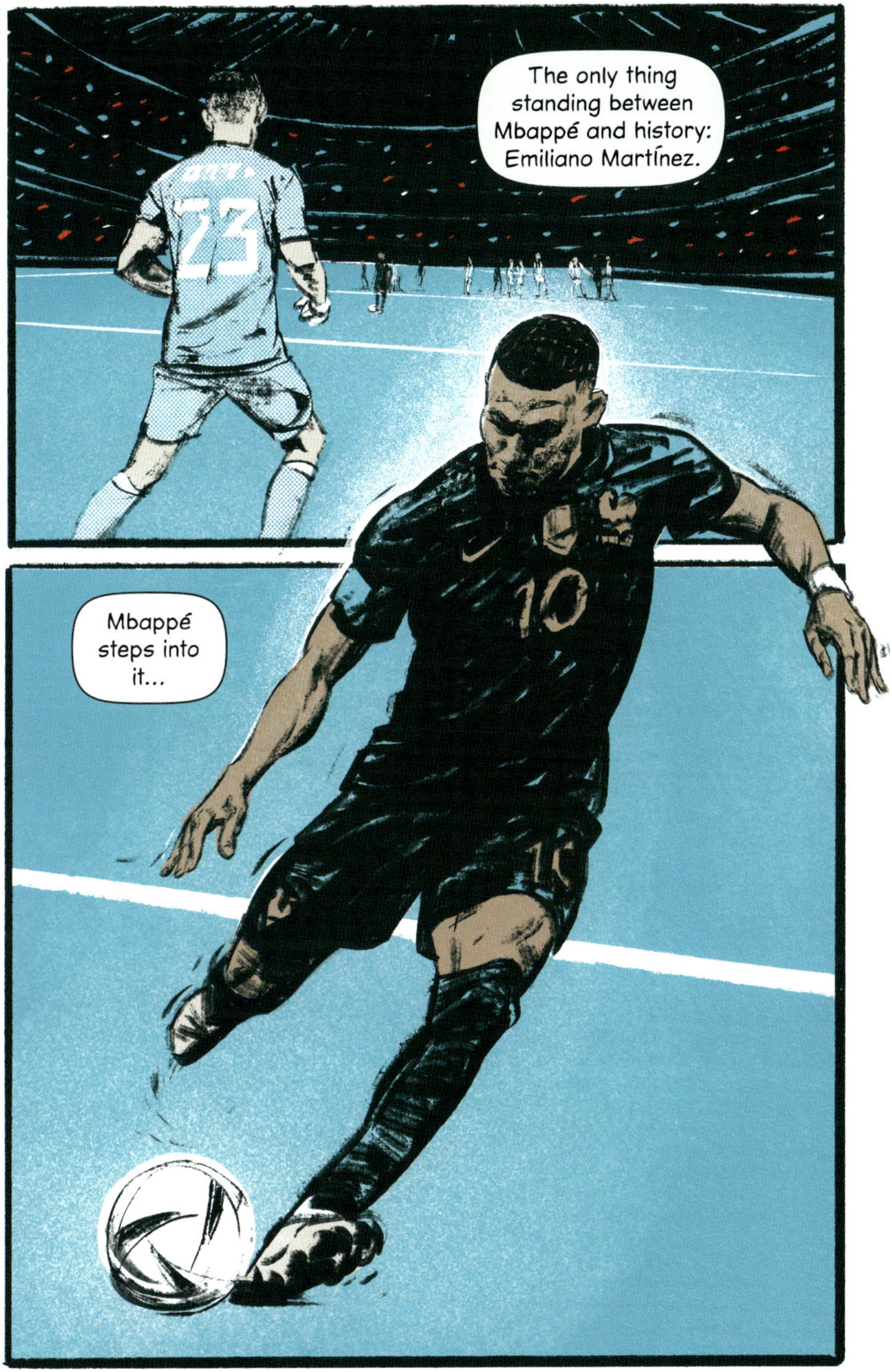
The only thing standing between Mbappé and history: Emiliano Martínez.
Mbappé steps into it...

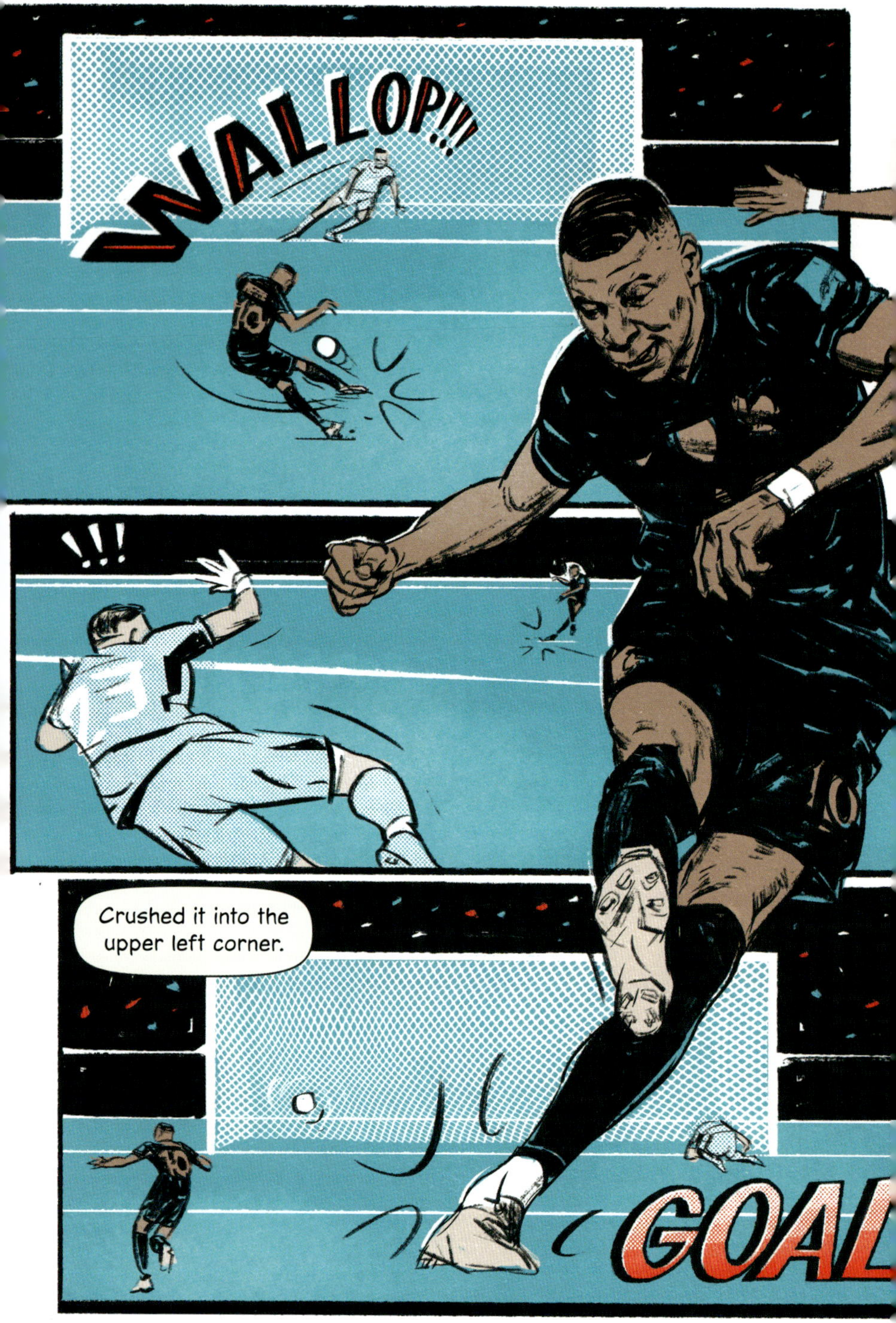
WALLOP!!!
!!!
Crushed it into the upper left corner.
GOAL

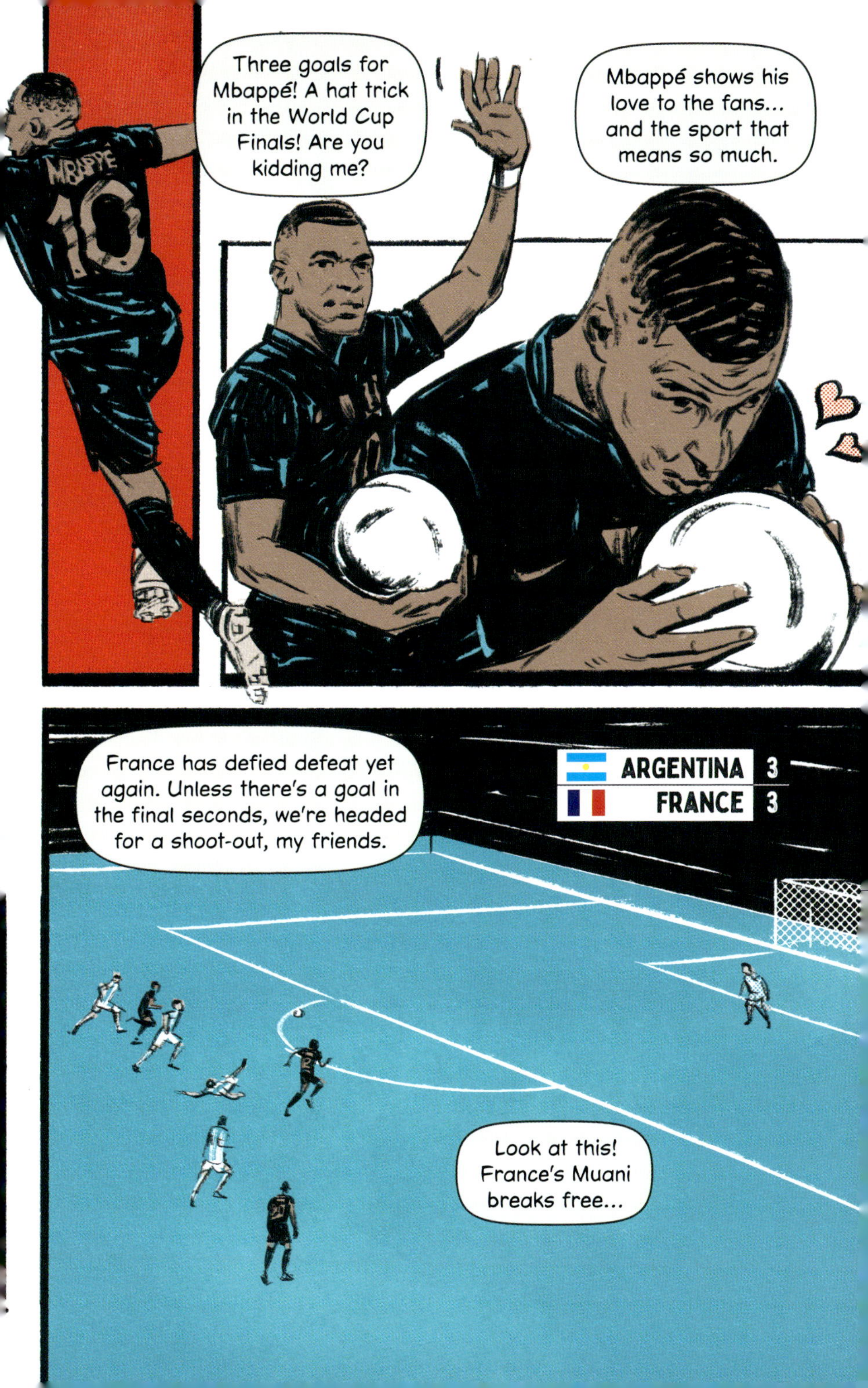
Three goals for Mbappé! A hat trick in the World Cup Finals! Are you kidding me?
Mbappé shows his love to the fans... and the sport that means so much.
France has defied defeat yet again. Unless there's a goal in the final seconds, we're headed for a shoot-out, my friends.
ARGENTINA 3
FRANCE 3
Look at this! France's Muani breaks free...

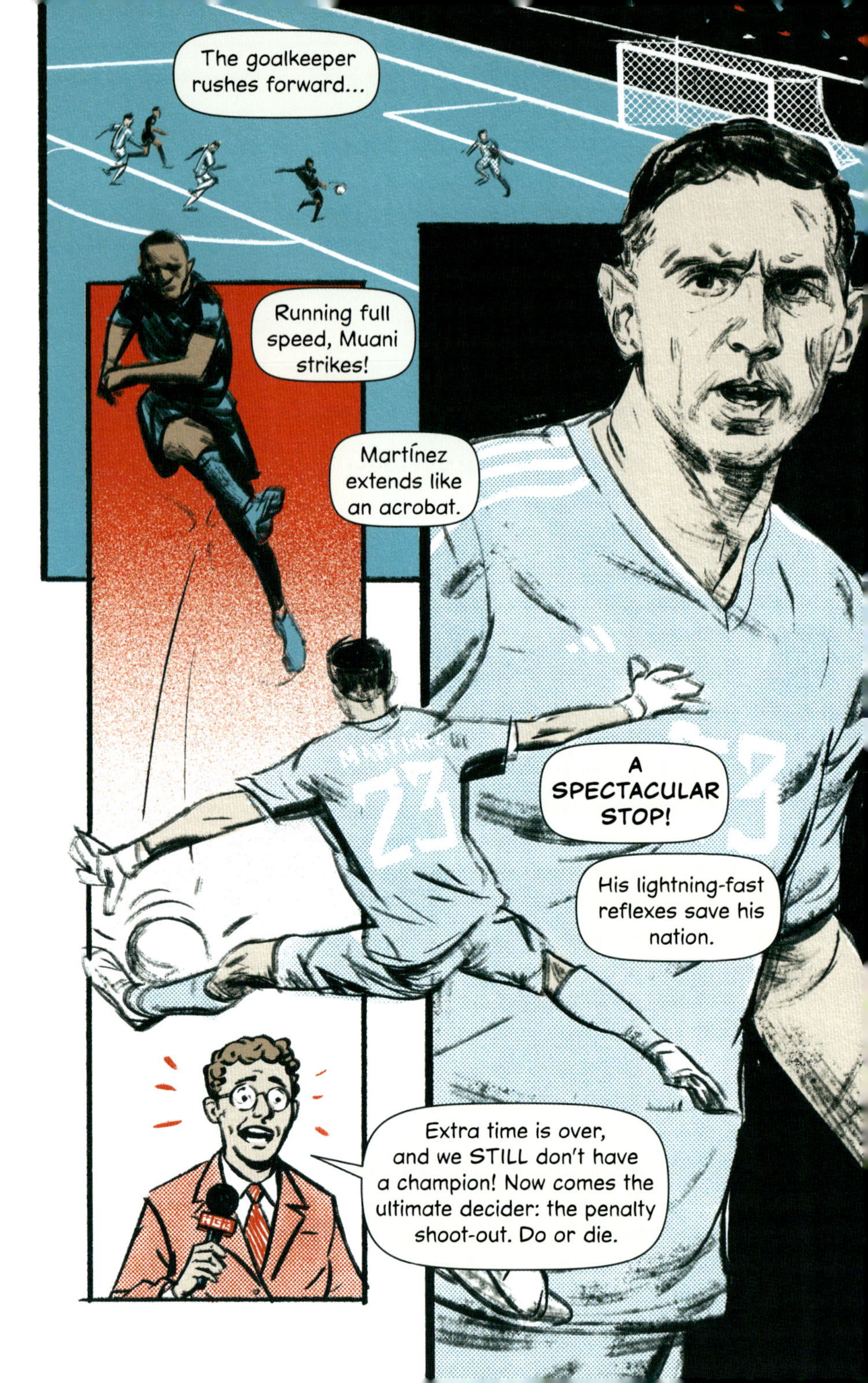

The goalkeeper rushes forward...
Running full speed, Muani strikes!
Martínez extends like an acrobat.
A SPECTACULAR STOP!
His lightning-fast reflexes save his nation.
Extra time is over, and we STILL don't have a champion! Now comes the ultimate decider: the penalty shoot-out. Do or die.

WATER BREAK!
THE PENALTY SHOOT-OUT. DO OR DIE.

In the 2022 World Cup Final, it all came down to a shoot-out, which is a tie-breaker where players shoot from the same spot as they would for penalty kicks. The first time a World Cup Final was decided by a penalty shoot-out was in 1994, when Brazil defeated Italy.

1994 FIFA WORLD CUP: JULY 17, 1994

BRAZIL 0 – 0 ITALY
PENALTIES: 3-2 FINAL

HOW IT WORKS:
Five players per side are pre-chosen to take the penalty kicks. They take individual turns against the opposing goalkeeper. Players may only kick once.

The team with the most scores after five shots wins the shoot-out. If a team gains a lead that cannot be overtaken before the five shots have been taken, they are announced the winner.

PENALTIES:	1	2	3	4	5
ITALY	✗	✓	✓	✗	✗
BRAZIL	✓	✓	✗	✓	

If the shoot-out is tied after five shots, teams get extra shots until there is a winner.

PENALTIES:	1	2	3	4	5	6	7	8	9	10	11	12	13	14	15
ITALY	✗	✓	✓	✗	✓	✓	✗	✓	✓	✗	✗	✓	✗	✓	✗
BRAZIL	✓	✓	✗	✓	✗	✓	✗	✓	✓	✗	✗	✓	✗	✓	✓

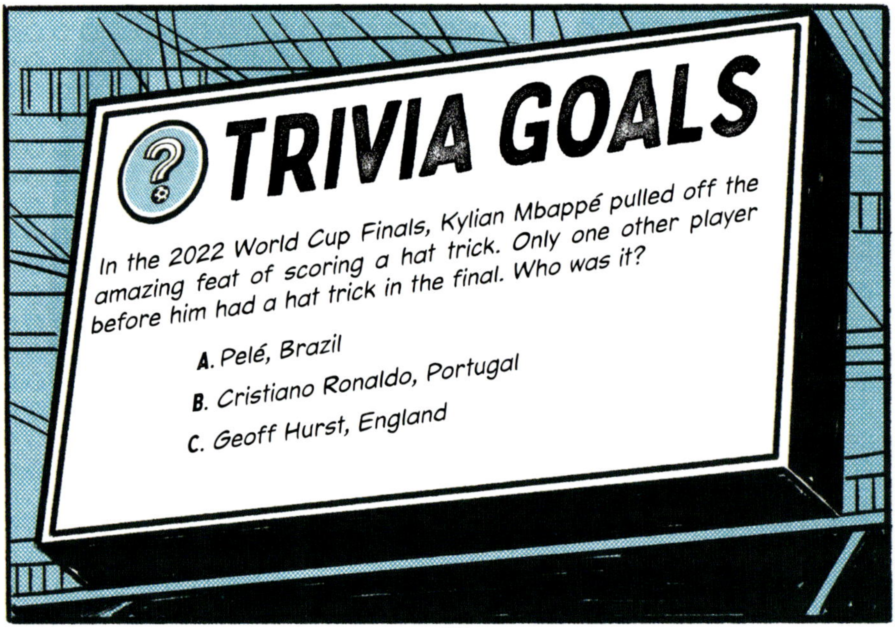
TRIVIA GOALS
In the 2022 World Cup Finals, Kylian Mbappé pulled off the amazing feat of scoring a hat trick. Only one other player before him had a hat trick in the final. Who was it?
A. Pelé, Brazil
B. Cristiano Ronaldo, Portugal
C. Geoff Hurst, England

PENALTY SHOOT-OUT

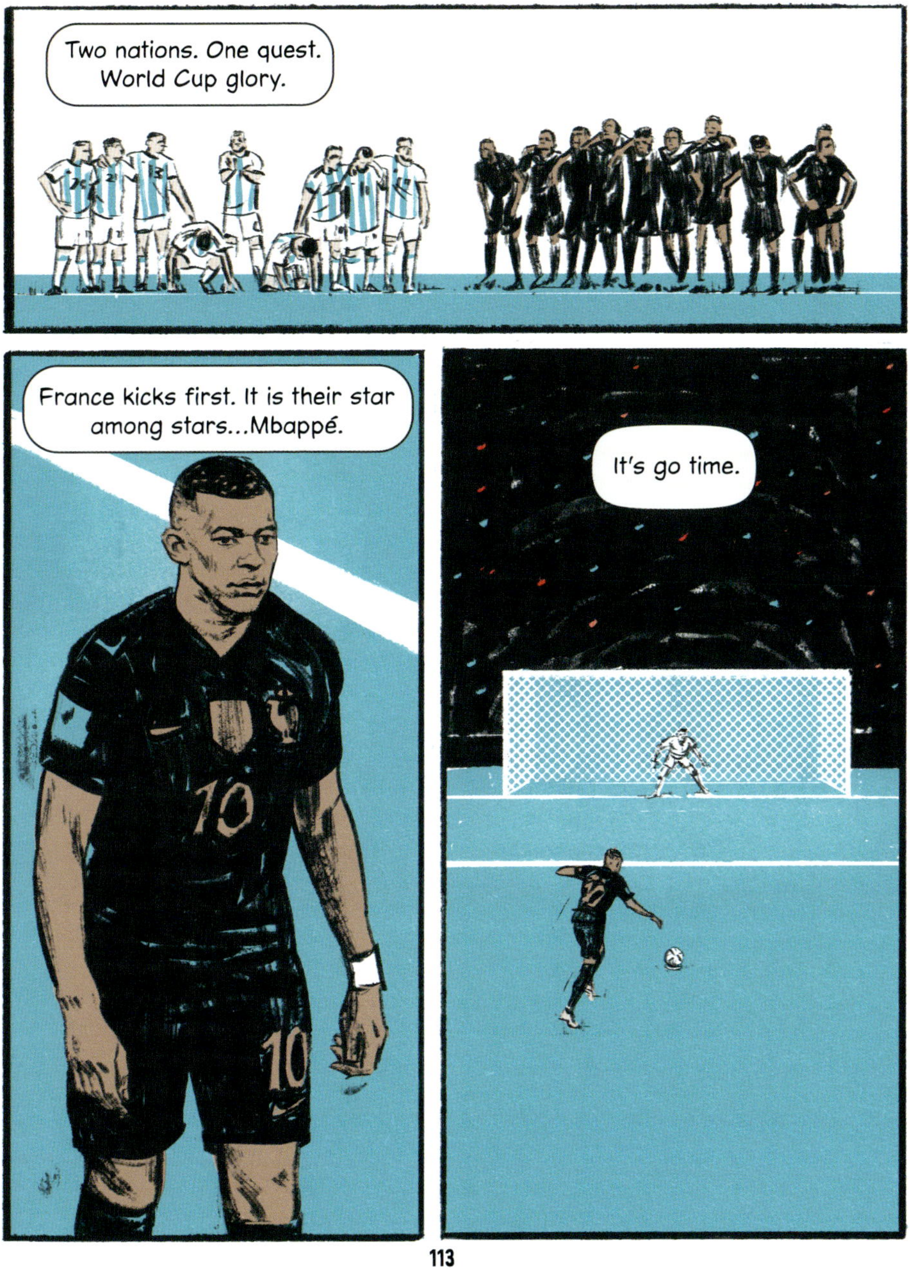

Two nations. One quest. World Cup glory.
France kicks first. It is their star among stars...Mbappé.
It's go time.

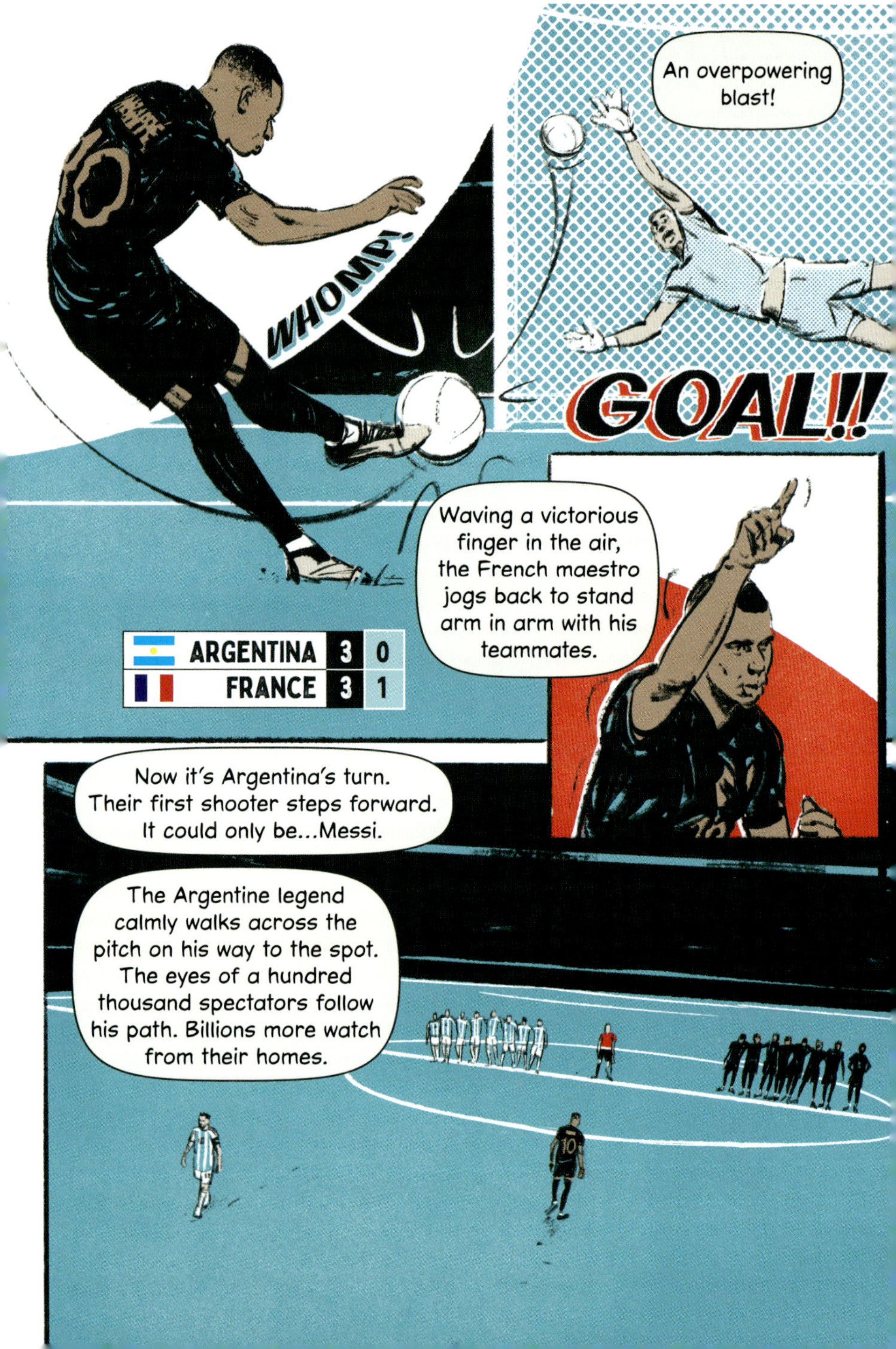
WHOMP!
An overpowering blast!
GOAL!!
ARGENTINA 3 0
FRANCE 3 1
Waving a victorious finger in the air, the French maestro jogs back to stand arm in arm with his teammates.
Now it's Argentina's turn. Their first shooter steps forward. It could only be...Messi.
The Argentine legend calmly walks across the pitch on his way to the spot. The eyes of a hundred thousand spectators follow his path. Billions more watch from their homes.

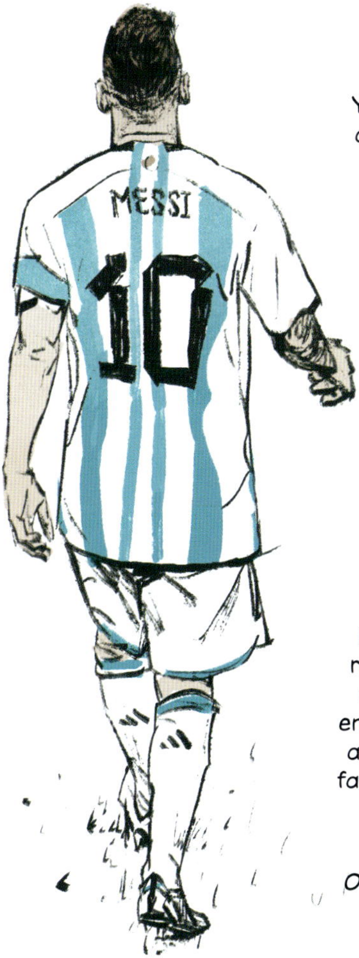

Yet in this moment, Messi is all alone. Alone with his thoughts. Alone with his legacy.

As he strides purposefully ahead, what runs through Leo's mind?

Is he remembering where his journey began? Those childhood soccer games in the yard with his family? Or about that invincible Machine of '87 squad, when he dreamed of this exact moment, like so many kids do, a World Cup Final shoot-out?

Maybe he's recalling all the Barcelona league trophies and records collected along the way, and how they were never quite enough? He still feels the sadness and disappointment of Argentine fans in his heart, like a heavy rock stuck deep in his chest.

Or maybe it's none of that.

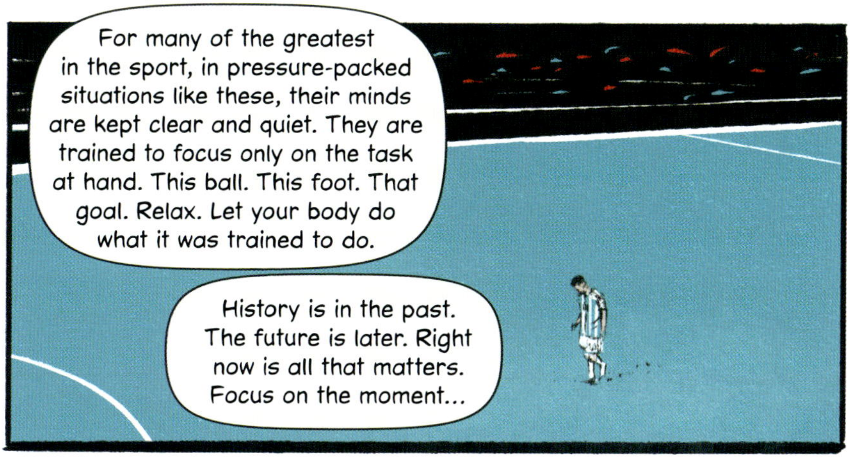
For many of the greatest in the sport, in pressure-packed situations like these, their minds are kept clear and quiet. They are trained to focus only on the task at hand. This ball. This foot. That goal. Relax. Let your body do what it was trained to do.
History is in the past. The future is later. Right now is all that matters. Focus on the moment...

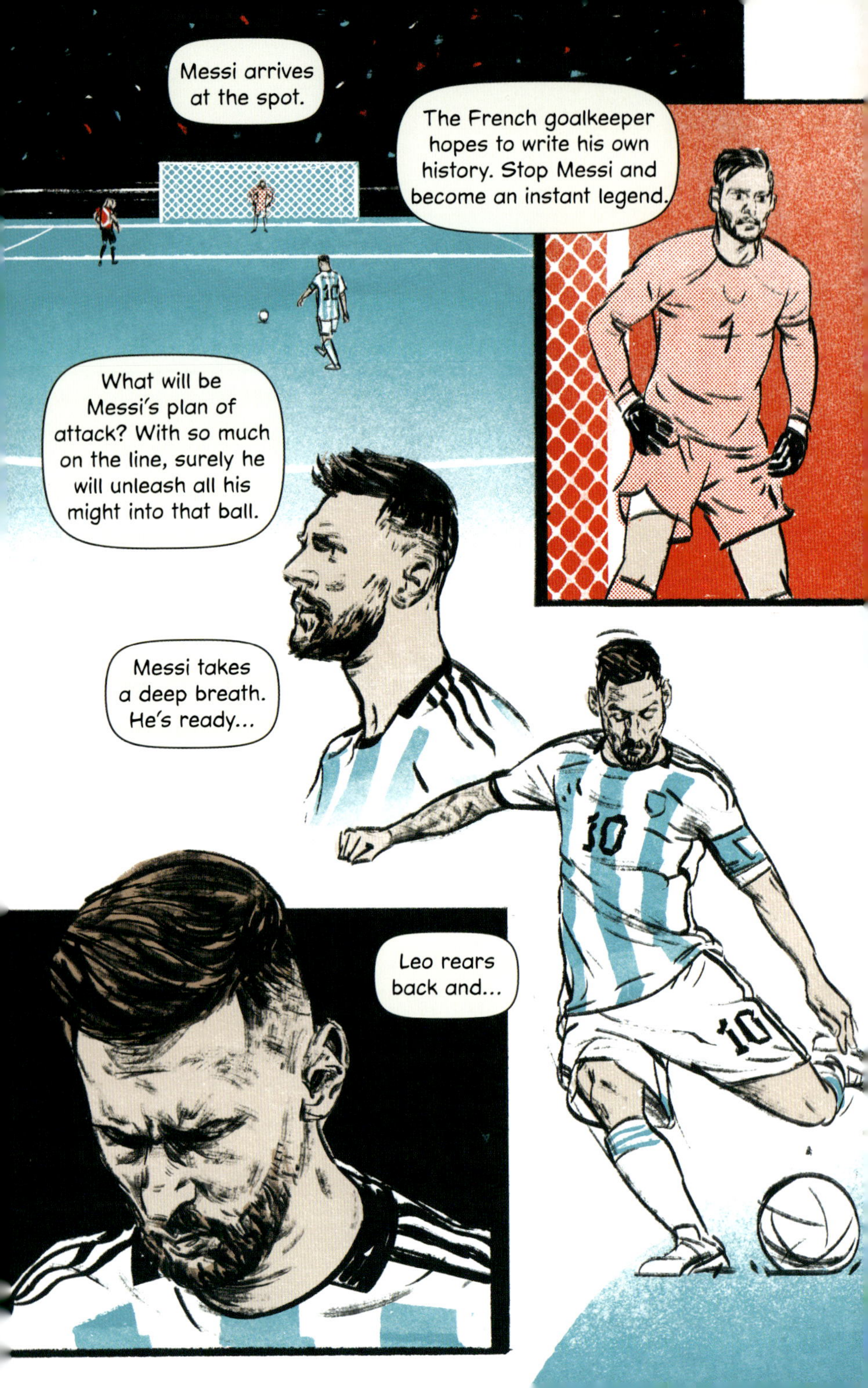
Messi arrives at the spot.
The French goalkeeper hopes to write his own history. Stop Messi and become an instant legend.
What will be Messi's plan of attack? With so much on the line, surely he will unleash all his might into that ball.
Messi takes a deep breath. He's ready...
Leo rears back and...

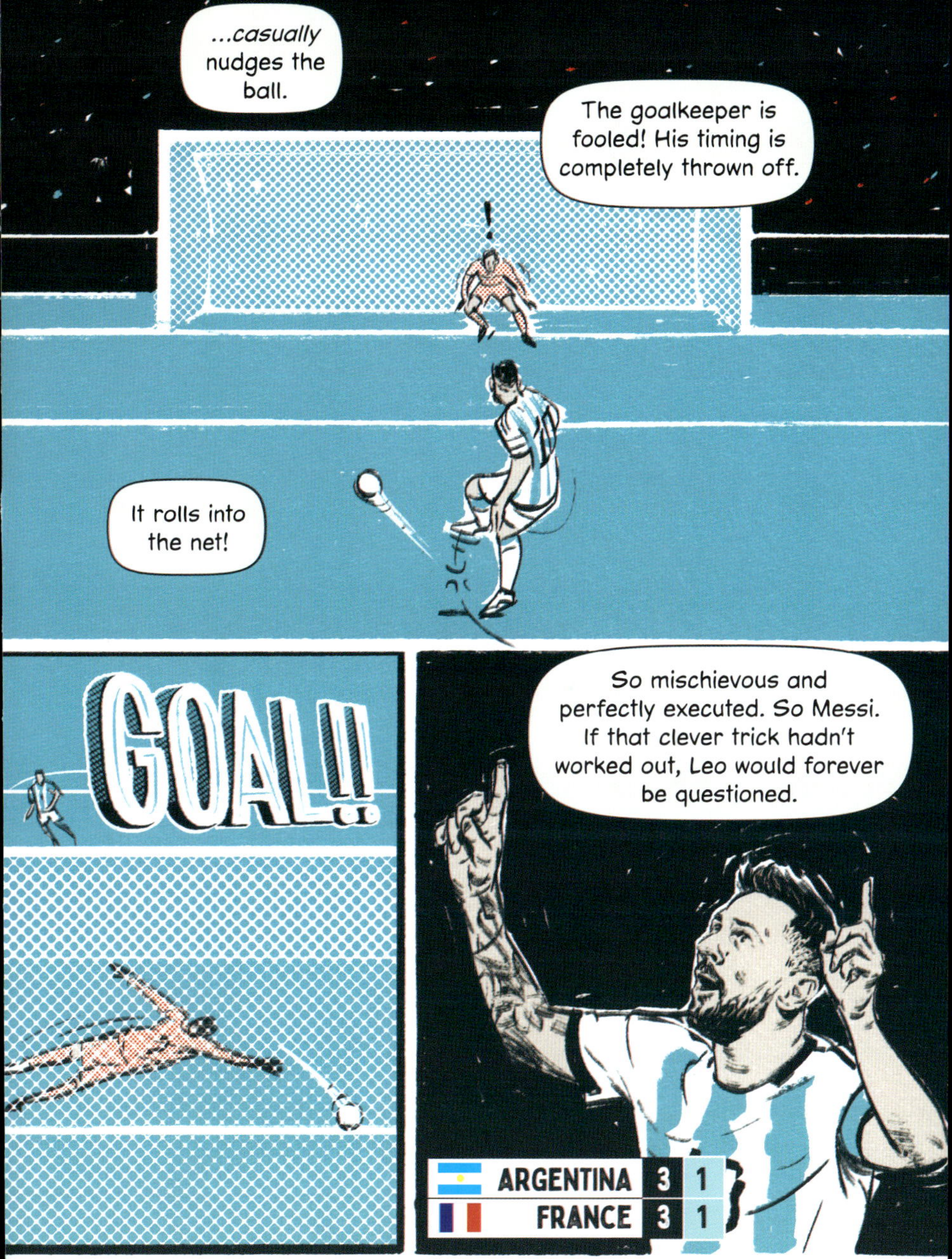
...casually nudges the ball.
The goalkeeper is fooled! His timing is completely thrown off.
It rolls into the net!
GOAL!!
So mischievous and perfectly executed. So Messi. If that clever trick hadn't worked out, Leo would forever be questioned.
ARGENTINA 3 1
FRANCE 3 1

Highlight reel of the next five penalty kicks...

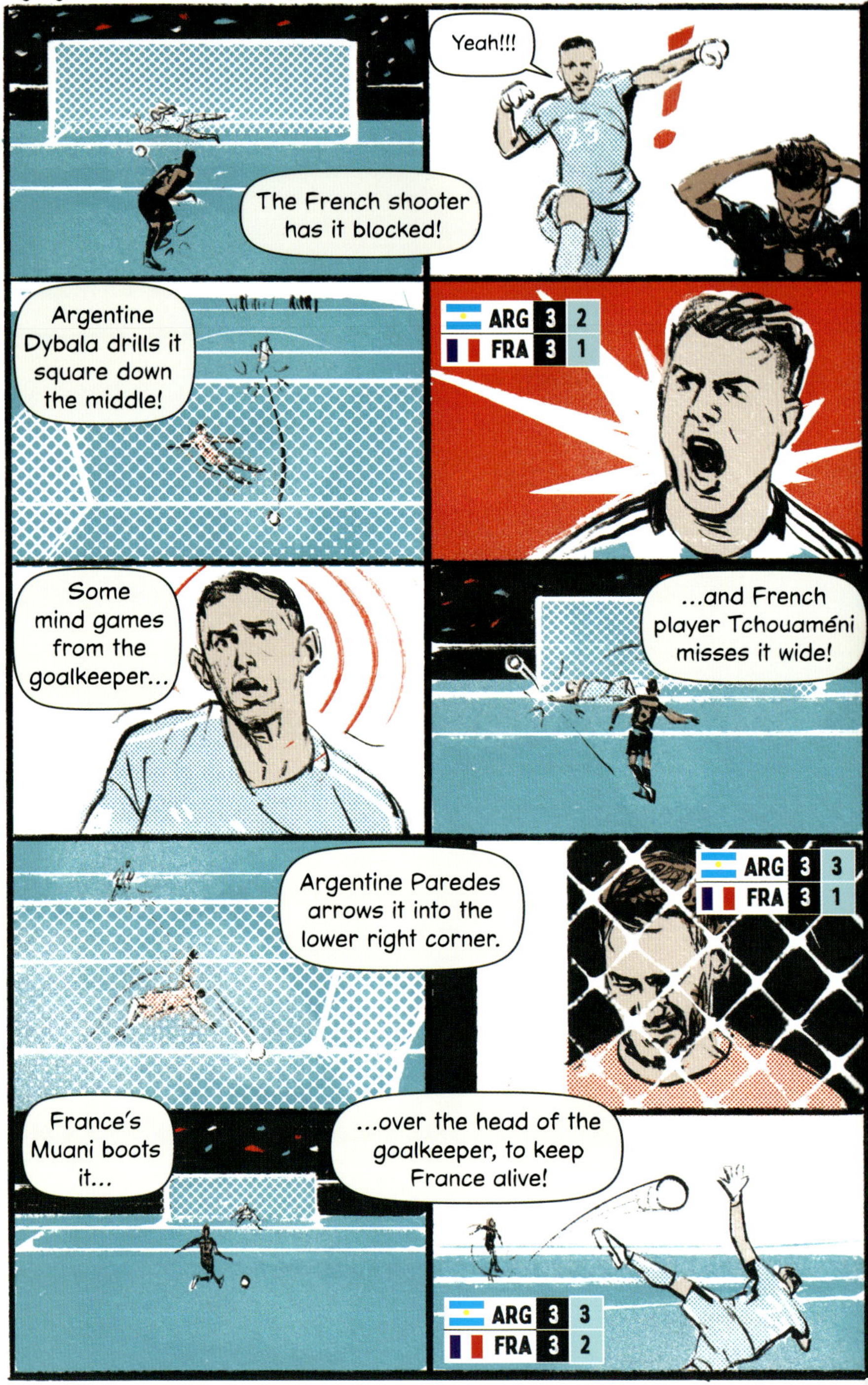

Yeah!!!
The French shooter has it blocked!
Argentine Dybala drills it square down the middle!
ARG 3 2
FRA 3 1
Some mind games from the goalkeeper...
...and French player Tchouaméni misses it wide!
Argentine Paredes arrows it into the lower right corner.
ARG 3 3
FRA 3 1
France's Muani boots it...
...over the head of the goalkeeper, to keep France alive!
ARG 3 3
FRA 3 2

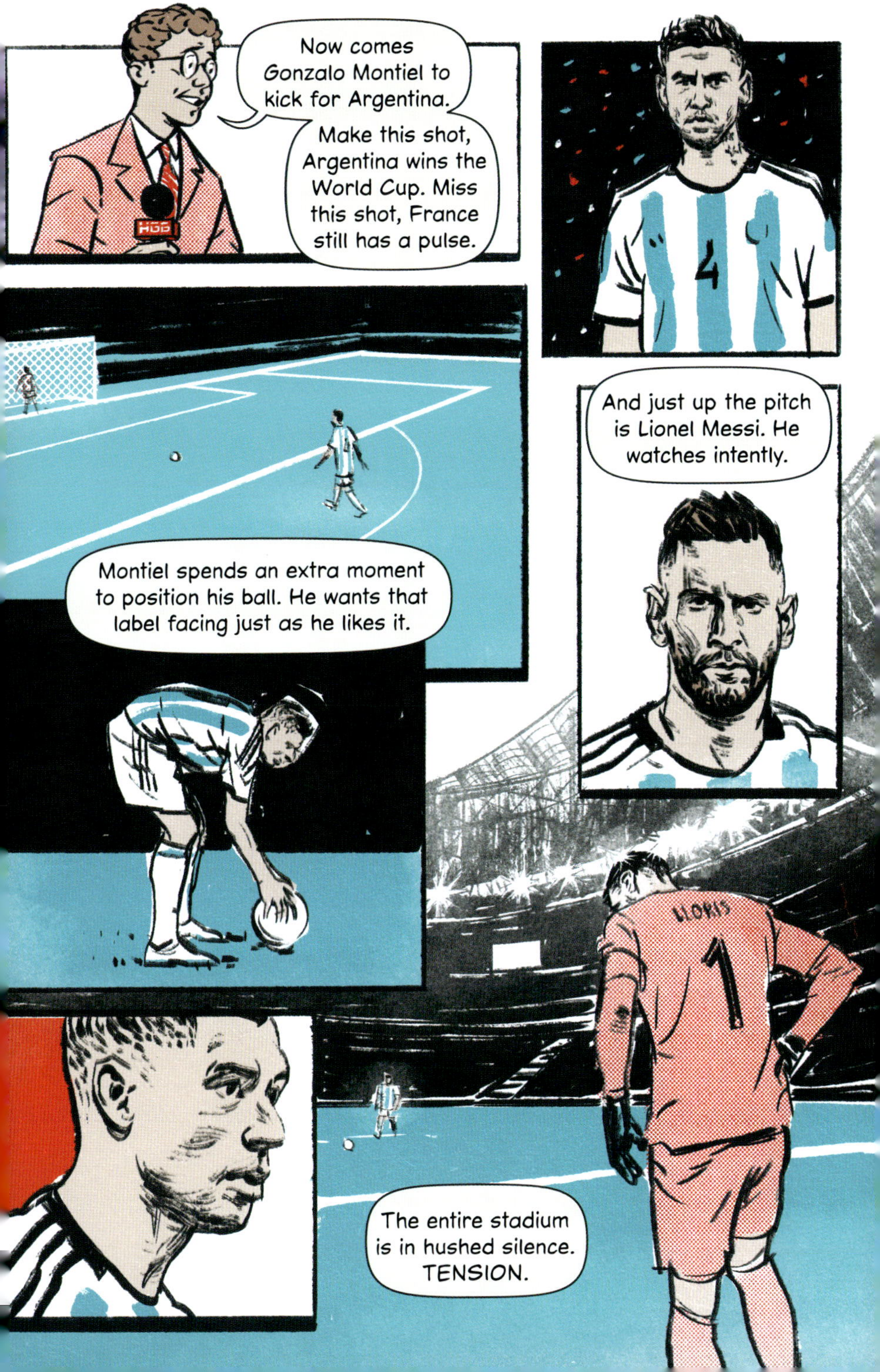
Now comes Gonzalo Montiel to kick for Argentina.
Make this shot, Argentina wins the World Cup. Miss this shot, France still has a pulse.
Montiel spends an extra moment to position his ball. He wants that label facing just as he likes it.
And just up the pitch is Lionel Messi. He watches intently.
The entire stadium is in hushed silence. TENSION.

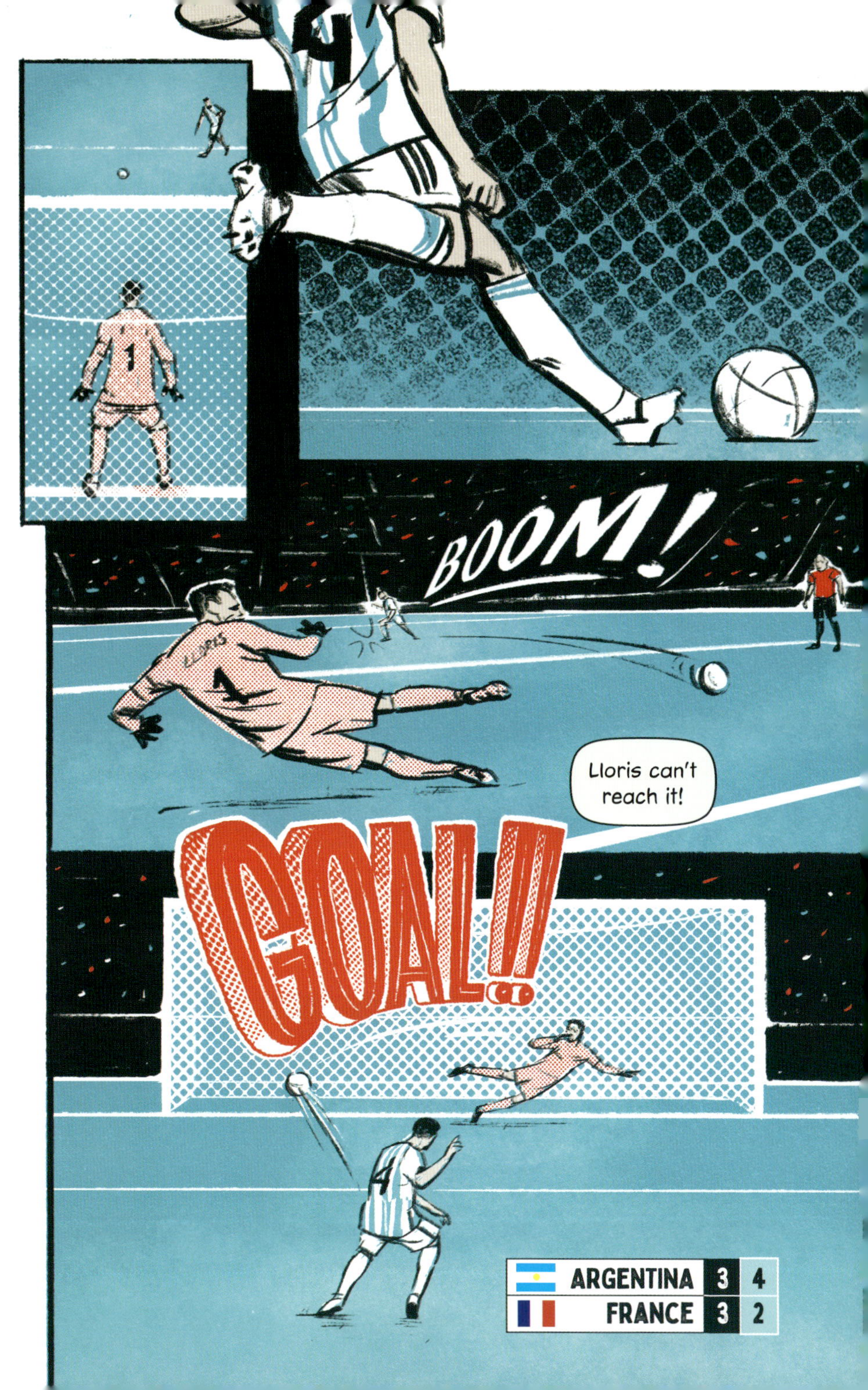
BOOM!
Lloris can't reach it!
GOAL!!
ARGENTINA 3 4
FRANCE 3 2

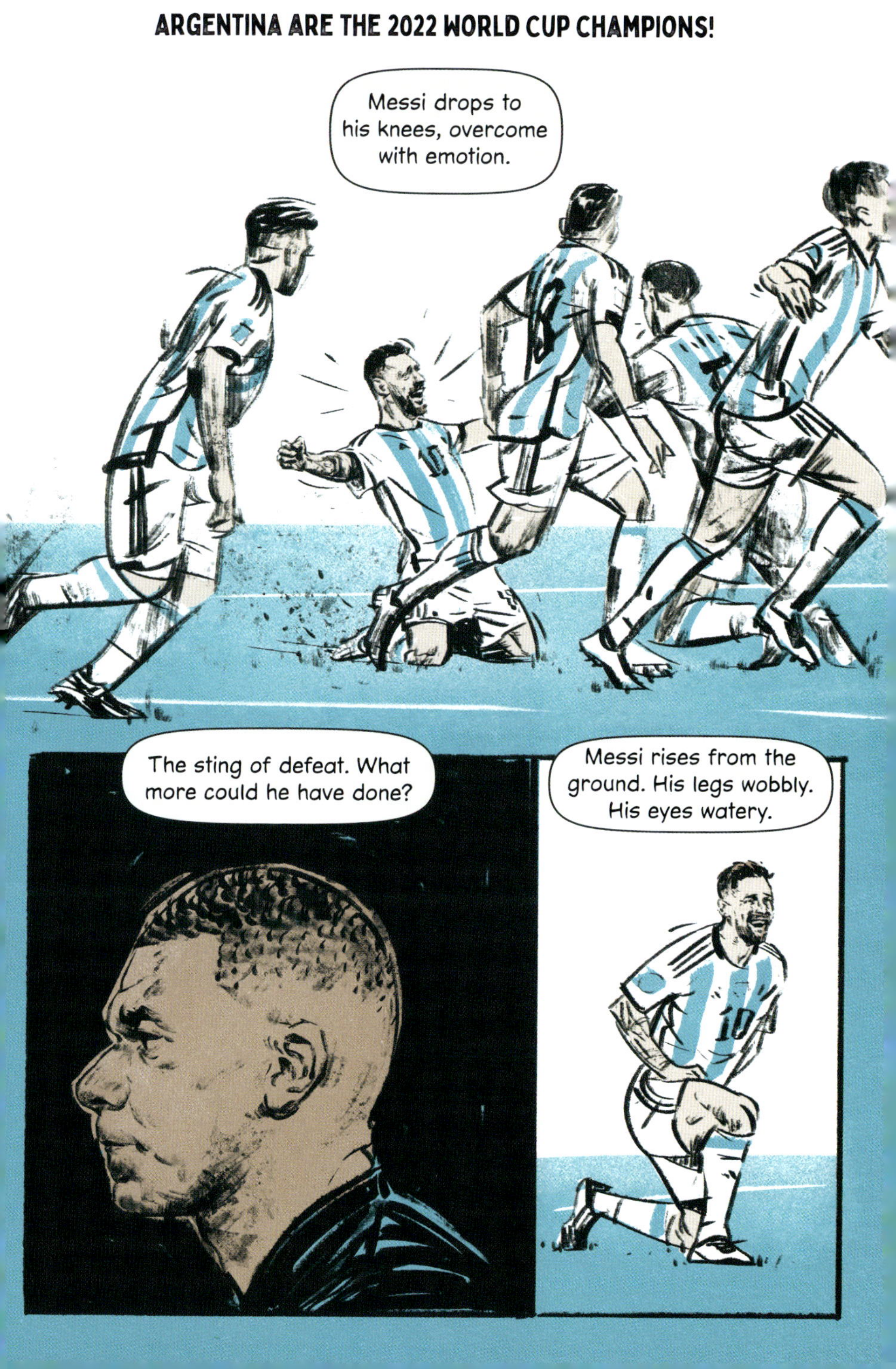
ARGENTINA ARE THE 2022 WORLD CUP CHAMPIONS!
Messi drops to his knees, overcome with emotion.
The sting of defeat. What more could he have done?
Messi rises from the ground. His legs wobbly. His eyes watery.

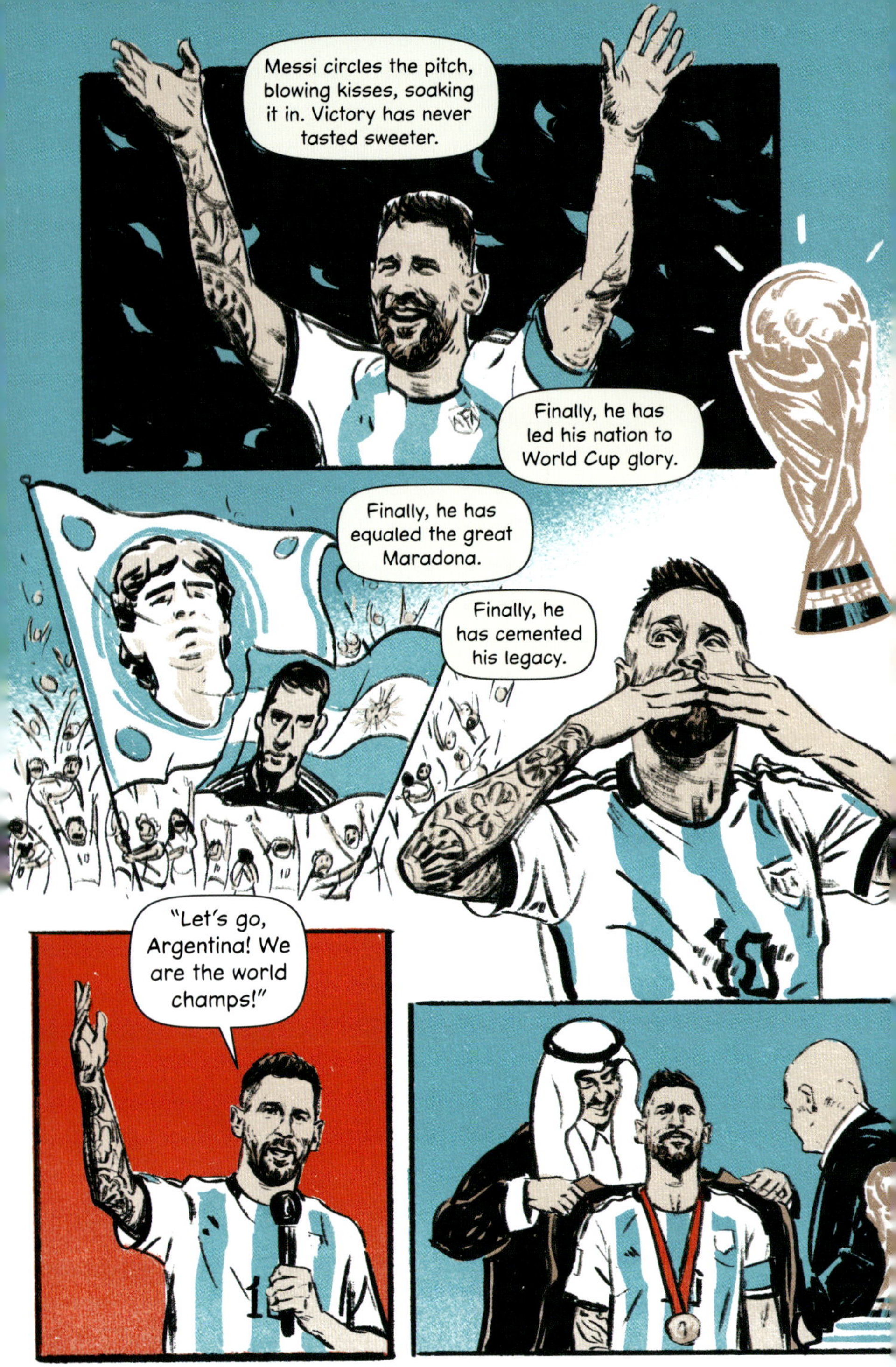
Messi circles the pitch, blowing kisses, soaking it in. Victory has never tasted sweeter.
Finally, he has led his nation to World Cup glory.
Finally, he has equaled the great Maradona.
Finally, he has cemented his legacy.
"Let's go, Argentina! We are the world champs!"

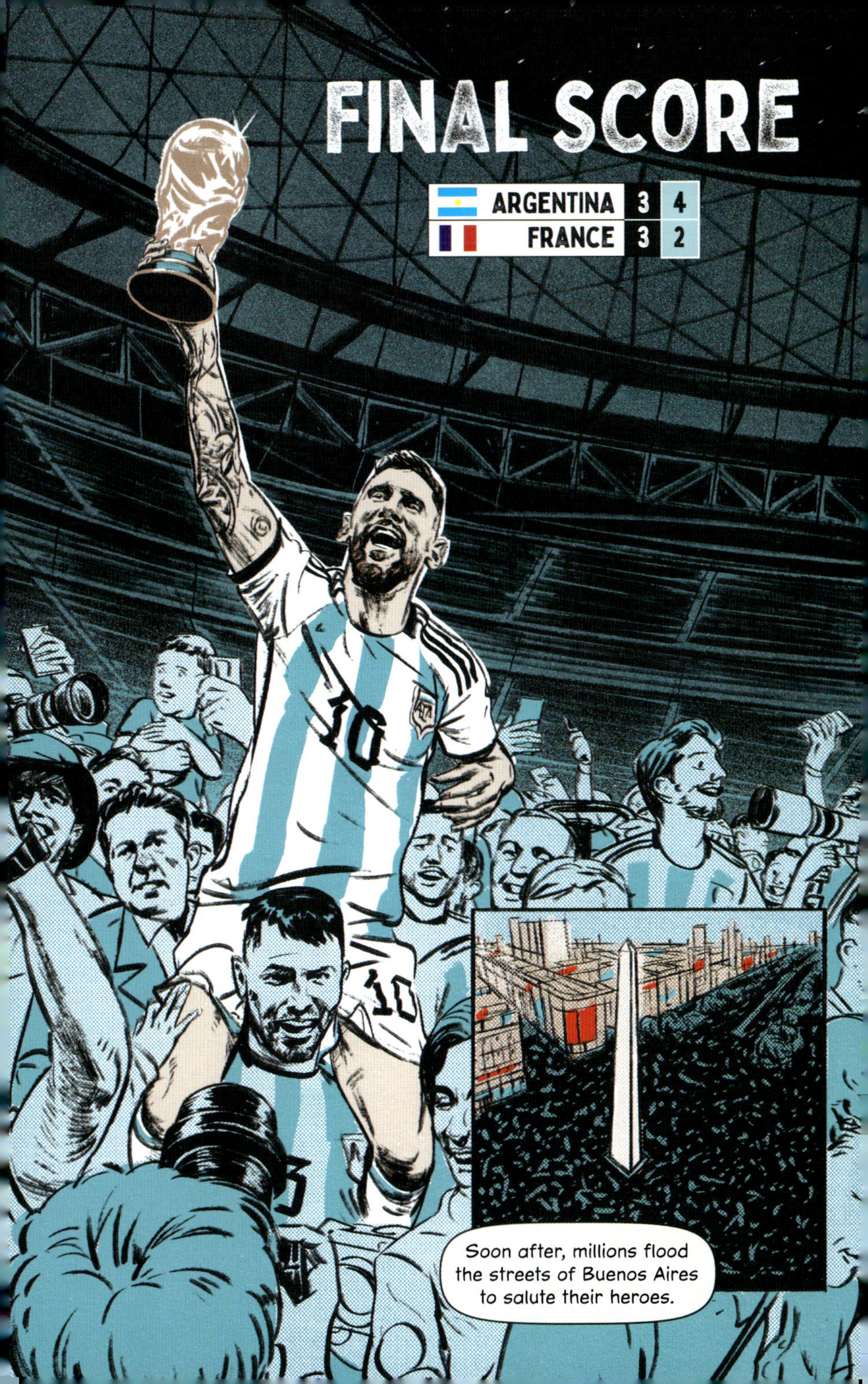
FINAL SCORE
ARGENTINA 3 4
FRANCE 3 2
10
10
Soon after, millions flood the streets of Buenos Aires to salute their heroes.

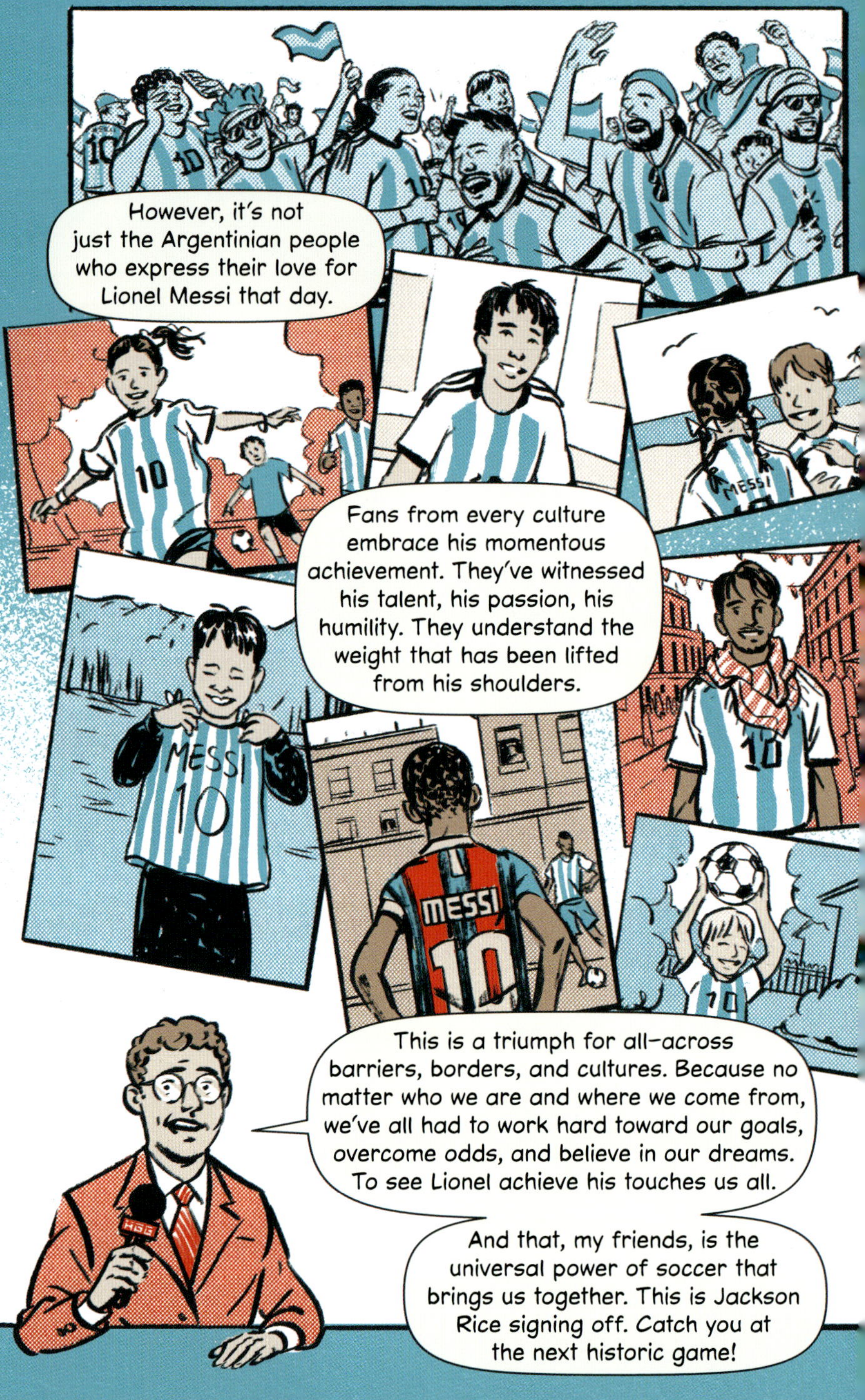

10
10
10
However, it's not just the Argentinian people who express their love for Lionel Messi that day.
10
MESSI
Fans from every culture embrace his momentous achievement. They've witnessed his talent, his passion, his humility. They understand the weight that has been lifted from his shoulders.
MESSI
10
10
MESSI
10
10
This is a triumph for all—across barriers, borders, and cultures. Because no matter who we are and where we come from, we've all had to work hard toward our goals, overcome odds, and believe in our dreams. To see Lionel achieve his touches us all.
And that, my friends, is the universal power of soccer that brings us together. This is Jackson Rice signing off. Catch you at the next historic game!

OVERTIME

FAN SHOWDOWN!

Today's topic: Maradona vs. Messi.

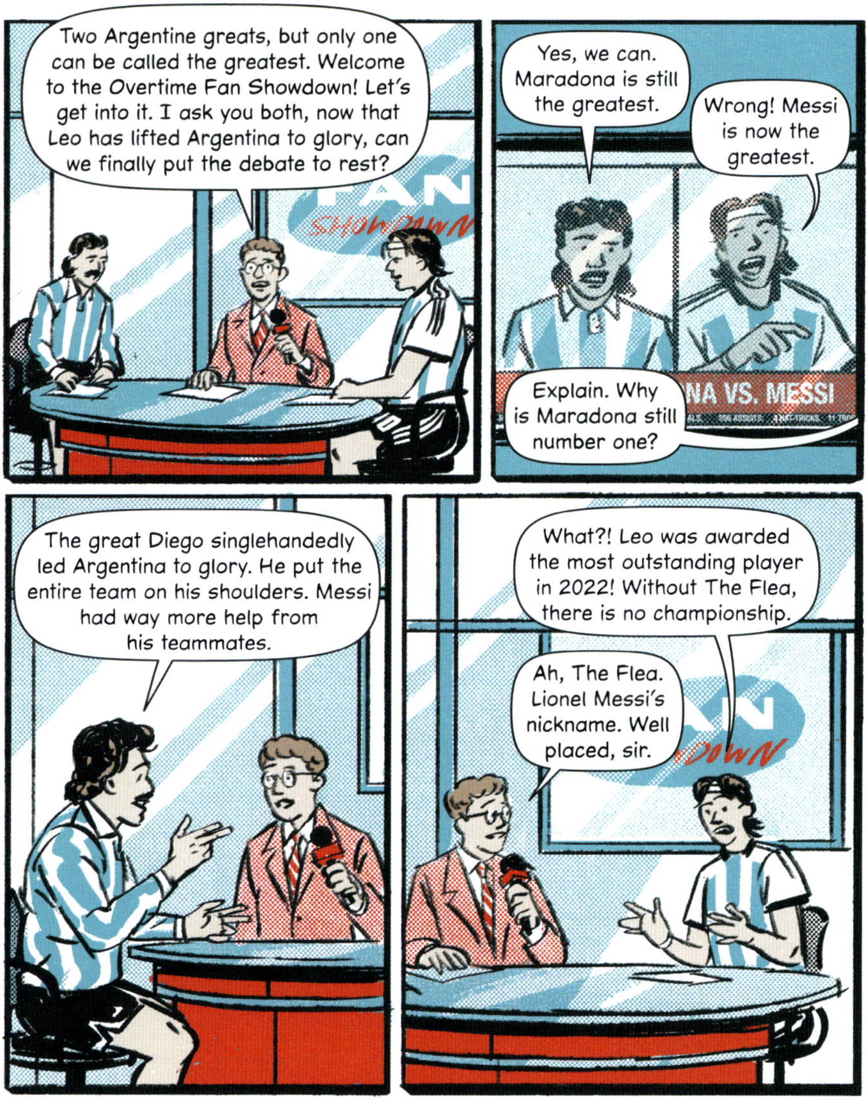

Two Argentine greats, but only one can be called the greatest. Welcome to the Overtime Fan Showdown! Let's get into it. I ask you both, now that Leo has lifted Argentina to glory, can we finally put the debate to rest?
Yes, we can. Maradona is still the greatest.
Wrong! Messi is now the greatest.
NA VS. MESSI
Explain. Why is Maradona still number one?
The great Diego singlehandedly led Argentina to glory. He put the entire team on his shoulders. Messi had way more help from his teammates.
What?! Leo was awarded the most outstanding player in 2022! Without The Flea, there is no championship.
Ah, The Flea. Lionel Messi's nickname. Well placed, sir.

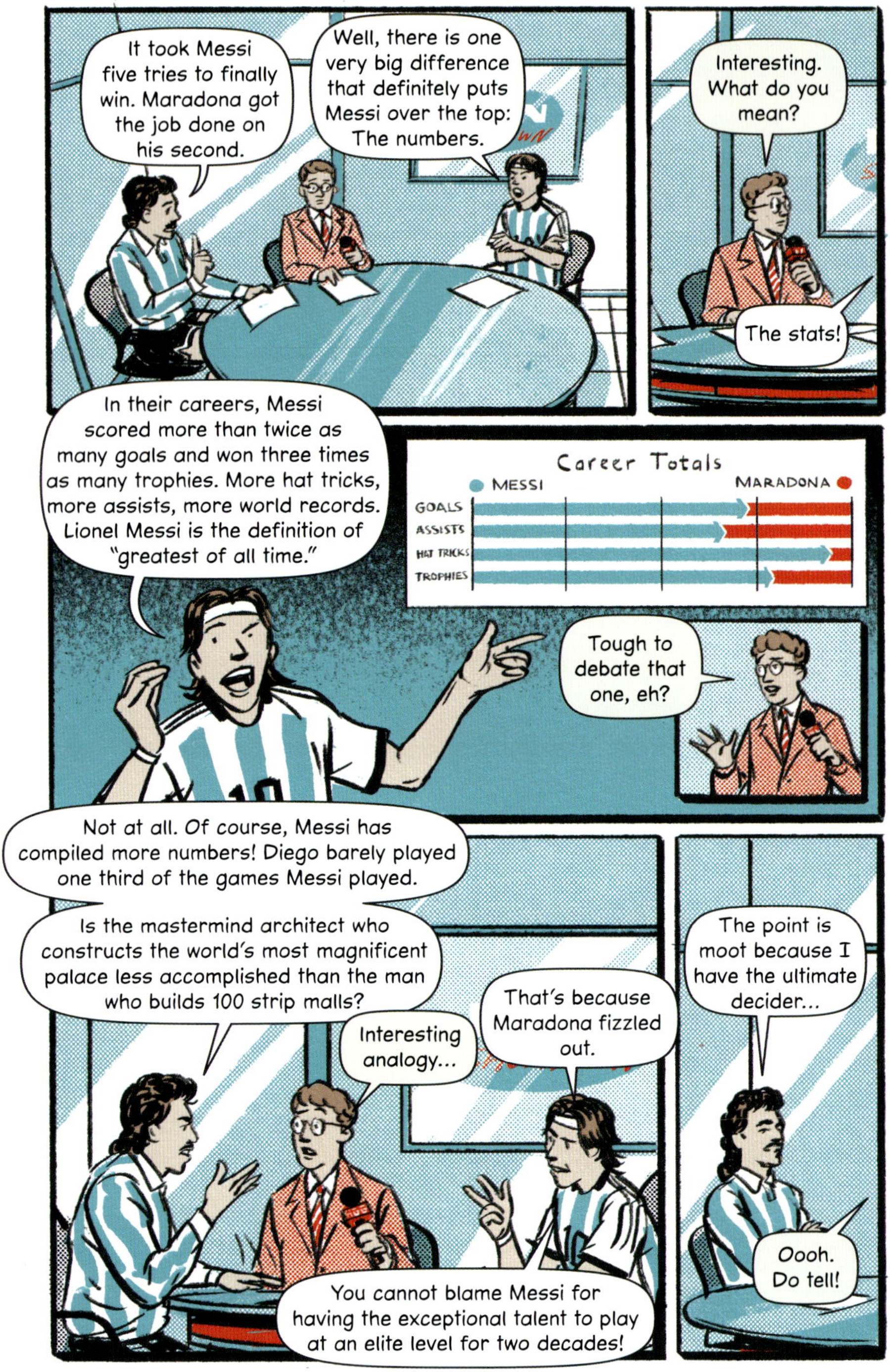
It took Messi five tries to finally win. Maradona got the job done on his second.
Well, there is one very big difference that definitely puts Messi over the top: The numbers.
Interesting. What do you mean?
The stats!
In their careers, Messi scored more than twice as many goals and won three times as many trophies. More hat tricks, more assists, more world records. Lionel Messi is the definition of "greatest of all time."
Career Totals
MESSI
MARADONA
GOALS
ASSISTS
HAT TRICKS
TROPHIES
Tough to debate that one, eh?
Not at all. Of course, Messi has compiled more numbers! Diego barely played one third of the games Messi played.
Is the mastermind architect who constructs the world's most magnificent palace less accomplished than the man who builds 100 strip malls?
Interesting analogy...
That's because Maradona fizzled out.
You cannot blame Messi for having the exceptional talent to play at an elite level for two decades!
The point is moot because I have the ultimate decider...
Oooh. Do tell!

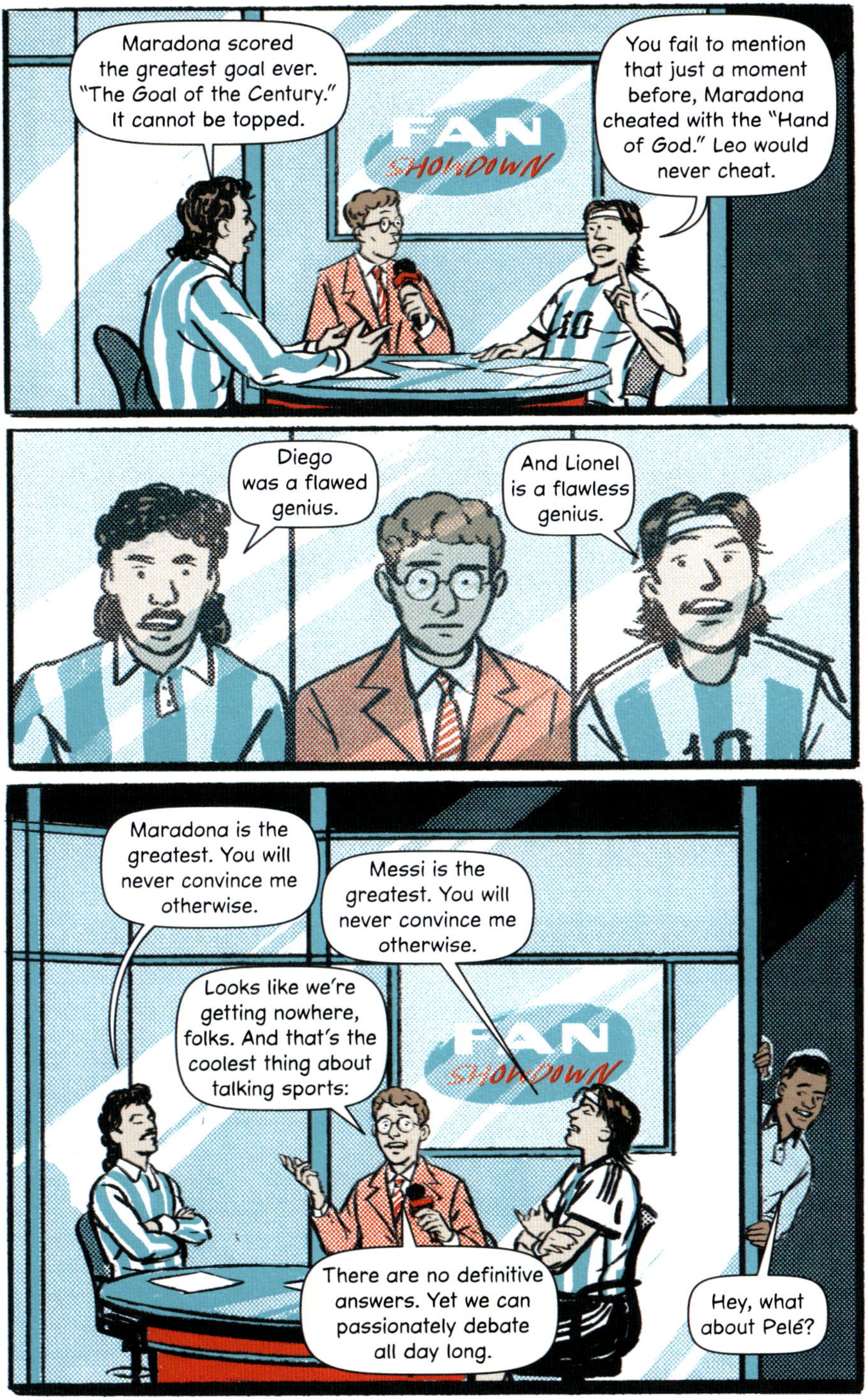
FAN SHOWDOWN
Maradona scored the greatest goal ever. "The Goal of the Century." It cannot be topped.
You fail to mention that just a moment before, Maradona cheated with the "Hand of God." Leo would never cheat.
Diego was a flawed genius.
And Lionel is a flawless genius.
Maradona is the greatest. You will never convince me otherwise.
Messi is the greatest. You will never convince me otherwise.
Looks like we're getting nowhere, folks. And that's the coolest thing about talking sports:
FAN SHOWDOWN
There are no definitive answers. Yet we can passionately debate all day long.
Hey, what about Pelé?

TRIVIA GOALS ANSWERS

p. 10: A
During a penalty kick in the 1938 semifinals, an Italian player named Giuseppe Meazza blasted a ball so hard that his pants dropped to his knees. No worries, he made the goal, and Italy made the finals.

p. 31: A
Just like your friends sometimes bicker over which ball should be used, both nations demanded their ball or nothing. One half was Argentina's ball, the other half was Uruguay's.

p. 43: B
Maradona was so explosive that he couldn't be contained and was often fouled. In fact, in the 1982 World Cup tournament, he was fouled 23 times.

p. 51: B
Barcelona was so excited to sign Messi to a contract that the deal was solidified over a meal at a restaurant. The napkin was the closest thing they had for paper.

p. 56: B
Messi has won the Ballon d'Or, which translates to "golden ball," a staggering eight times! Yet only once has this prestigious award been given to a goalkeeper.

p. 64: C
Mbappé donated his earnings, nearly a half million dollars, to a charity for children. He said, "It doesn't change my life, but it changes theirs. And if it can change theirs, it is a great pleasure." However, the French striker is a big sneaker-head, too.

p. 71: B
Robots become jockeys and are placed onto the backs of camels. Then they are remotely controlled by competitors as fans cheer them on.

p. 88: A
Ángel Di María was born on February 14, 1988. He comes from Rosario, Argentina, the same hometown of his teammate, Lionel Messi.

p. 102: A
According to reports, the telegram that the Italian prime minister Benito Mussolini sent to his team had a very foreboding message: "Vincere o Morire." Coming from a leader whom many consider one of the most terrifying dictators in modern history, this sounds like a threat he would follow up on. Though the literal English translation is "Win or Die," to Italians, it may have meant simply, "Win or nothing."

p. 112: C
The 3 goals for Geoff Hurst led his England squad to a 4-2 victory in the 1966 World Cup over West Germany.

HOW MANY GOALS DID YOU SCORE? SEE WHERE YOU RANK:
9-10 goals: World Cup Champion
6-8 goals: League Star
3-5 goals: Varsity Player
0-2 goals: Junior Up-and-Comer

SOURCES

"Argentina v France | Final | FIFA World Cup Qatar 2022 | Full Match Replay." FIFA+. Lusail Stadium, Lusail, Qatar, December 18, 2022. https://www.plus.fifa.com/en/player/9cb7e8df-0828-4c67-8549-8648eff419b7?catalogId=7047fe21-4af1-476c-9fb8-e4655c5668e2&entryPoint=Slider.

Benjamin, Brian. "The Story of the 1930 World Cup." *These Football Times*, April 9, 2014. https://thesefootballtimes.co/2014/09/04/the-story-of-the-1930-world-cup/.

Bisset, Simon, Ben Jones, Eddie Mallia-Rourke, and Caio Correa, dir. *FIFA World Cup Qatar 2022: A Historic World Cup*. Aired December 19, 2023, on FIFA+. https://www.plus.fifa.com/en/player/a1b1fa66-a271-450d-8796-c07123662720?catalogId=82aceda3-9c71-4fd5-b462-e3088d3700f9&entryPoint=CTA.

Blanchette, Rob. "Germany vs. Argentina: Analyzing Lionel Messi's Impact on the 2014 World Cup Final." Bleacher Report, July 14, 2014. https://bleacherreport.com/articles/2128712-germany-vs-argentina-analysing-lionel-messis-impact-on-2014-world-cup-final.

Brown, Paul. "World Cup 1930: 'The So-Called World's Association Football Championship.'" Medium, May 9, 2018. https://medium.com/soccer-stories/the-so-called-worlds-association-football-championship-3f825e7b10e6.

Burns, Ashley. "Great Moments in Humanity: A Letter Has Surfaced Detailing the 1914 Christmas Truce." Uproxx, January 2, 2013. https://uproxx.com/sports/christmas-truce-letter-soccer-world-war/.

Carlisle, Jeff, and Kyle Bonagura. "An Oral History of USA-Iran at the 1998 World Cup: Political Tension, Teammate Betrayal, and Humiliation." ESPN, November 28, 2022. https://www.espn.com/soccer/story/_/id/37634212/oral-history-usa-iran-1998-world-cup-interviews-photos.

Dawson, Gavin. "Unforgettable World Cup Moments: Mussolini's 'Win or Die' Telegram to Italy's 1938 Team." Football Whispers, September 22, 2024. https://footballwhispers.com/blog/unforgettable-world-cup-moments-mussolinis-win-or-die-telegram-to-italys-1938-team/.

"Diego Maradona Goal of the Century I Argentina v England I 1986 FIFA World Cup." FIFA, March 9, 2018. YouTube video, 2 min., 34 sec. https://www.youtube.com/watch?v=Da_CDPRG2j0.

Duggan, Michael. "The Catholic Visionary Who Founded the World Cup." *The Catholic Herald*, June 14, 2018. https://catholicherald.co.uk/the-catholic-visionary-who-founded-the-world-cup/.

Fitzpatrick, Richard. "The Machine of '87: Messi's Boyhood Teammates Recall Early Signs of Greatness." Bleacher Report, June 23, 2017. https://www.bleacherreport.com/articles/2717227-the-machine-of-87-messis-boyhood-teammates-recall-early-signs-of-greatness.

Gadsby, Paul. "World Cup Mystery: What Happened to the Original Jules Rimet Trophy?" *The Guardian*, June 13, 2014. https://www.theguardian.com/football/2014/jun/13/world-cup-mystery-what-happened-jules-rimet-trophy.

Langton, James. "'Dead' Player Gatecrashing Own Wake Capped Off the First and Weirdest World Cup." *The National*, December 2, 2022. https://www.thenationalnews.com/fifa-world-cup-2022/2022/12/02/dead-player-gatecrashing-own-wake-capped-off-the-first-and-weirdest-world-cup/.

Lichfield, John. "Jules Rimet: The Man Who Kicked Off the World Cup." *The Independent*, June 5, 2006. https://www.independent.co.uk/news/people/profiles/jules-rimet-the-man-who-kicked-off-the-world-cup-481145.html.

Lowe, Sid. "Lionel Messi: How Argentinian Teenager Signed for Barcelona on a Serviette." *The Guardian*, October 15, 2014. https://www.theguardian.com/football/blog/2014/oct/15/lionel-messi-barcelona-decade.

"Maradona 'Hand of God' Goal 1986 World Cup." ClassicEngland, April 27, 2012. YouTube video, 59 sec. https://www.youtube.com/watch?v=-ccNkksrfls.

Mora y Araujo, Marcela. "How Diego Maradona Redefined Football in the Space of Less than Five Minutes." CNN, November 15, 2022. https://www.cnn.com/2018/06/11/football/world-cup-argentina-england-1986-diego-maradona/index.html.

Pilger, Sam. "Lionel Messi vs. Diego Maradona: Why the Winner Is Obvious." Bleacher Report, June 8, 2018. https://bleacherreport.com/articles/1796916-lionel-messi-vs-diego-maradona-why-the-winner-is-obvious.

Rampling, Ali. "The Best Quotes About Diego Maradona." 90min, November 25, 2021. https://www.90min.com/posts/the-best-quotes-about-diego-maradona.

Razo, Eduardo. "Messi Has 'Everyone' Rooting for Him to Win World Cup, Former PSG Boss Believes." PSGTalk, November 30, 2022. https://psgtalk.com/2022/11/messi-has-everyone-rooting-for-him-to-win-world-cup-former-psg-boss-believes/.

SFCAdmin. "Parou Guerra, Foi Campeão, Nasceu o Messias." Santos FC, April 2, 2019. https://www.santosfc.com.br/parou-guerra-foi-campeao-nasceu-o-messias/.

Uncredited. "Jules Rimet and the Birth of the World Cup." Sky History. https://www.history.co.uk/article/jules-rimet-and-the-birth-of-the-world-cup.

Uncredited. "Leo Messi Becomes the Most Decorated Player in History." FC Barcelona, August 20, 2023. https://www.fcbarcelona.com/en/news/3642383/leo-messi-becomes-the-most-decorated-player-in-history.

ABOUT THE AUTHOR AND ILLUSTRATOR

When **Chris Barish** is not reading about sports or history, he's writing about sports history. Much like the first person who ever put together the chocolate and the marshmallow, he realized that it was possible to combine his two favorite things to make an even cooler thing. In addition to authoring graphic novels, he has also written award-winning campaigns for sports superstars like Aaron Judge, Joel Embiid, and Derrick Henry. Chris currently lives in New York with his family, in a house filled with sports gear, books, instruments, and lots of muddy boots.

Nate Sweitzer became an illustrator shortly after he could hold a pencil. His work bridges the past and present, blending techniques from art history with fresh approaches from the digital world. He brings human stories to life with dynamic illustrations full of action, suspense, and striking perspectives. A lifelong fan of history and sports, Nate draws inspiration from the drama of real-life events and athletes competing at the highest level. He works out of his studio in New York, creating artwork for books, magazines, and posters. When he's away from his desk, you'll likely find him exploring the outdoors, watching sports, or stubbornly refusing to change his guitar strings.

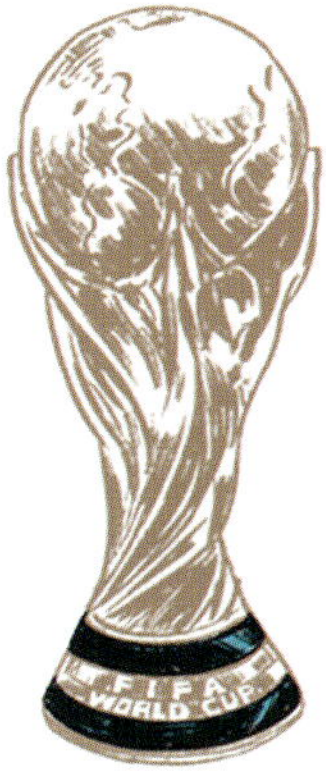
FIFA
WORLD CUP